D1053612

**Creating a
Company for
Customers**

FINANCIAL TIMES

Prentice Hall

In an increasingly competitive world, it is quality
of thinking that gives an edge – an idea that opens new
doors, a technique that solves a problem, or an insight
that simply helps make sense of it all.

We work with leading authors in the fields of
management and finance to bring cutting-edge thinking
and best learning practice to a global market.

Under a range of leading imprints, including
Financial Times Prentice Hall, we create world-class
print publications and electronic products giving
readers knowledge and understanding which can then
be applied, whether studying or at work.

To find out more about our business and professional
products, you can visit us at www.business-minds.com

For other Pearson Education publications, visit
www.pearsoned-ema.com

Pearson
Education

Creating a Company for Customers

How to build and lead a market-driven organization

Malcolm McDonald

Martin Christopher

Simon Knox

Adrian Payne

Edited by Jane Simms

The Marketing ©ouncil

FINANCIAL TIMES
Prentice Hall

An imprint of **Pearson Education**

London • New York • San Francisco • Toronto • Sydney • Tokyo • Singapore
Hong Kong • Cape Town • Madrid • Amsterdam • Munich • Paris • Milan

PEARSON EDUCATION LIMITED

Head Office:
Edinburgh Gate
Harlow CM20 2JE
Tel: +44 (0)1279 623623
Fax: +44 (0)1279 431059

London Office:
128 Long Acre
London WC2E 9AN
Tel: +44 (0)20 7447 2000
Fax: +44 (0)20 7240 5771
Website: www.business-minds.com

First published in Great Britain in 2001

© Pearson Education Limited 2001

The right of Malcolm McDonald, Martin Christopher, Simon Knox and
Adrian Payne to be identified as authors of this work
has been asserted by them in accordance with the
Copyright, Designs and Patents Act 1988.

ISBN 0 273 64249 9

British Library Cataloguing in Publication Data
A CIP catalogue record for this book can be obtained from the British Library

10 9 8 7 6 5 4 3 2 1

Typeset by Northern Phototypesetting Co Ltd, Bolton
Printed and bound in Great Britain by Biddles Ltd, Guildford & King's Lynn

The Publishers' policy is to use paper manufactured from sustainable forests.

About the authors

Martin Christopher is Professor of Marketing and Logistics and Deputy Director of Cranfield School of Management with special responsibility for management development programmes. He is also Chairman of the Cranfield Centre for Logistics and Transportation and head of The Marketing Group.

He has worked as a consultant for major international companies in North America, Europe, the Far East and Australasia, and is a non-executive director of a number of companies.

He has held appointments as Visiting Professor at the Universities of British Columbia, Canada; New South Wales, Australia; and South Florida in the USA.

Martin Christopher is a Fellow of The Chartered Institute of Marketing, and a Fellow and council member of The Institute of Logistics and Transport, which in 1987 awarded him the Sir Robert Lawrence medal for his contribution to the development of logistics education in Britain.

(E-mail: m.g.christopher@cranfield.ac.uk)

Simon Knox is Professor of Brand Marketing at Cranfield School of Management, and consultant to a number of multinational companies including McDonald's, Levi Strauss, DiverseyLever and the Ocean Group. Before joining Cranfield he worked for Unilever, where he held a number of senior roles marketing international brands in both detergents and foods.

Since joining Cranfield, Simon Knox has published over 60 papers on branding and customer purchasing styles and is a regular speaker at international conferences. He is the Director of the Institute for Advanced Research in Marketing at the School and is currently leading a research team on Customer Relationship Management on behalf of Computer Science Corporation (CSC). He is the co-author of the book *Competing on Value* (http://www.competingonvalue.com) published by Financial Times Pitman Publishing in the UK, Germany and the USA.

(E-mail: s.knox@cranfield.ac.uk)

Malcolm McDonald is Professor of Marketing Strategy and Deputy Director of Cranfield School of Management with special responsibility for e-business.

He has extensive industrial experience, including a number of years as marketing director of Canada Dry. During the past 20 years he has run marketing seminars and workshops in the UK, Europe, Japan, India, the Far East, Australia, South America, South Africa, Brazil and the USA.

He has written 30 books, including the best selling *Marketing Plans: How to prepare them; how to use them*, and many of his papers have been published.

His current interests centre around the use of information technology in advanced marketing processes.

(E-mail: m.mcdonald@cranfield.ac.uk)

Adrian Payne is Professor of Services and Relationship Marketing and Director of the Centre for Relationship Marketing at Cranfield School of Management. Before joining Cranfield he held a number of positions in industry, including that of chief executive officer (CEO) of a manufacturing company and senior roles in corporate planning and marketing.

He is an authority on customer relationship management, relationship marketing, customer retention and services marketing, and has written nine books on these subjects. He works internationally as a consultant, keynote speaker and educator in marketing.

(E-mail: a.payne@cranfield.ac.uk)

About the editor

Jane Simms is a freelance writer and editor, specializing in marketing, management and business. She was previously editor of *Marketing Business*, the magazine of The Chartered Institute of Marketing, and before that edited *Financial Director*. She has contributed to a wide range of publications, including the national newspapers, and now writes regularly for *Marketing* and *Director*.

(E-mail: janesimms@btinternet.com)

Contents

Figures

Tables

Foreword

by Sir Michael Perry, CBE, *President of The Marketing Council*

This book sets out a new blueprint for marketing. The onset of global competition has put marketing at the top of the CEO's agenda in many leading companies. For these companies marketing is viewed as the strategic task of winning customer preference.

For this reason alone it is timely that the team of Cranfield marketing professors should publish this book on pan-company marketing. It is quite rightly targeted at CEOs and their boards. The questions it poses are supremely important. Is our company designed and led to win customer preference? Is marketing represented at the board-room table? Does our agenda prioritize customer insight, relevant differentiation, and the acquisition and retention of customers? Pan-company marketing properly supported by the CEO and his or her board answers these questions.

Pan-company marketing is also critical to understanding and designing the key processes of the business: innovation, supply chain management and customer management. And it lies at the heart of e-business.

It is no longer enough to have a great marketing or brand department, or an entrepreneurial spirit or a strong brand identity. It is not enough to design business processes around the customer. In this book marketing is recognized as the force which unifies the whole company in the unremitting quest for customer preference.

Acknowledgements

The authors have been helped and advised by John Stubbs of The Chartered Institute of Marketing, and we are all extremely grateful to him for his wisdom and worldly advice.

Jane Simms, however, took on the major burden of managing four marketing professors, keeping them to their deadlines, editing out anything that was over-academic, joining the chapters together in a truly masterly way, and contributing parts of the text.

We should like to thank Jane for her patience and for her professionalism. This book is the better for her involvement.

Professors   Malcolm McDonald
             Martin Christopher
             Simon Knox
             Adrian Payne

Part 1

Overview

1

Why are you in business?
The value-driven CEO

In a market-driven company everyone, from the CEO to the telephone salesperson, is preoccupied with what the customers need and delivering it to them.

'A good big 'un will always beat a good little 'un', according to aficionados of the noble art of pugilism. They are undoubtedly correct, because their experience confirms this to be true. But two very important unspoken assumptions colour this thinking: the contest is limited to the confines of a boxing ring, and it is conducted under the Marquess of Queensberry rules.

In such conditions the heavier fighter will always triumph over his lighter-weight adversary. David, had such a handicap been imposed upon him, would never have been able to overcome Goliath. And Sir Francis Drake could never have defeated the vastly superior Spanish Armada.

Both of these apparently disadvantaged competitors succeeded by doing something unexpected. Each refused to play the game on their opponent's terms, slogging it out toe to toe. Instead they turned their lack of physical strength into the strategic advantage of nimbleness, speed of attack and surprise.

The commercial equivalent of this approach is manifested in the large number of organizations listed on the world's stock exchanges that did not even exist 20 years ago. Companies such as Dell and Microsoft, First Direct and Direct Line, once considered to be the 'Davids' of their industries, have become 'Goliaths', changing the entire business landscape as they have developed.

This is a book for business leaders. It is intended as a guide for CEOs and their fellow board members to help them achieve outstanding growth, to transform their organizations in the marketplace, to challenge the status quo, to search for new insights and to lead their companies to be innovative and customer focused. Above all, we want to encourage them to aspire to consistent growth in shareholder value through getting customers to prefer their products and services to those of their competitors. In simple terms, this means inspiring the whole organization to be market driven – creating a company for customers.

But there is no Aladdin's lamp, no simple formula or panacea, which can make an organization's dreams come true. This book is all about what being market driven means, what it involves, how it works, the impact on stakeholder value and, crucially, the role of the business leader in creating a market-driven company. It is *not* a book about marketing, which is just another function like finance, human resources, information technology (IT), production and research and development (R & D). But it will, inevitably, focus on customers and the processes involved in delivering to them the kind of value that makes them loyal, thus creating a company that suppliers, employees, the community and shareholders – as well as customers – all love and admire.

But *Creating a Company for Customers* also seeks to clarify what the term 'marketing' actually means and how it should be defined, designed, managed and integrated into market-driven operations. The word is currently used willy-nilly to describe any number of activities from strategic market thinking to tactical marketing activities such as advertising and promotions. This can be confusing for a business leader who is told his or her company should be 'marketing led', when it should, of course, be 'market led'.

The concept of marketing as it has classically been practised in the traditional bastion of fast-moving consumer goods, with its emphasis on product, promotion, price and place, is becoming if not redundant, then less relevant. Competitive advantage comes increasingly from the service and 'added value' elements of a product or service. Moreover, business itself is moving from a manufacturing to a service economy. As such, the focus is shifting from the historic emphasis on products to people – both employees and customers. Consequently customer focus and service – to the end of winning customer preference – is taking over from brand management as the new marketing paradigm. This shift is being underpinned by the huge growth of 'direct' marketing, characterized by databases, call centres and Internet activities, which is transforming the marketing landscape. The very important fifth 'P' of people should be added to the existing four. Indeed, much of Chapter 3 of this book, on relationship management, is devoted to people management and internal marketing.

The Marketing Council in the UK has coined the term 'pan-company marketing' to describe this new paradigm, in which marketing as a philosophy pervades the entire organization, with customer focus as its tangible manifestation. In a market-driven company everyone, from the CEO to the telephone salesperson, is preoccupied with what the customers need and delivering it to them. The role of the marketing department is to add value to the rest of the organization by practising its disciplines to the highest professional standards, and using its expertise to gather customer insights and intelligence in order to give customers the products and services they need.

> Only when we grasp the nettle of what it means to be market driven can we begin to work backwards and build an organization designed for customers.

But this market-driven approach has to be led and managed by the CEO, supported by his or her board. Many business leaders remain wedded to the financial husbandry or accountancy-led school of management that, through paring to the bone, has caused so many companies to go to the wall. Pan-company marketing is not an attempt to fuel the historic tension between finance and marketing – and increasingly human resources – by seeking to place marketing above other disciplines in the company hierarchy. Rather, it is a way of breaking down restrictive functional silos by focusing everyone on the same goal: winning customer preference.

Pan-company marketing, or the market-driven approach, is emphatically not another fad – the latest panacea to be hungrily seized on by companies desperate for a quick-fix solution to their problems. It is a total company philosophy which can not only happily coexist with other management initiatives – business process reengineering, total quality management, balanced scorecards and the like – but dramatically increase their chances of succeeding. It simply needs to be integrated into the 'DNA' of the way the organization goes about its business – just like sound financial management.

A search through the literature on what being market driven involves in excellent companies reveals a fascinating array of findings and advice. Nonetheless, from the iconoclastic, such as Tom Peters, to the more sober and serious, such as Philip Kotler and former Unilever chairman Sir Michael Perry, there is remarkable commonality and agreement about what creates excellent, market-driven performance. These common elements are shown in Box 1.1.

Box 1.1

Key elements of world-class market-driven performance

1 Profound understanding of the marketplace
2 Creative segmentation and selection
3 Powerful differentiation, positioning and branding
4 Effective marketing planning processes
5 Long-term integrated marketing strategies
6 Institutionalized creativity and innovation
7 Total supply chain management
8 Market-driven organization structures
9 Careful recruitment, training and career management
10 Vigorous line management implementation

Even a cursory glance at the list in Box 1.1 reveals a heavy emphasis on understanding the market as a key success factor in being market driven. Indeed, organizations are increasingly including phrases such as 'market driven' and 'customer responsive' in their publicly promulgated mission statements.

Before getting into too much depth about what the term 'market driven' means, business leaders should think carefully about the answers to the questions in Box 1.2 concerning the deliverables from all their managerial and planning efforts.

In our experience of working with some of the world's biggest organizations, the responses of CEOs, directors and senior managers to these questions are generally disappointing. This demonstrates just how difficult it is to translate the desire to be market driven into practice. It is a gap identified by Jean-Claude Larréché, professor of marketing at French business school INSEAD, in ongoing research into the fundamental capabilities which influence the sustainable competitiveness of firms. Larréché has found that even among the top global firms innovation and marketing operations are weak compared with other capabilities. But the biggest threat to their competitiveness is top managers' inability to get close to customers and employees.

Box 1.2

Thought starters

- Can you list your key target markets (in order of priority)?
- Can you describe (quantitatively and qualitatively) the value each of your key target markets requires?
- In each of these key target markets, can you describe how your organization creates better value than your competitors?
- Do the relevant senior people in your organization understand and support the three points above?
- Does your strategic plan spell out how your organization is going to create superior profits (sustainable competitive advantage)?
- Are all the relevant functions in your company organized in a way that supports delivering the value customers require?

It is also clear from the above checklist of market-driven performance that, while it is the role of the marketing specialists to quantify the present and future value required by the different groups in a market, it is the role of *everyone* in the organization to deliver it, not just those involved in marketing. All customer-interfacing people have a key role to play in creating customer value. But so do all those who provide support internally and externally to these customer-facing functions, such as IT specialists, accountants, economists, human resource (HR) and R & D personnel. Creating customer value goes even further than this, of course, and is influenced by supply chain management and the attitudes of shareholders and opinion leaders, among others.

But the CEO is the linchpin: unless value creation is led from the top and managed proactively from the board downwards, more junior executives are unlikely to be able to effect the necessary co-ordination and integration.

But if they are to make things happen, business leaders need the kind of practical guidance that is difficult to cull from the wealth of literature pumped out during the past 40 years. This ranges from the iconoclastic – covering techniques such as managing by wandering around (MBWA) and the Peter Principle (promoting people beyond their level of competence) – to the more serious offerings of Michael Porter, Peter Drucker, Philip Kotler and literally thousands of other scholars. It is easy to make emotional pleas for organizations to be market driven. It is more difficult to outline in a reasonably structured way how to achieve it.

So the purpose of this book is to provide business leaders with a route map and a set of actionable propositions for creating superior customer value, hence superior shareholder and stakeholder value. Action boxes are provided at the end of each of the succeeding chapters.

Why being market driven has become so important

Why has being market driven emerged as the number one priority for organizations today? This is not a theoretical book and, as far as possible, we will steer clear of academic language. But there is nothing so practical as a good theory, and it seems appropriate to explain this particular point by referring to a nice little piece of theory.

Consider for a moment how anything 'new' gets adopted in the market. The US researcher Everett Rogers did some ground-breaking research in the 1960s that is as valid today as it was then. He discovered that when something revolutionary is developed – televisions, computers, direct banking, for instance – the process of commercialization usually follows a pattern that resembles a bell-shaped curve, as shown in Figure 1.1.

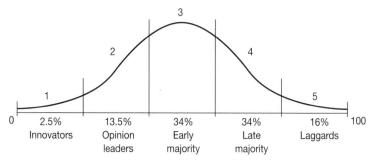

Fig. 1.1   The process of commercialization
Source: Rogers (1962)

Put simply, there is a small proportion of people who are so innovative and unusual that they tend to try anything new, irrespective of its likely eventual general appeal. But just because this group adopts the product or service does not mean there is a market for it, as these people are often cranks. Rogers referred to them more kindly as 'innovators' and estimated them to represent about 2.5 per cent of the population.

The next group, the 'opinion leaders', are crucial to the success of any new product or service. These people tend to be influential, have money, are fiercely independent and generally do not care what others think of them. They could, in vernacular terms, be called 'the Jones'. The Jones are always ahead of 'the Smiths' and the Smiths are forever trying to keep up with the Jones. This group gives social approbation to the product or service and kick-starts the market. Rogers estimated they make up around 13.5 per cent of the population, and unless they take up the new product or service, it is unlikely to be more generally adopted.

The next group, the 'early majority' (the Smiths), begins to adopt the product or service and the market starts to grow exponentially, until the 'late majority' enters the market. At this stage price tends to become important, as by now there is plenty of choice and this group is less well-off than earlier groups.

Finally the last group, the 'laggards', enters the market, until everyone who could have one has now got one. For example, in Western Europe most households have cars, washing machines, televisions, calculators and so on, which means that these markets are mature, or replacement, markets. This is shown in Figure 1.2.

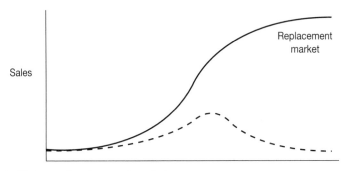

Fig. 1.2   Mature and replacement markets

In mature markets, the only way to grow business is by growing market share. At this stage market growth depends on gross domestic product, population growth and other macroeconomic factors. For example, in Western Europe we are making too many cars every year, we have too many farms, airlines are subsidized, we have too many insurance companies and banks, and competition is intense. We will return to this theme in Chapter 2. For now, let us consider what happens to organizations at each stage of market development.

In the early stage, *technology* is paramount: if we do not have a boat we cannot go to the island.

By stage 2, demand tends to outstrip supply, so *production* becomes the overriding consideration, as the race is on to meet demand. During this phase the barons of the organization are the technical people, whether they be production engineers, lawyers, architects, chemists or whatever.

In stage 3, the market is established and new entrants join to take advantage of the high sales and profits growth. Consequently, markets begin to fragment, or segment, and the response is *promotion*, which now becomes a priority, often in the form of advertising and proactive selling.

By the time stages 4 and 5 are reached, there is still growth, as new users are still entering the market, but there are fewer of them, so the rate of growth begins to decline, often leading to overcapacity and price wars.

It is usually at this stage that *financial husbandry* takes over: costs are cut and ratio management is introduced. The trouble with this is that it tends to create delusions of success and often leads to what the UK journalist Andrew Lorenz has described as

'Anorexia Industrialosa' – an excessive desire to be leaner and fitter, leading to emaciation and, eventually, death.

It is interesting to note that, of Peters and Waterman's 43 so-called 'excellent' companies cited in *In Search of Excellence* in 1982, there were only six that could be considered excellent just eight years later, according to Richard Pascale (1990) in *Managing on the Edge*.

Financial husbandry on its own can have disastrous consequences, and success today, unless anchored in real customer satisfaction, is likely to be transitory. You only have to look at the problems that have been dogging the once blue-chip UK retailer Marks & Spencer (M & S) to see the price of ignoring the customer.

M & S's profits were slashed and its confidence dashed in the biggest shock in its 116-year history. The official story was that it got its fashion line wrong, but in fact the company's problems had been accruing over many years. For example, it was only recently that customers could use debit and credit cards in the stores. If a food line was out of stock, the story goes that customers blamed themselves for arriving too late! Until recently customers could not try on clothes, and changing-booths were introduced very reluctantly. Such arrogance was bound to have detrimental consequences – particularly as other high street stores such as Gap and Next were offering attractive, high-quality merchandise at reasonable prices, together with good customer service.

Marks & Spencer's experience, of course, begs the question as to whether long-term market leadership and domination leads inevitably to arrogance and complacency, and whether this militates against new ideas, products, processes and regeneration. Virgin's 'tracker' funds, Yahoo!, Amazon.com and the like are forcing well-established leaders to re-examine traditional management models and outmoded formulae for success.

But during the past ten years, many companies have sought a remedy for their declining fortunes by retreating into faddism, hungrily adopting one fad after another as they were peddled by eager consultants. In most cases these initiatives have failed, as organizations have treated them as a quick-fix bolt-on without addressing their underlying problems. The International Standards Organization's ISO 9000 quality initiative, for example, very laudable when used sensibly, has, in the main, only been a guarantee that organizations can produce rubbish perfectly and consistently. We use the word 'rubbish' judiciously, because there is little point in producing perfectly something that people do not buy.

Most boards are spending too much of their valuable time on internal operational efficiency (doing things right) at the expense of external operational effectiveness (doing the right things).

Another fad has been business process reengineering (BPR). This has been an outstanding success in those companies which have used it to redesign their processes to create value for customers. But in those organizations which have not grasped the nettle of customer satisfaction, it has achieved merely cosmetic productivity improvements. Yet another has been balanced scorecards. This too, for

CEOs who understand the need to balance the requirements of all the stakeholders in a company delivering customer value, has been very successful. It is a strategy used with great success by BAA, for example, for managing its complex web of stakeholder relationships, as we shall discover in Chapter 3. But for those CEOs who do not understand the importance of being market driven, it has proved to be just another fad.

Of course all of these initiatives are fabulous and do work, but only when they are seen in the context of providing superior customer value as a means to providing superior shareholder value. Alas, even in those organizations committed to 'relationship' and 'one-to-one' marketing, too often customers remain the Cinderellas. As Harvard Business School's Susan Fournier has pointed out, rapid development of relationship techniques in the USA has been accompanied by growing customer dissatisfaction. The much vaunted relationship that companies were so eager to forge with their customers involved not so much delighting them as abusing them, suggested Fournier.

The problem is that companies have become so internally focused they have got carried away with supply-side issues and taken their eye off the customer ball. Until organizations make a serious effort to lift their heads above the parapet and understand their markets and their customers better, all the great initiatives referred to above will amount to expensive, time-consuming mistakes. Most boards are spending too much of their valuable time on internal operational efficiency (doing things right) at the expense of external operational effectiveness (doing the right things).

In many cases managerial attitudes and corporate cultures became ingrained during the heady years of success, so companies persevere with the old tried and tested formulae, usually with disastrous results. But more of this in Chapter 2.

We will now turn our attention to what being market driven means, and to an explanation of how 'marketing' – a word which causes a lot of confusion – fits into the market-driven, customer-focused approach. The term 'marketing' is frequently used to describe a customer-driven organization's philosophy. As mentioned above, The Marketing Council has coined the expression 'pan-company marketing' to describe its philosophy of making the entire organization, not just the marketing department, focus on the customer. But the word 'marketing' is most frequently used to describe the function of marketing, which received its fair share of criticism during the 1990s.

Marketing: veneer or substance?

What is most worrying about the flurry of articles and reports over recent years claiming that marketing has failed is the evident confusion about the marketing concept and the marketing function. The marketing function (or department) never has been and never will be effective in an organization with a technical, production, operations or financial orientation. Such enterprises adopted the vocabulary of marketing a long time ago and applied a veneer of marketing techniques.

Many of the high street banks have spent fortunes on hiring marketing people, often from fast-moving consumer goods (FMCG) companies, producing expensive television commercials and creating a multiplicity of products, brochures and leaflets.

But most customers still cannot distinguish between the major players, so what competitive advantage have any of these organizations gained? Is this marketing in the sense of understanding and meeting customers' needs better than the competition, or is it old-fashioned selling with the name changed, where we try to persuade customers to buy what we want to sell them, how, when and where we want to sell it?

The computer industry provides even clearer examples. For years IT companies used the word 'marketing' indiscriminately as they tried to persuade customers to buy the ever more complex outpourings of their technology. Racked by recession, decline and huge losses, the industry was transformed by new customer-oriented entrants like Microsoft and Dell, which forced it to change root and branch the way it went about its business.

> *Tinkering with existing processes and current organizational structures just won't do. What's required is a root and branch reappraisal.*

Generally marketing departments never have, nor ever will, actually *do* marketing. The reasons are obvious. If the term 'marketing' embraces all those activities related to creating and satisfying demand and the associated intelligence, then it is clear that most marketing takes place during the delivery of the service and during contact with customers. While marketing supports and reflects this process, it is not the sole preserve of those people in the organization who happen to work in the marketing department.

As business writer Alan Mitchell has put it in *Marketing Business:* 'To say the marketing department is responsible for marketing is like saying love is the responsibility of one family member.' It is equally absurd to suggest that personnel issues are the sole preserve of the HR department, as though nobody else in the organization need concern themselves with people. The same could be said for finance and information systems. Indeed, it is such myopic functional separation that got many organizations into the mess they are in today. In our experience organizations that have always been focused on the market rather than preoccupied with their own functional hierarchies have few of the problems referred to in the 1994 Coopers and Lybrand report that severely criticized marketing and judged it to be going through a 'mid-life crisis'.

Marketing's role in business success

Long-term success, by which we mean a continuous growth in earnings per share and in the capital value of the shares, depends on four elements.

1   An excellent core product or service along with associated R & D. Customer insight is critical to this process. Companies with average products deserve average success.
2   Excellent, world-class, state-of-the-art operations. Inefficiency today is likely to be punished. Differentiation and scale, of course, help to determine operational efficiency in customer satisfaction terms. Where corporate culture prevents it from doing so, quality becomes a sterile ISO activity.

3   A culture which encourages and creates an infrastructure which allows employees to be creative and entrepreneurial within the prescribed company procedures. Boring people, for whom subservience and compliance are the norm, cause average performance.

4   Professional marketing departments, staffed by qualified professionals (not failed engineers, failed salespeople or, indeed, failures from any other function). Companies which recruit professionally qualified marketers with appropriate experience are far more likely to succeed than those whose marketing departments are staffed by just about anybody who fancies themselves as a marketer.

Given these ingredients and, above all else, a corporate culture which is not dominated, for historical reasons, by either production, operations or finance, the evidence suggests that customer preference is central to achieving corporate objectives. But companies that succeeded when there was little competition are unlikely to sustain that success today with a 'let's try a bit of marketing' attitude.

Again, the banks provide a good example. Most people hold banks in contempt, and any organization that believes that marketing is something people 'do' on the sixth floor in London's Lombard Street deserves to fail. It is not the fault of the marketing department if an organization is not commercially successful, and to believe it is is to misunderstand and misappropriate the role of marketing.

Is marketing really at the crossroads?

Fast-moving consumer goods manufacturers are facing real challenges to their brand supremacy from increasingly powerful retailers and, in particular, own labels. But this is not a new phenomenon: the threat has been mounting for at least 15 years. It is interesting to note, however, that leading retailers are succeeding by adopting the same marketing approaches that traditionally drove the growth of the packaged goods manufacturers.

The classic and often simplistic marketing approaches were developed in consumer goods in the 1950s, but much of industry and commerce (financial services, hotels, IT and industrial manufacturing, for example) introduced fundamental marketing processes and activities much more recently. It is wrong to generalize, given that every industry sector is facing its own particular set of circumstances. But in our experience marketing in most organizations has not yet reached 'the crossroads', as some commentators suggest, largely because they remain wedded to their old production, technical or financial orientations.

The organizations themselves may be at the crossroads, but until they really come to understand what a marketing orientation or culture is and create an environment in which marketing professionals can operate effectively, all we are really witnessing are the growing pains or, in some cases, the birth pangs of marketing. It may not look like this to the casual observer because, as we have already indicated, most companies have adopted a superficial marketing veneer.

Understanding what marketing really is

We are not trying to exonerate the marketing community from all blame for corporate failure. As UK Prime Minister Tony Blair discovered after trying to 'rebrand' Britain, words can get in the way of meaningful communication and action. This, perhaps, is the most valid criticism of marketers. They have failed to define effectively what marketing is, what it can achieve, and how it must be supported in order to stand any chance of fulfilling its mission of leading the corporation in understanding and satisfying the needs of all of its consumers and customers – through innovation, R & D, production, purchasing, logistics and so on – to create competitive advantage.

For marketing to work, it must flourish at three different levels in the enterprise.

1   The board of directors must understand and enthusiastically embrace the notion that creating and maintaining customer satisfaction is the only route to long-term profitable success. Only when the top management team share this common vision is there any chance of inculcating an organization-wide marketing culture where everyone, including the telephonists, van drivers, order clerks and so on, believes in and practises the concepts of superior customer service. This corporate top-down driven vision of what marketing is can create significant and sustainable success, as companies like General Electric, 3M and Unilever have demonstrated.

2   The business strategies of the company must start with and be evaluated against what the market wants. Unless marketing has a strategic input in order to ensure the future of the company is planned from the marketplace inwards, any subsequent marketing activity is likely to be unsuccessful.

3   Tactical marketing activities must be implemented within the context of the market-led strategies. They must meet high professional standards across the spectrum of functions such as market research, product development, pricing, distribution, advertising, promotion and selling.

The marketing community already has specific names for different aspects of marketing – advertising, selling, market research and the like – but we might need to invent a new glossary to express these three very distinct dimensions of marketing. The single word 'marketing' is used indiscriminately to cover one or more of these levels in different contexts, and the confusion arising does little for the cause of strategic marketing or the market-driven approach.

There is a genuine and widespread concern about the role, function and future of marketing.

After all, other major business functions, such as finance, clearly define the different dimensions of their activities. Even outsiders can see that there is a distinct difference between the roles and functions of the auditor, the cost and works accountant, the management accountant and the finance director. So we do not blame the cost and works accountant for his or her company's failure owing to reckless business or financial strategy. But we tend to criticize the whole of 'marketing' when, for example, the 'cost and works marketer' – perhaps a hotel marketing executive –

fails to generate demand for a hotel built in the wrong place, with the wrong facilities, by operations management who felt they knew better than the marketplace and did not bother to consult it.

There is a genuine and widespread concern about the role, function and future of marketing. But in most companies we know and work with, it is not that marketing has been successfully practised and is now failing; it is that marketing has been imperfectly or partially implemented (even in FMCG). Most corporations do not need to 'reinvent' the function, but to more rigorously and creatively implement the concepts, tools and methodologies which underlie the notion of identifying and satisfying customer needs better than the competition.

> *... it is not that marketing has been successfully practised and is now failing; it is that marketing has been imperfectly or partially implemented.*

Growing pains and teenage excesses need sympathetic and careful handling by parents if offspring are to mature successfully. The life stage analogy seems more appropriate to the state of marketing than viewing it as being at the crossroads or critically ill, which may lead us to try to replace something which, in most companies, has not yet had a proper chance to function.

But how should marketing be managed and integrated into well-formed market-driven corporate infrastructures?

Operationalizing marketing

Fundamentally, marketing is simply a process, with a set of underlying tools and techniques, for understanding markets and for quantifying the present and future value required by the different groups of customers within these markets – what marketers refer to as segments. It is a strictly specialist function, just like accountancy or engineering, which is proscribed, researched, developed and examined by professional bodies such as The Chartered Institute of Marketing in Europe and Asia and the American Marketing Association in the USA. Sometimes customer-facing activities such as customer service, selling, product development and public relations are controlled by the marketing function, but often they are not, even though many of them are included in the academic marketing curriculum.

We can define these strategic and tactical aspects of marketing as 'the market understanding process', and we go on to examine this in detail in Chapter 2. The market understanding process can be represented as in Figure 1.3.

In the model in Figure 1.3 representatives from appropriate functions are members of market planning teams, with the main body of work being done by the marketing representative who has the professional skills to accomplish the more technical tasks of data and information gathering and market analysis. The team might also include a representative from product development, brand managers, key account managers and so on, depending on circumstances.

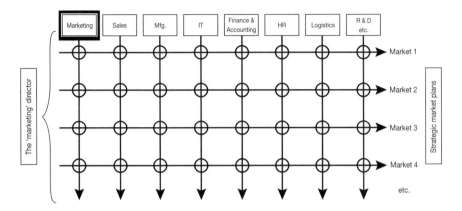

Fig. 1.3 Organizing for marketing planning

The advantages of this approach are as follows:

1 any plans emerging are based on a deep understanding of the organization's asset base and capabilities;
2 members of the team 'own' the plan, thus preventing implementation problems later on;
3 the marketing director, or whoever is responsible to the board for integrating and co-ordinating all the plans emanating from this process, can be sure that he or she is not foisting unwanted plans on to reluctant functional heads;
4 any strategic functional plans, such as IT, Logistics, Purchasing, R & D and so on, will be genuinely market driven or customer needs driven rather than production driven;
5 any business or corporate plans that emerge at a higher level will also be market driven.

But this is not how most organizations plan for creating superior customer value. Too often marketing plans emerge from a marketing 'department' and are developed in isolation and largely ignored by the power brokers.

A model for creating a company for customers

Now we have addressed the issue of understanding markets and demonstrated a process for doing so, we must turn to the question of how to create the value demanded by customers and the critical role the CEO and board play in this.

The model in Figure 1.4 depicts very simply the process of creating value for customers. This is a useful simplification of the above discussion, but the more detailed model in Figure 1.5 provides the business leader with more guidance on how to build a company for customers.

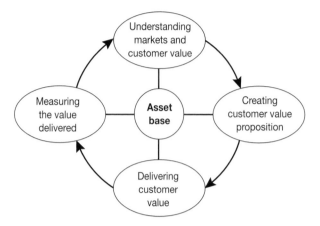

Fig. 1.4   The value-creating process

It is clear from the model in Figure 1.5 that the business leader's role is to drive key processes that are designed to position and brand the organization, create customer value and create shareholder (hence stakeholder) value.

This is what leading-edge organizations are doing to create sustainable competitive advantage. There is no other way to cope with the uncertainty and increased competition in the new millennium.

The most important person in the process is the CEO. He or she has ultimate responsibility for guiding the processes that will:

- position and brand the organization in the market;
- create superior value for the chosen customer groups by meeting their needs better than competitors;
- create excellent profits (sustainable competitive advantage);
- create the requisite stakeholder value for groups other than shareholders, such as employees and suppliers, and influence groups such as local and international communities, governments and the like.

The model shows five key processes, but there could be others, depending on organizational circumstances. For example, organizations whose only resource is people may have a people, or internal management, process. The five listed are, however, the main processes we have observed in our dealings with thousands of world-class companies each year, so we have chosen these as the basis for this book.

We also recognize that other models are possible. For example, you could appoint a functional head as the principal leader of a particular process. The IT director could well become 'director of knowledge management', responsible for managing the infrastructure for information flows both internally and externally. Alternatively, you might decide to appoint a separate director of knowledge management to manage this process.

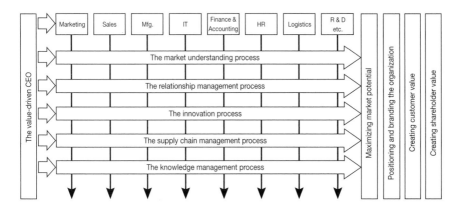

Fig. 1.5 Detailed model of the value-creating process

Likewise, the R & D director could well be asked to manage the innovation process, but this could equally be done by the marketing director or another specially appointed director.

But processes do not involve people 'doing' things in isolation. Rather, processes embrace a series of behaviours that become ingrained in the way the business is conducted.

Creating a Company for Customers will not promote organization charts and organizational theories. We have had these for many years, to little effect. The purpose of the book is to encourage all business leaders to build their organizations around their customers and their customers' preferences. Only when we grasp the nettle of what it means to be market driven can we begin to work backwards and build an organization designed for customers. Tinkering with existing processes and current organizational structures will just not do. What's required is a root and branch reappraisal, along the lines of that carried out by Jack Welch, who turned General Electric into the legendary organization it is today, or by Colin Marshall, who, over ten years ago, transformed British Airways from an ailing airline into one of the world's most successful companies (though the exercise probably needs repeating now). More recent examples of spectacular success resulting from total customer focus include Bill Gates's Microsoft, UK retailer Tesco under its CEO Terry Leahy, and European logistics and parts business Unipart, under its CEO John Neill.

The first process we will examine, in Chapter 2, is market understanding. Only by understanding markets, quantifying the present and future value required by the different customer groups within those markets and communicating the required value to everyone in the organization, does any company have a chance of creating and delivering the required value. Organization charts only make sense in this context. Organizations and organizational processes should be designed around delivering customer value. There can be no other way.

So, the hierarchy is as shown in Figure 1.6. This model does not put other stake-holders on the same level as customers, despite the obvious link between satisfied stakeholders and satisfied customers. Nor does it imply that the interests of customers should be met at the expense of other stakeholders, which is why the balanced score-card concept and the logic behind organizations such as the European Foundation for Quality Management – both of which seek to integrate corporate processes in a bal-anced manner around the creation of customer value – are absolutely accurate. But a company needs to focus on satisfying customers because it is customers – *not* employ-ees, suppliers, environmentalists and the like – who are the ultimate arbiters of qual-ity. Satisfied customers lead to satisfied shareholders and other stakeholders.

As the model in Figure 1.5 shows, the market understanding process is separate from the relationship management process. This is because so many of the organi-zation's functions and activities involve contact with customers. These include sales, key account management, telephone sales, direct mail, exhibitions, the web site, advertising campaigns, sales promotion campaigns, logistics, manufacturing, credit control, after-sales service and so on. Many of these functions and activities are not controlled by marketing people.

Fig. 1.6   The value hierarchy

It is not appropriate here to stipulate what should or should not be included within the remit of the marketing function. But we have always contended that the marketing director should control both marketing and sales. There is always friction when the powerful groups who are responsible for calling on customers also decide the actual product and customer mix, which frequently varies considerably from the desired mix stipulated in the marketing plan. This is a classic case of 'the tail wagging the dog'.

Clearly, in such cases, if there is no one director co-ordinating both of these key activities, the CEO should be responsible for ensuring that what is planned is imple-mented. But asking the CEO to act as marketing and sales director is going too far.

However, sales and marketing are frequently separated, which is why the process for preparing marketing plans outlined in Figure 1.3 is so important. At least this way the sales team, along with other functions, should understand and buy into the proposed plan. The same logic applies to other value-creating functions, such as R & D, distribution, customer service and the like.

But we do not wish to be didactic about organizational responsibilities: we merely want to describe the processes involved in understanding, creating, delivering and measuring customer satisfaction as a route to shareholder and other stakeholder satisfaction.

The structure of the book

The model for building a company for customers is repeated in Figure 1.7, but this time incorporating chapter numbers.

The logic of the book has now been explained. The structure is as shown in Table 1.1.

We have racked our brains to find a suitable title for the kind of CEO who must drive these processes. Eventually we settled on the title 'the value-driven CEO'. The job of the value-driven CEO is to rethink business strategy, processes, organization and culture in order to win customer preference by providing superior customer value. The role is quite distinct from that of marketing, whose job is to understand and track markets, segment customers and consumers in order to understand their changing needs and wants, and to develop plans for the brand and for communicating the business strategy. But none of this marketing activity can be effective without the leadership and support of the value-driven CEO.

At the end of every chapter you will find an interview with a top business leader. These interviews provide fascinating insights from the people who are actually *doing* in their companies what we are advocating in this book – practising what Cranfield is preaching, if you like!

We hope you enjoy reading *Creating a Company for Customers*. It is a book written especially for CEOs and their board colleagues. We enjoyed writing it, and learned a lot from the experience and wisdom of those business leaders who contributed to it and from others mentioned in the text.

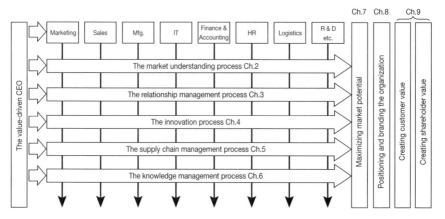

Fig. 1.7   Model of the value-creating process and relevant chapters in this book

Table 1.1   Structure of this book

Part 1	*Overview*
Chapter 1	The value-driven CEO
Part 2	*Managing value-creating processes*
Chapter 2	The market understanding process
Chapter 3	The relationship management process
Chapter 4	The innovation process
Chapter 5	The supply chain management process
Chapter 6	The knowledge management process
Part 3	*Delivering customer value*
Chapter 7	Maximizing market potential
Chapter 8	Positioning and branding the organization
Chapter 9	Creating stakeholder value

References and further reading

Pascale, R. T. (1990) *Managing on the Edge*. New York: Simon and Schuster.
Peters, T. J. and Waterman, R. H. (1982) *In Search of Excellence*. New York: Warner Books.
Rogers, E. (1962) *Diffusion and Innovations*. New York: The Free Press.

Part 2

Managing
value-creating
processes

Getting back to basics:
the market understanding process

How can any organization achieve customer focus while it continues to organize itself around what it makes, rather than around its customers or its markets?

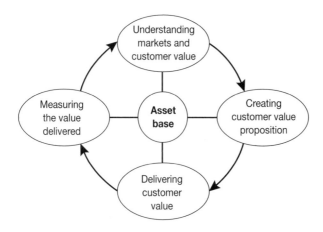

Fig. 2.1 The value-creating process

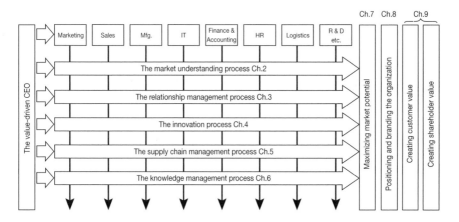

Fig. 2.2 Model of the value-creating process and relevant chapters in this book

Many corporate cultures are hostile to the marketing ethic. Managing directors who got their jobs as a result of behaviours which were appropriate in the latter part of the twentieth century do not know how to respond to increased competition and static or declining markets. Their natural reaction is to resort to their old behaviours, one of which is to cut costs without addressing the fundamental issue of growth. Growth is, admittedly, more difficult than cutting costs, as it requires customers who want to buy things from us rather than from our competitors. It also takes real intellect to adopt a strategic rather than a tactical approach.

Unsuccessful organizations do not bother with strategic marketing planning at all, relying instead on sales forecasts and the associated budgets. But many salespeople sell the products they find easiest to sell (usually at a maximum discount) to those customers who treat them the best. So, by developing short-term budgets first, and then extrapolating them, companies only succeed in extrapolating their own stupidity. Preoccupation with short-term forecasts and budgets is typical of companies that confuse this approach with strategic marketing planning. Ironically, despite this financial orientation, most companies still fail to properly allocate attributable customer interface costs, and hence have little idea which are their profitable and unprofitable customers.

> *Marketing is an attitude of mind that manifests itself in the management process whereby the whole organization organizes itself to satisfy the objectives of both company and customers.*

The depth of ignorance about what marketing is is neatly summed up by one managing director's declaration at a public seminar: 'There's no time for marketing in my company until sales improve!' The truth, of course, is that marketing is an attitude of mind that manifests itself in the management process whereby the whole organization organizes itself to satisfy the objectives of both company and customers. Marketing as a philosophy will never take hold in companies that persist in organizing themselves around tribes of human resource specialists, accountants, engineers, IT, salespeople and so on, or around products or technologies. Such tribes will never subjugate their own tribal goals to the broader aims of customer satisfaction. And how can any organization achieve customer focus while it continues to organize itself around what it makes, rather than around its customers or its markets?

But such companies are being left behind by organizations headed by visionary business leaders. These CEOs and their fellow board members lead the effort to understand their markets and their customers, and understand that only by creating superior customer value will they survive and thrive in this new millennium. They also recognize that strategic marketing planning makes a major contribution to growth in profits. Indeed, there is now a substantial body of evidence to show that thorough marketing planning results in greater profitability and stability over time, as well as helping to reduce friction and operational difficulties within organizations.

Over 20 scholarly research studies have identified corporate culture and financially-driven systems and procedures as the main barriers to effective marketing planning. It is clear that, until organizations learn to grasp the nettle of customer orientation, financial husbandry will continue to dominate corporate life, even though it caused many companies to fail during the 1980s and 1990s and will create more casualties during the first decade of the new millennium.

This chapter explains how business leaders can ensure they have a robust strategy regarding both what and to whom they sell. It also sets out clear guidelines on marketing planning and the marketing inputs business leaders should expect to the business plan.

Until organizations learn to grasp the nettle of customer orientation, financial husbandry will continue to dominate corporate life, even though it caused many companies to fail during the 1980s and 1990s.

Marketing as a competitive weapon

A principal role for marketing in any organization is to define and understand markets and to quantify the present and future value required by the different groups of customers within those markets. Particularly in large, complex organizations, this is best done through a process which results in strategic and marketing plans.

The purpose of such plans is to create sustainable competitive advantage, or 'super profits'. Other terms used include 'positive net present value' and 'economic value added', but whatever the terminology, the effect is continuous growth in earnings per share and in the capital value of the shares in excess of the industry- or sector-weighted average return.

Before focusing on how to develop world-class marketing strategies, we need to explore a few concepts. The first is financial and business risk, represented in the matrix in Figure 2.3. Box 1 in the figure shows high financial risk combined with high business risk, an often lethal combination. Consider Sir Freddie Laker's SkyTrain venture in the 1980s. The capital cost of entering the airline business is high, so Sir Freddie needed a very high financial gearing to enter the most competitive market in the world – the London/North Atlantic route. Moreover, he adopted a low-price strategy against the mighty global airlines, which, given Laker's high breakeven point, became unsustainable against special price promotions mounted by the competition to counter the SkyTrain threat.

Millions of individual consumers were dealt a similar blow in the late 1980s and early 1990s: they had geared themselves up to the hilt against the hope that house prices would rise – only to be left with negative equity when they fell.

Box 2 in Figure 2.3 shows low financial risk and high business risk. Richard Branson entered the airline market with very few planes – which he initially leased – and, therefore, low financial gearing. Like Laker, he entered the lucrative North Atlantic route, but his strategy was one of differentiation, something he has sustained very successfully ever since. His service remains fundamentally different from that of other airlines, especially Virgin Upper Class, which is particularly popular among younger travellers, and Virgin Airlines goes from strength to strength.

Box 3 in Figure 2.3 shows low financial risk and low business risk. Any organization in this delightful position would be ill advised to hoard the cash! For many

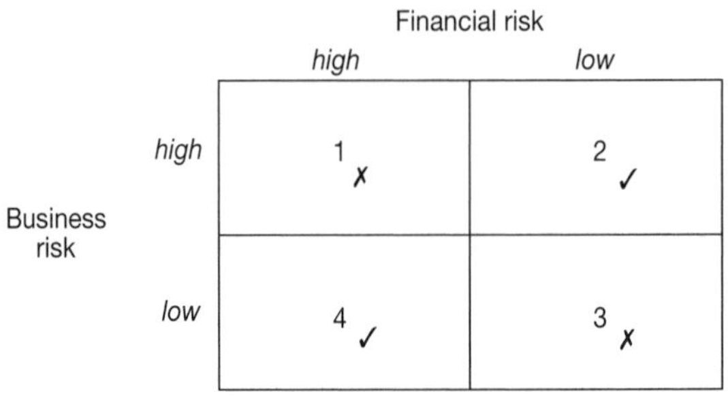

Financial risk

	high	low
high	1 ✗	2 ✓
low	4 ✓	3 ✗

Business risk

Fig. 2.3   Financial and business risk matrix

years, Marks and Spencer fell into this category, and it cleverly used the money to invest in higher business risk ventures, so moving to Box 2. On the other hand, if the financial risk is high, it would seem prudent to invest at least some of the cash in low-risk businesses (Box 4). An example of a low business risk, high financial risk organization is Olympia and York before the property market fell drastically in the late 1980s.

It is easy, then, to see why some businesses perform better than others over long periods of time.

The world's stock exchanges can be represented by the 'line of best fit' in Figure 2.4. The diagram shows return plotted against risk. Successful organizations produce either the same return for a lower perceived risk, or a higher return for the same risk, or both. Being north-west of the line year after year is the mark of organizations whose shares continuously outperform their sectors. Using the cost of capital as a discount rate against future earnings to produce a positive net present value is indicative of super profits, or sustainable competitive advantage.

This is not to be mistaken for producing super profits in one single year, which an organization can achieve relatively easily by cutting costs, cutting capital expenditure, or even by selling off some of the assets. Financial markets are much too sophisticated these days to be taken in by this approach, and you will often see the share price fall after an increase in a single year's profits and an increased dividend. We looked at the

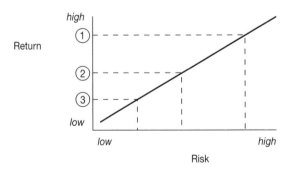

Fig. 2.4   The 'line of best fit'

effect of such behaviours in Chapter 1, where we highlighted the penalties of adopting a purely financially oriented approach to managing the business.

The fragile future profitability of many organizations is illustrated in the two following examples.

Table 2.1 shows the performance of a fictitious company, InterTech, which appears to be excelling in nearly every business dimension. Table 2.2 shows the same company's performance compared with the market as a whole. This clearly shows a severe underperformance, indicating the company is heading for disaster.

Table 2.1   InterTech's five-year performance

Performance (£million)	Base year	1	2	3	4	5
Sales revenue	£254	£293	£318	£387	£431	£454
– Cost of goods sold	135	152	167	201	224	236
Gross contribution	£119	£141	£151	£186	£207	£218
– Manufacturing overhead	48	58	63	82	90	95
– Marketing & sales	18	23	24	26	27	28
– Research & development	22	23	23	25	24	24
Net profit	£16	£22	£26	£37	£50	£55
Return on sales	6.3%	7.5%	8.2%	9.6%	11.6%	12.1%
Assets	£141	£162	£167	£194	£205	£206
Assets (% of sales)	56%	55%	53%	50%	48%	45%
Return on assets	11.3%	13.5%	15.6%	19.1%	24.4%	26.7%

Table 2.3, taken from Hugh Davidson's (1997) *Even More Offensive Marketing*, shows two companies making the same return on sales on the same turnover. But even a cursory glance at the two sets of figures shows clearly that the Dissembler company is heading for disaster. Financial institutions around the world are rarely fooled by so-called 'successful' annual results.

Table 2.2   InterTech's five-year market-based performance

Performance (£million)	Base year	1	2	3	4	5
Market growth (%)	18.3	23.4	17.6	34.4	24.0	17.9
InterTech sales growth (%)	12.8	17.4	11.2	27.1	16.5	10.9
Market share (%)	20.3	19.1	18.4	17.1	16.3	14.9
Customer retention (%)	88.2	87.1	85.0	82.2	80.9	80.0
New customers (%)	11.7	12.9	14.9	24.1	22.5	29.2
% Dissatisfied customers	13.6	14.3	16.1	17.3	18.9	19.6
Relative product quality (%)	+10	+8	+5	+3	+1	0
Relative service quality (%)	+0	+0	−20	−3	−5	−8
Relative new product sales (%)	+8	+8	+7	+5	+1	−4

Table 2.3 (a)   Quality of profits

%	Virtuous plc (%)	Dissembler plc (%)
Sales revenue	100	100
Cost of goods sold	43	61
Profit margin	57	39
Advertising	11	3
R & D	5	–
Capital investment	7	2
Investment ratio	23	5
Operating expenses	20	20
Operating profit	14	14

Key trends →
- Past 5-year revenue growth 10% pa
- Heavy advertising investment in new/ improved products
- Premium-priced products, new plant, so low cost of goods sold

- Flat revenue, declining volume
- No recent product innovation, little advertising
- Discounted pricing, so high cost of goods sold

Table 2.3 (b)   The make-up of 14 per cent operating profits

Factor	Virtuous plc (%)	Dissembler plc (%)
Profit on existing products over 3 years old	21	15
Losses on products recently launched or in development	(7)	(1)
Total operating profits	14	14

Source: Davidson (1997)

Why do we need marketing plans?

It's more difficult today

Organizations need to agree on what to sell, to whom, how and the desired results, and this is often encapsulated in a strategic marketing plan. But running a business today is not the comparatively simple matter it was in 1990. We were invited to run a seminar for the managing directors (MDs) of a construction company in the heady days when the industry was extremely profitable. This particular group had just turned in a 65 per cent increase in net profits and the MDs attending were obviously not too pleased to have to spend a day listening to a professor of marketing holding forth. We asked one MD, who had just achieved particularly good results for his region, the following questions:

- Did your market increase last year and, if so, how much of your net profit growth came from this?
- Did you increase your market share last year and, if so, how much of your net profit growth came from this?
- Did you increase your prices last year at a rate greater than inflation and, if so, how much of your net profit growth came from this?
- Did you increase your productivity last year and, if so, how much of your net profit growth came from this?

There were other questions too, but he could not answer any of them. He clearly was not managing anything.

The mix of product and market types

Figure 2.5 represents a version of US guru Michael Porter's 'generic strategies' matrix (Porter, 1980). It shows that it is easier to differentiate products and services in some markets than others. It is obviously more difficult to differentiate products such as flat glass, chlorine and car insurance policies than, say, perfume, beer and clothes. In low-differentiation markets the corporate goal must be low costs in order to make adequate margins. But costs are rarely the driving force in an organization whose products or services are substantially different from those of the competition.

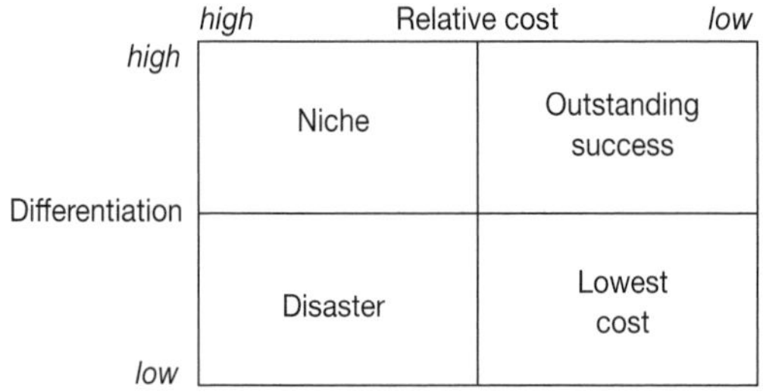

	high	Relative cost	low
high			
		Niche	Outstanding success
Differentiation			
		Disaster	Lowest cost
low			

Fig. 2.5   The generic strategies matrix
Source: Porter (1980)

In reality, most organizations have a mix of products or services that could be classified in all four boxes – disasters, 'lowest cost' products, niche products and products that are outstandingly successful.

For example, Canada Dry used to have to sell fizzy soft drinks products such as large bottles of lemonade even though it made its profits on mixer drinks such as tonic water and ginger ale. It needed a full line of soft drinks in order to be a serious player in the market.

... costs are rarely the driving force in an organization whose products or services are substantially different from those of the competition.

Accountants are always tempted to de-list such products, but they play a role in making profits. The strategic marketing plan has to spell out at least three years in advance what the mix will be between products and services in each of the four boxes in Figure 2.5.

The mix of margins and sales

All organizations also have products and services that produce different levels of sales and profit margin.

Figure 2.6 shows the make-up of return on net assets (RONA), illustrating that profit occurs because of a mix of different margin products and different levels of turnover for each of these products. Again, the marketing plan has to spell out at least three years in advance the desired mix of low-margin, high-turnover, high-margin, high-turnover products and all variations in between. It is not enough just to do the accounts at the end of the fiscal year and hope you get the right net profit.

$$\frac{\text{Operating income}}{\text{Net assets}} = \text{RONA}$$

$$(\text{RoS}) \ \frac{\text{Operating income}}{\text{Sales revenue}} \ \text{X} \ \frac{\text{Sales revenue}}{\text{Net assets}} \ \begin{array}{c}(\text{Asset} \\ \text{turnover})\end{array}$$

Fig. 2.6   The make-up of return on net assets and return on sales

You could argue that the short-sighted belief in the supremacy of return on sales (RoS) has led to the destruction of the manufacturing base in countries like the UK. As we pointed out in Chapter 1, markets fragmented as new entrants invaded high-margin markets, forcing industry after industry to escape to smaller, higher-value niche markets. The British motorcycle industry, attacked by the Japanese with small, low-priced bikes, is a case in point. The British had a policy that every motorcycle, in every market where it was sold, should yield a given margin over the costs incurred in taking it to market, and that if it did not, either the price should be raised or it should be taken off the market.

British motorcycle manufacturers kept moving to more expensive, higher-margin products with a lower turnover, until the Japanese, with enormous economies of scale, introduced superbikes that easily outperformed their British rivals. The result? Yet another industry was sacrificed by those who failed to understand the importance of balancing low-margin, high-turnover products with high-margin, low-turnover products.

Apart from which, it has always been *markets*, rather than *products*, that make profits, as it is the costs of serving customers after the product has left the factory that make or break a company – a point that still escapes many CEOs.

Many of those who presided over the mass destruction of British industry were promoted to the boards of other companies, so preserving and promoting this narrow, financially-driven approach.

This state of affairs is a far cry from the brilliant performance of companies like Rentokil, General Electric, Unilever and the like, whose CEOs have continuously increased their shareholders' wealth. These CEOs understand that unless they create value for customers there can be no business. They also understand that their businesses cannot be driven solely by margin management.

Managerial reasons for a marketing plan

Aside from the need to cope with increasing turbulence, environmental complexity, more intense competition and the sheer speed of technological and market change, a strategic marketing plan is essential for a number of reasons:

- for managers – to help identify sources of competitive advantage;
- for superiors – to force an organized approach;
- for non-marketing functions – to develop specificity;
- for subordinates – to ensure consistent relationships;
- to inform;
- to obtain resources;
- to obtain support;
- to gain commitment;
- to set objectives and strategies.

The business leader and marketing planning

The role of marketing planning

Marketing planning is essential to business success because it analyzes in detail future opportunities to meet customer needs and takes a professional approach to making available to well-defined market segments those products or services that deliver the sought-after benefits.

But marketing planning should not be mistaken for budgets and forecasts, which we have always had. Marketing planning identifies what and to whom sales are going to be made in the longer term to give revenue budgets any chance of succeeding.

There is no such thing as a 'market' – only people with needs and money. Any organization must offer something to those people, which will make them want to buy from it rather than from anyone else who just happens to be around. Nowadays, because markets are generally over-supplied and customers have a wide choice, if companies want to persuade people to part with their money they have to understand their needs in depth and develop specific 'offers' with a differential advantage over the competition. These offers are not just physical products or services, but involve the entire relationship between supplier and customer, including factors such as the company's reputation, brand name, accessibility and service levels.

> *Marketing planning should not be mistaken for budgets and forecasts, which we have always had.*

Here strategic marketing planning comes into its own. (Turn to p. 46 to discover how John Condron, CEO of Yell, uses marketing planning to liberate creativity in his organization.)

What marketing planning is

> *Marketing planning identifies what and to whom sales are going to be made in the longer term to give revenue budgets any chance of succeeding.*

Marketing planning is a logical sequence of activities leading to the setting of marketing objectives and the formulation of plans for achieving them. It is a conceptually simple management process. It is a way of identifying a range of options, of making them explicit, of formulating marketing activities which are consistent with the organization's overall objectives and of scheduling and costing out the specific activities most likely to achieve objectives.

Marketing planning, then, is a managerial process, from which there are two outputs:

- the strategic marketing plan, which covers a period of between three and five years;
- the tactical marketing plan, which is the scheduling and costing out of the specific activities necessary to achieve the first year's objectives in the strategic marketing plan.

A brief summary of the process

Marketing planning starts with the organization's mission and financial objectives, moves on to the marketing audit stage, which includes summaries in the form of SWOT (strengths, weaknesses, opportunities and threats for main products/markets) analyses, then progresses to making assumptions and setting draft marketing objectives and strategies for a three- to five-year period. At this stage, functional managers other than the one responsible for marketing become involved, to ensure that the organization is capable of resourcing the market's requirements. Alternative plans are considered, one is chosen and budgets are then finalized, and eventually, tactical marketing plans are prepared. Headquarters will often consolidate both the strategic plans and the tactical plans into business or corporate plans. At the start of the organization's fiscal year the tactical marketing plan is implemented and monitored via the management information system, until the whole process begins again.

This process can be represented as a circle, as shown in Figure 2.7, which obviates the question about whether the process is top down or bottom up, for clearly it is a continuous process. The process can be as formal or informal as required, depending on circumstances, but it should always combine thoroughness with creativity.

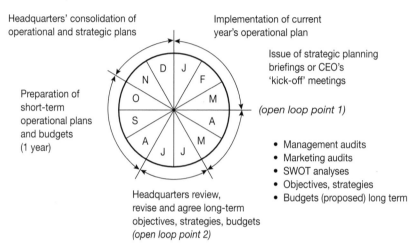

Headquarters' consolidation of operational and strategic plans

Implementation of current year's operational plan

Issue of strategic planning briefings or CEO's 'kick-off' meetings

Preparation of short-term operational plans and budgets (1 year)

(open loop point 1)

- Management audits
- Marketing audits
- SWOT analyses
- Objectives, strategies
- Budgets (proposed) long term

Headquarters review, revise and agree long-term objectives, strategies, budgets *(open loop point 2)*

Fig. 2.7   Strategic and operational planning

A strategic marketing plan should be a clear and simple summary of key market trends, key target markets, the value required by each of them, how the organization intends to create value superior to that provided by competitors, and it should clearly prioritize marketing objectives and strategies and their financial consequences.

All too often, though, strategic marketing plans are diffuse, confusing compilations of unconnected sections with a budget stuck on the end.

At Cranfield we have formally critiqued more than 200 strategic marketing plans from the strategic business units of multinational companies. Based on our analysis, the list below sets out the most frequent errors CEOs should guard against when reviewing their strategic marketing plans.

1   Market overviews contain substantially more information than is necessary, with no hint of the implications for marketing activity.
2   Key segments are rarely identified. 'Segments' are often sectors or products, rather than groups of customers with similar needs.
3   The competitive situation is not well analyzed and plans appear to assume no activity or reaction by competitors.

4 SWOT analyses rarely pin down convincingly the value that is required by segments. They are frequently too general to lead to any actionable propositions.
5 An organization's distinctive competences are rarely isolated and built on.
6 SWOT analyses are rarely summarized clearly and logically, categorizing the portfolio of products and services and the relative potential and strengths of each.
7 Marketing objectives are frequently confused with marketing strategies and do not follow logically from the portfolio summary.
8 The resource implications of effecting the marketing plans are not always clear.

Organizing for marketing planning

In Chapter 1 we included a diagram illustrating how marketing planning should be organized. This is repeated in Figure 2.8.

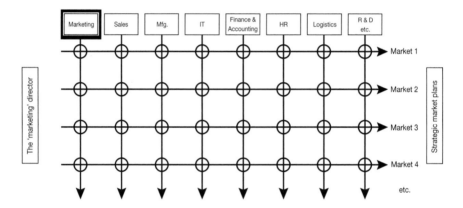

Fig. 2.8   Organizing for marketing planning

We also spelled out the advantages of doing it this way. Principal among these were:

- the involvement and buy-in of other functions to the resulting plans;
- the market-driven nature of the resulting functional plans, such as the IT plan, the R & D plan and so on;
- the market-driven nature of the resulting business or corporate plans as a result of the co-ordinated inputs of the 'marketing' director.

Providing a realistic context for strategic marketing planning

Much paper has been wasted on the topic of mission (or purpose, or vision) statements. Yet our experience of working with many of the world's best companies has taught us that organizations need some realistic guidelines as a context for strategic marketing planning, or they tend to flit from one idea to another, depending on the current fad or mood of the CEO.

Too many mission statements look like the following meaningless 'generic mission statement', which could apply to virtually any organization in the world:

> Our organization's primary mission is to protect and increase the value of its owners' investments while efficiently and fairly serving the needs of its customers. Generic plc seeks to accomplish this in a manner that contributes to the development and growth of its employees, and to the goals of countries and communities in which it operates.

The purpose of the mission statement should be to state clearly the *raison d'être* of the business unit and should briefly cover the following points:

- the role or contribution of the unit – for example, profit generator, service department, opportunity seeker;
- definition of the business – for example, the needs the unit satisfies or the benefits it provides, without being too specific or general;
- the distinctive competence of the unit – a statement that could equally apply to any competitor is unsatisfactory;
- considerations for future direction, such as a move into a new market. This should include what the organization will do, might do and will never do.

We see too many business units which plan for the wrong objective. An example of this is the case of a business unit which is really there principally for the purpose of supporting another, more profitable, unit. Making training units into profit centres is a fairly typical 'macho' response from so-called 'hard' CEOs. One CEO even made the company's library into a profit centre with the result that everyone stopped borrowing books! Units should not deliberately make a loss, of course, and there is nothing wrong with them being cost-effective, even to the point of breaking even or making a small surplus. But it is not helpful to suggest that their primary role in the business is to make a profit.

Market definition and segmentation

It is increasingly important to understand the needs of major customers, and planning to satisfy these needs can be integrated with marketing and corporate planning. But before we turn to those issues, we need to address two crucial starting points for business leaders to manage their organizations as outlined above: market definition and segmentation. It is growing increasingly difficult to define markets correctly, and creative market segmentation is becoming more and more important. These two factors, above any other, are driving corporate policy as the pace of change accelerates and business boundaries blur.

In the mid-1990s Cranfield School of Management conducted a study on the future of marketing, focusing on the challenges businesses were going to face in the new millennium. These challenges and the responses of successful companies are summarized in Boxes 2.1, 2.2, 2.3, 2.4 and 2.5.

Box 2.1

The challenge of rapid change

Pace of change
- Compressed time horizons
- Shorter product life cycles
- Transient customer preferences

Marketing challenges
- Ability to exploit markets more rapidly
- More effective new product development (NPD)
- Flexibility in approach to markets
- Accuracy in demand forecasting
- Ability to optimize price setting

Box 2.2

Refining the process

Process thinking
- Move to flexible manufacturing and control systems
- Materials substitution
- Developments in microelectronics and robotization
- Quality focus

Marketing challenges
- Dealing with microsegmentation
- Finding ways to shift from single transaction focus to the forging of long-term relationships
- Creating greater customer commitment

Box 2.3

The challenge of the marketplace

Market maturity
- Over capacity
- Low margins
- Lack of growth
- Stronger competition
- Trading down
- Cost-cutting

Marketing challenges
- Adding value leading to differentiation
- New market creation and stimulation

Box 2.4

The customer

Customers' expertise and power
- More demanding
- Higher expectations
- More knowledgeable
- Concentration of buying power
- More sophisticated buyer behaviour

Marketing challenges
- Finding ways of getting closer to the customer
- Managing the complexities of multiple market channels

Box 2.5

The international dimension

Internationalization of business
- More competitors
- Stronger competition
- Lower margins
- Larger markets
- More customer choice
- More disparate customer needs

Marketing challenges
- Restructuring of domestic operations to compete internationally
- Becoming customer-focused in larger and more disparate markets

Market definition

The problem of correctly defining markets is endemic to most industries. The days of neat markets, constrained by Standard Industrial Classification (SIC) codes, have all but disappeared. The automotive industry and its associated value chains is typical. The industry is being driven by more complex technology, stricter environmental legislation, mature markets, more sophisticated customers and globalization. This has forced it to become less vertically integrated in order to become leaner, leading to partnerships with a small number of tier-one suppliers. These tier-one suppliers are no longer just component manufacturers, but are system and integrated module suppliers, servicing their clients seamlessly on a global basis through alliances, joint ventures and acquisitions.

This leaves a massive question mark over the future direction of major corporations like SKF, the global bearings company. Does an organization like this become a tier-two, or even a tier-three supplier? The same issue faces organizations like BT: the trends suggest the possibility of such organizations becoming second-tier suppliers to service organizations which can form alliances in the value chain to deal with the entire communications problems of major companies.

This not only clouds the issue of market definition, but affects many of the long-established tenets of management education – including market share.

Market share

Most business people understand the direct relationship between relatively high share of any market and high returns on investment, as shown in Figure 2.9.

But since, for example, BMW is not in the same market as Ford, you need to be careful about how you define 'market'. Correct market definition is crucial for measuring market share and market growth, specifying target customers, recognizing relevant competitors and, most importantly, formulating marketing strategy, as it is this, above all, that delivers differential advantage.

> *... a market should be defined as all the different products or services which customers regard as being capable of satisfying a particular need.*

The general rule is that a market should be defined as all the different products or services which customers regard as being capable of satisfying a particular need. For example, the in-company caterer is only one option when it comes to satisfying lunch-time hunger. This need could also be met at external restaurants, pubs, fast-food outlets and sandwich bars. The emphasis in the definition, therefore, is clearly on the word 'need'.

But it is not just existing products that can satisfy a customer's need: new products, yet to be developed, could satisfy that need even better. For example, the button manufacturer which believed its market was the 'button market' would have been very disappointed when zips and Velcro began to satisfy the need for fastenings. Had this company adopted a needs-based definition of its market, its management would have recognized how transient current products are, and accepted that one of its principal

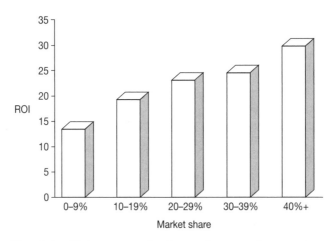

Fig. 2.9   The relationship between market share and return on investment
Source: PIMS database

tasks was to seek out better ways of satisfying its market's needs and to evolve its product offer accordingly. Likewise, Gestetner might have avoided its problems had it not defined its market as 'duplicators'. IBM, too, could have saved itself a lot of bother had it realized that mainframes were products, not markets.

To summarize, correct market definition is crucial for:

- measuring share;
- measuring growth;
- specifying target customers;
- recognizing relevant competitors;
- formulating marketing objectives and strategies.

The chairman of one – now bankrupt – European airline told his general managers that he wanted his airline to be the best in the world and to provide customer service to the point of obsession. But his airline did not compete in many markets, and the company's unfocused customer obsession policy led it to provide service it could not afford. Such heroic and woolly statements do more harm than good.

Market segmentation

Markets usually fall into natural groups or segments which contain customers who exhibit the same broad requirements. These segments form separate markets in themselves and can be quite large. Taken to its extreme, each individual consumer is a unique market segment, because everyone has different requirements.

But it is clearly uneconomical to make unique products for every individual, except in the most unusual circumstances. So products are made to appeal to groups of customers who share approximately the same needs, and there are universally accepted criteria governing what constitutes a viable market segment. For example:

- segments should be big enough to provide the company with the desired return for its effort;
- members of each segment should have very similar requirements, yet be distinct from the rest of the market;
- criteria for describing segments must be relevant to the purchase situation;
- segments must be reachable.

While these criteria might appear obvious, market segmentation is one of the most difficult marketing concepts to put into practice. But unless organizations succeed they will become just another company selling 'me too' products, with price being the purchase criterion. This can decimate profits, unless an organization happens to have lower costs, hence higher margins, than competitors.

There are three stages to market segmentation.

1   A detailed examination of the way a market operates, identifying where decisions are made about competing products or services. Successful segmentation is based on a detailed understanding of decision-makers and their requirements.
2   Looking at how customers behave in the marketplace – who is buying what?

3   Addressing why customers buy what they do and then searching for market segments based on analysis of their needs.

Once an organization clearly understands the structure of the market and how it works, segmentation should take place at each major buying decision point and a separate strategic plan should be prepared for each.

A fertilizer company that grew and prospered during the 1970s and 1980s on the back of superior products reached its farmer consumers via merchants (wholesalers). But as other companies copied the technology, the merchants began to stock competitive products and drove prices and margins down. Had the fertilizer company paid more attention to the needs of its different farmer groups and developed products especially for them, based on farmer segmentation, it would have continued to create demand pull through differentiation. As it was, its products became commodities and the power shifted almost entirely to the merchants. The company is no longer in business.

> *... segmentation consists of building a representative model of the market at each junction by recording all the unique combinations of what is bought and identifying the different customer characteristics for each of these microsegments.*

There are countless other examples of companies which, because they paid insufficient attention to the needs of users further down the value chain, eventually ceased to provide any real value to their direct customers and went out of business.

An example of excellent practice is Procter and Gamble (P & G) in the USA, which supplies, among others, WalMart, the giant food retailer. Figure 2.10 shows that P & G creates demand (hence high turnover and margins) by paying detailed attention to the needs of consumers *and* to its direct customer, WalMart. WalMart can operate on small margins because only as the bar code goes across the till does P & G invoice it, manufacture another product and activate the distribution chain – all through an integrated IT process. Procter and Gamble has reduced WalMart's costs by hundreds of millions of dollars.

In a nutshell, segmentation consists of building a representative model of the market at each buying decision point by recording all the unique combinations of what is bought and identifying the different customer characteristics for each of these microsegments. This often produces a lot of microsegments, each of which should have a volume or value figure attached. The number of microsegments can be reduced by separating the important from the unimportant features and by removing anything that is superfluous.

Fig. 2.10   Procter and Gamble's demand focus

The final step consists of looking for clusters of microsegments that share the same or similar needs and applying the company's minimum volume/value criteria.

This usually results in ten or fewer actionable segments that now form the basis of, or the inputs to, the strategic marketing planning process. (A full explanation of this procedure can be found in McDonald and Dunbar, 1998).

The following three short case histories illustrate how successful market segmentation leads to superior profitability.

Bottoms Up: how Threshers segmented its market

In the early 1990s Threshers, a top UK liquor chain with outlets in major shopping centres and local shopping parades, was experiencing a decline in both customer numbers and average spend. The original formula for success of design, product range and merchandising, meticulously copied in each outlet, no longer appeared to be working.

The chain had become a classic example of a business sitting comfortably in the middle ground, attempting to be all things to all people, but satisfying very few.

Rather than sit back in the belief that the business was just passing through a difficult patch, and what worked yesterday was bound to work again, the company embarked on a project designed to help it understand its actual and potential customer base.

The first stage of this study used one of the more sophisticated geodemographic packages (CCN's Mosaic) to understand the residential profiles of each shop's catchment area. This revealed many geodemographic differences, and the business quickly accepted that the same retail formula was unlikely to appeal to the different target markets it had identified.

Instead of looking at each shop separately, the company subjected catchment area profiles for each shop to a clustering routine in order to place similar catchment areas together. This resulted in 21 different groupings, each of which was then profiled, using purchasing data from national surveys, in terms of its potential to buy different off-licence products. (The company's own in-house retailing data would only have reflected the purchasing pattern of existing customers or, at worst, only a proportion of their requirements if these were limited by the company's existing product range.)

But stocking the requisite range of products in their correct geographical location would not necessarily attract the company's respective target markets. The chain was already associated with one type of offer which, in addition to a particular range of drinks, included the basic design of the shops and overall merchandising.

So the project moved into a second phase, in which the market's attitudes and motivations to drinking were explored and relative values attached to the various dimensions uncovered. The company commissioned an independent piece of market research to do this, and it resulted in the market being categorized into a number of psychographic groups. These included 'happy and impulsive' shoppers, 'anxious and muddled' shoppers, 'reluctant but organized' shoppers, and 'disorganized, extravagant' shoppers.

The attitudinal and motivational findings were then put together with the demographic data, allowing the original 21 clusters to be condensed into five distinct segments, each requiring a different offer. The company now had to decide between two strategies: to focus on one segment using one brand and relocate its retail outlets; *or* to develop a manageable portfolio of retailing brands, leave the estate relatively intact, and rebrand, refit and restock as necessary.

It opted for the second strategy.

Realizing that demographic profiles in geographic areas can change over time, and that customer needs and attitudes can also evolve, the company now monitors its market carefully and is prepared to modify its brand portfolio to suit changing circumstances. For the time being its five retail brands – Bottoms Up, Wine Rack, Threshers Wine Shop, Drinks Store from Threshers and Food and Drinks Store – sit comfortably within the five segments. They also sit comfortably together in the same shopping centre, enabling the group to meet effectively the different requirements of the segments within that centre's catchment area.

This strategy is also consistent with the financial targets set for the business.

Source: Based on Thornton (1993)

How STPP showed its teeth

Sodium Tri-Poly Phosphate (STPP) was once a simple, unexciting, white chemical cleaning agent. Today, one of its uses is as the major ingredient in toothpaste. The toothpaste business is sophisticated and profitable, with many different brand names competing for a share of what has become a cleverly segmented market.

Have you ever wondered how the toothpaste marketers classify you in their segmentation of the market? Table 2.4, which presents the main segments, may assist you. It is not up to date, but it is a good historical example of market segmentation.

Brewer's droop: how Amber Nectar got it wrong

A privately owned brewery in the UK – let's call it Amber Nectar – was enjoying exceptional profitability for its industrial sector, despite being far from the largest brewery in the UK and operating only within a particular metropolitan area.

Table 2.4   The segmentation of the toothpaste market

		Worrier	*Sociable*	*Sensory*	*Independent*
Who buys	Socio-economic demographics	C1, C2	B, C1, C2	C1, C2, D	A, B
	Psychographics	Large families 25–40 Conservative: hypochondriosis	Teens Young Smokers High sociability: active	Children High self-involvement: hedonists	Males 35–50 High autonomy Value oriented
What is bought	% of total market	50%	30%	15%	5%
	Product examples	Crest	Macleans Ultra Bright	Colgate (stripe)	Own label
	Product physics Price paid Outlet Purchase	Large canisters Low Supermarket	Large tubes High Supermarket	Medium tubes Medium Supermarket	Small tubes Low Independent
	frequency	Weekly	Monthly	Monthly	Quarterly
Why	Benefit sought	Stop decay	Attract attention	Flavour	Price
Potential for growth		Nil	High	Medium	Nil

Source: Adapted from Haley (1968)

At one of its regular meetings the board agreed that the company had developed a very successful range of beers and it was time to expand into new geographic areas. Other brewers, particularly the very large ones, vigorously opposed the company's expansion programme. This came as no great surprise to the board, who knew their successful range of beers would guarantee product trial and customer loyalty in the new areas. They had built up a large reserve, largely made up of past profits, to finance the expansion plan.

As in all good market-focused companies, a specially appointed task force headed by the CEO monitored the progress of the marketing plan against its target. In addition, the sales and marketing director, a key member of the task force, held regular meetings with his staff to continuously evaluate the sales and marketing strategies being followed.

The plan badly underperformed and was eventually abandoned.

In the subsequent post-mortem, the brewery discovered why it had been so successful in the past, and why this success could not be replicated in other areas of the UK. To its loyal customers, a key attraction of the brewery's beers was the 'local' flavour. The company's market was the metropolitan area it already operated in, and its competitors were other local brewers in the same area. So trying to export this success was clearly not going to work. It could only expand by setting up new local breweries in other areas, or by acquiring already established local breweries.

Without this brewer realizing it, the UK beer-drinking market had already segmented itself. This brewer's segment was the 'Regional Chauvinist', and the company already had an overwhelming market share in the particular region it operated in. Hence its profitability.

Had the company understood this segmentation structure earlier on, it would have spent its reserve more effectively and achieved its growth objectives.

Case history conclusion

The three case histories illustrate the importance of intelligent segmentation in guiding companies towards successful marketing strategies. But it is easy to be wise after the event, and defining and segmenting markets as a route to creating superior customer value presents a real challenge to most companies.

It is a challenge they must grasp, however. In today's highly competitive world, few companies can afford to compete only on price, for there is no product that someone, somewhere, cannot sell cheaper. In any case, in many markets the cheapest product rarely succeeds. So organizations have to find some way of differentiating themselves from the competition, and the answer lies in market segmentation.

... few companies can afford to compete only on price ...

Very few companies can afford to be all things to all people. The main aim of market segmentation is to enable a firm to target its marketing effort on the most promising opportunities. But an opportunity for firm A is not necessarily an opportunity for firm B, so a firm needs to develop a blueprint of the customer or segment it prefers, which can significantly help its productivity in the marketplace.

All key members of the company should clearly understand the differential benefits of its product or service.

To reiterate, market definition is crucial for:

- measuring share;
- measuring growth;
- specifying target customers;
- recognizing relevant competitors;
- formulating marketing objectives and strategies.

The objectives of market segmentation are:

- to help determine marketing direction through analyzing and understanding trends and buyer behaviour;
- to help determine realistic and obtainable marketing and sales objectives;

- to help improve decision-making by forcing managers to consider in depth the options ahead.

We go on to explore how the business leader can exploit his or her organization's marketing activities to best effect in Chapter 7.

 Checklist for CEOs of essential deliverables

CEOs should ask themselves the following questions to ensure they avoid the pitfalls listed above and to determine whether they are getting real value from their organization's marketing efforts.

Market structure and segmentation

- Is there a clear and unambiguous definition of the market we are interested in serving?
- Is it clearly mapped, showing product/service flows, volumes/values in total, our shares and critical conclusions for our organization?
- Are the segments clearly described and quantified? These must be groups of customers with the same or similar needs, not sectors.
- Are the real needs of these segments properly quantified with the relative importance of these needs clearly identified?

Differentiation

- Is there a clear and quantified analysis of how well our organization satisfies these needs compared with competitors?
- Are the opportunities and threats clearly identified by segment?

Prioritization of objectives and strategies

- Are all the segments classified according to their relative potential for growth in profits over the next three years and according to our organization's relative competitive position in each?
- Are the objectives consistent with their

position in the portfolio (volume, value, market share, profit)?

- Are the strategies (including products, services, solutions, etc.) consistent with the objectives?
- Are the key issues for action for all departments clearly spelled out as key issues to be addressed?

Value capture

- Do the objectives and strategies add up to the profit goals required by our organization?
- Does the budget follow on logically from all of the above, or is it merely an add-on?

And overall, does the marketing plan

- demonstrate a clear understanding of market structure?
- list, in order of priority, key target markets (segments)?
- describe the value that is required by each target market?
- describe how our organization creates better value than competitors?
- spell out how our organization is going to create sustainable competitive advantage (super profits)?
- Finally, is it creative, interesting and believable?

Interview: John Condron, CEO, Yell

How Yell uses marketing planning to liberate creativity

Yellow Pages is the UK's premier source of accurate, comprehensive and classified business information across a range of media. It was recently rebranded as Yell, one of BT's four operating businesses that came about as a result of its recent restructuring. John Condron joined Yellow Pages as marketing manager in 1980, and has progressed through the company, becoming managing director six years ago and, in May 2000, CEO of Yell.

When I joined Yellow Pages the marketing department comprised four people, including two clerical staff. In those days people thought you bought marketing by the metre or the kilo. Yellow Pages was a production-driven company, which concentrated on producing and selling directories. Order-taking and printing were the two main priorities, and we had no marketing strategy and we didn't understand our customer base. So the business was very back-end production-driven.

We had to reorganize the company around business priorities – that is, our customers and our customers' needs, rather than processes and products. We had to become demand driven, not supply led. Your future is with your customers' needs, not with what you produce.

As such, when I became marketing and sales director, marketing quite deliberately came before sales in the title to reflect the importance of marketing over sales. And we introduced a formal marketing planning model to help us to focus on our customers.

Our ideal scenario was to be able to provide an optimum product for every customer – their own directory designed specifically for them. But we obviously couldn't do that, so what we did was try to meet the bespoke requirements of as many different groups of customers as possible. We had been segmenting our market by customer group (primarily business and domestic) and geography (regional boundaries) for years. But we started separating out products from the generic business. For example, the industrial business-to-business market had many different needs from the business-to-consumer market, and the direct marketing industry had its own particular requirements, so we opened the Business Database, which specialized in a whole new range of data products.

Once we had done that segmentation we had to change the way the business was run. Instead of the very blanket approach the sales team used to take, marketing started to direct the sales operation to sell products that marketing had identified as being relevant for particular target markets.

The sales force were understandably suspicious – and not a little resentful – when we told them who they should be targeting. They had rough and calloused hands from ten years' experience out in the field, whereas we were the new boys. We had to work hard to convince them that we were right, and that by following our lead they would sell more and therefore earn more.

At that stage many people took the view that marketing and strategic business plans were interesting documents, but they tended to languish in a drawer while the sales force carried on as they had before.

To overcome that resistance we worked very hard to get all the business operations, including sales and production, to buy in to the marketing planning process in order to secure the commitment of the whole organization to what we were collectively trying to do. So the sales manager and the production manager had to sign off the marketing plan, and the marketing manager had to sign off the sales plan. The overall aim was to have a strategic, as well as a tactical, view of where our business was going – what were we going to do next year and the year after that, and what were the key marketplace trends that were going to influence us?

We adopted a very disciplined and rational approach to marketing planning, analyzing and segmenting our customer base. A clear and scientific approach to our markets allowed us to chart the demographic changes that were happening, and as a result make our product offerings more relevant than they had been in the past. We redesigned our business model from being based on where people lived to where they went to buy: there had been a big growth in out-of-town shopping malls, for instance. And we were able to plot the rise of the financial services and other key sectors.

The sales force started to realize that marketing planning worked: it saved them more customers, it earned them more money, and the things they sold the year before worked, so the customers saw the benefits too. The sales force were then able to feed back information into the marketing planning process.

And the marketing planning process is ongoing: it doesn't have a beginning and an end. We set ourselves the target that on any Monday morning I could walk in and ask to see an updated marketing plan on a Friday. So our marketing plan was being continually refreshed to take account of changing customer requirements.

The budget is just one output from the planning process. Planning is to do with predicting and dealing with customer requirements on a daily basis. Marketing planning directs our product development people by, for example, highlighting what we believe are going to be the next key sectors, and the sales force goes out and sells to those target customers.

Selling more to current customers is more cost-effective than winning new customers, but you have to sell to new customers too to grow your business. You need a balance, and a sensible approach to good financial husbandry.

One of the early lessons we learned was to integrate marketing planning into strategic business planning. We used to have marketing planning standing alone in the marketing department. But having a separate marketing plan is counter-productive: it confirms the prejudice that marketing is a luxury and it reinforces 'Marketing' as a functional silo. Marketing planning *has* to feed into strategic business planning. Equally important is to integrate planning into implementation – which is why it is so critical to have all the support structures and services buying into and signing off plans. You have to build in implementation at every stage – what and when and how are you going to deliver, and with what resources?

We took marketing out of the marketing department and put it into the business at large. Our marketing department now comprises a specific set of disciplines, and everyone in the organization is involved in developing the strategic marketing plan.

A key measure of the success of this business is that everyone feels part of marketing – or 'customer improvement'. Feedback shows that 96 per cent of employees (and that figure is growing all the time) feel that improving the customer's position is part of their everyday job.

Our objective is to increase long-term shareholder value, and you only do that by supplying customers' needs in a cost-effective way. Strategic marketing planning allows you to direct your resources in order to achieve that. We have had much higher customer retention across our product portfolio, and our cost base has certainly benefited from targeted marketing.

Our core belief is that we have to organize around customers today and tomorrow, while practising sound financial husbandry. We use the balanced scorecard approach to manage our competing interests to the end of creating long-term sustainable stakeholder value. But we think 'customers', not 'profits', because profit accrues from putting your customers first. You need good business disciplines, but the first and critical step is to know your customers and to get very close to them. You stick together. Our job is about building customers' businesses with them.

We won the European Quality Award this year, and the judges kept coming back to our disciplined approach to our markets. We use the marketing planning process not to constrain or choke people but to free them of mundane tasks and liberate their creativity.

Yellow Pages has always been managed as a separate organization within BT, but the new restructuring gives us more focus. It will also show shareholders the value that has been hidden away inside our business – Yellow Pages has been a jewel in BT's crown for years, not least because of the way we have organized our business around our customers and markets.

References and further reading

Davidson, H. (1997) *Even More Offensive Marketing*. Harmondsworth: Penguin.

Haley, R. (1968) 'Benefit segmentation: a decision-oriented research tool', *Journal of Marketing*, 32, July.

McDonald, M. and Dunbar, I. (1998) *Market Segmentation: How to Do It; How to Profit from It*. London: Macmillan.

Porter, M. (1980) *Competition Strategy*. New York: The Free Press.

Thornton, J. (1993) 'Market segmentation from Bottoms Up', *Research Plus*, December.

3

Building bridges: the relationship management process

Organizations must understand that their relationship-building activities directed at customers are necessary but not sufficient on their own. The organization also needs to identify the other relevant market domains and the groups or segments within them and to develop strategies for all of them.

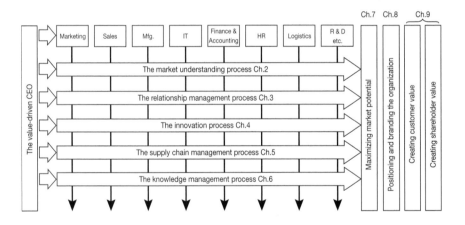

Fig. 3.1 Model of the value-creating process and relevant chapters in this book

This chapter is about how the CEO and the board should manage relationships with stakeholders. While the focus of both this chapter and the book is on customers, other stakeholders play an important role in 'creating a company for customers'.

Any organization has a large and diverse range of stakeholders. These include suppliers, the financial community, employees, customers, the government, trade unions, environmentalists, alliance partners, and so on. As we pointed out in Chapter 1, business leaders have a key role to play in managing these relationships in order to maximize customer and shareholder value.

But though ultimate responsibility for managing these groups lies with the CEO, in practice they are typically managed on a day-to-day basis within different parts of the organization. For example, the marketing department tends to be 'responsible' for customers, the purchasing department for suppliers and the finance department for managing relations with the financial community. The human resources department, in conjunction with line management, manages relationships with internal staff, potential recruits, unions and so on, while it falls to the public relations and corporate affairs departments to manage many of the other external stakeholders. Because so many different parts of the organization are involved, the various stakeholder groups tend to be managed in an unco-ordinated, disparate manner with the result that customer and shareholder value is not maximized.

> **Because so many different parts of the organization are involved, the various stakeholder groups tend to be managed in an unco-ordinated, disparate manner with the result that customer and shareholder value is not maximized.**

Some marketing practitioners use the term 'relationship marketing' to describe the management of these relationships. The use of this term begs two important issues. First, you can only optimize relationships with customers if you understand and manage relationships with other stakeholders. Most businesses appreciate the critical role their employees play in delivering superior customer value, but other stakeholders may also play an important part. Second, the tools and techniques used in marketing to customers, such as marketing planning and market segmentation, which we explained in Chapter 2, can also be used effectively in managing non-customer relationships. This broad concept of marketing has been endorsed by many leading business pundits including Philip Kotler, the US marketing expert.

It is familiar among the marketing fraternity, but the term 'relationship marketing' may not be the best descriptor, for a general audience, of the management of relationships with all these stakeholders. This is especially so in the context of pan-company marketing (making everyone in the company customer focused, as we described in Chapter 1), as the term might be taken to imply all these stakeholders should be managed by the marketing department, rather than on a cross-functional basis. Accordingly, a CEO may wish to use the term 'relationship management' to describe the management of his or her different stakeholders.

However, for the purposes of this book, we will use the term 'relationship marketing' to describe a customer-driven approach to managing an organization's stakeholder groups and the application of marketing tools to them. We consider that using the term in this context is justified because it emphasizes the use of marketing tools to manage relationships with a wide range of stakeholders, and because it is gaining increasing acceptance – more than six books have now been written advocating this approach and using this term. Ultimately, though, it is up to the individual business leader to use a term they feel comfortable with when describing the way their organization manages its stakeholders.

What is relationship marketing?

Before examining the way to build relationships with these stakeholders in greater detail, let us look at the concept of relationship marketing.

Increasingly the transactional approach to marketing, with its short-term focus on the 'sale' and on the 'acquisition' of customers, is being challenged. There are a number of reasons for this: relationships are built over time, products and services are becoming more complex and bespoke, interdependencies between customers and suppliers are intensifying and the competitive environment is growing increasingly global.

Since the 1950s the formal study of marketing has evolved across a range of sectors, as shown in Figure 3.2. In the 1950s, marketing interest focused primarily on consumer goods. In the 1960s, interest also started to be directed at industrial markets. In the 1970s, considerable attention started to be paid to non-profit or 'societal marketing'. In the 1980s, services came into the marketing limelight – an area that hitherto had received remarkably little attention, given its importance to the overall economy. And then, in the 1990s, a new emphasis started to emerge – relationship marketing – to be followed a few years later by customer relationship management, or CRM. Some consider relationship marketing and CRM to be identical, but we believe CRM is best described as 'relationship marketing enabled through information technology'.

> *Marketing should not begin and end with clinching the deal – it must also concern itself with maintaining and improving the relationship with the customer.*

One of the key themes of relationship marketing is that attracting new customers is only the first step in the marketing process. The critical factor is retaining that customer. Marketing should not begin and end with clinching the deal – it must also concern itself with maintaining and improving the relationship with the customer. It is this focus on customer retention that distinguishes relationship marketing from traditional marketing approaches which concentrate on customer acquisition.

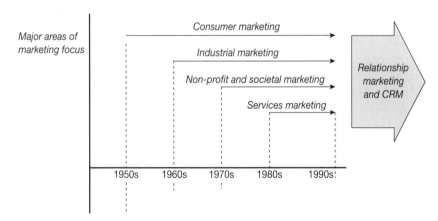

Fig. 3.2   The changing focus of marketing

The purpose of relationship marketing strategy is to shape the market in your favour – indeed, to create the market if necessary. Relationship marketing, and its association with quality and customer service, seeks to create enough value in the sale to bring customers back for more. That may sound similar to any other form of marketing, but though it may be so in theory, it is not necessarily so in practice. The strategic emphasis in relationship marketing is as much on keeping customers as it is on attracting them in the first place.

The key elements of this relationship marketing approach include the following:

- The emphasis in the interaction between supplier and customer shifts from a transaction focus to a relationship focus. Box 3.1 illustrates the main differences between these two approaches.
- The relationship marketing approach focuses on maximizing the lifetime value of desirable customers and customer segments.
- Relationship marketing is concerned with developing and enhancing relationships with six 'key markets' or market domains. It is concerned with the 'internal market' within the organization, as well as with building substantial external relationships with customers, suppliers, referral sources, influence markets and recruitment markets – all of which are explained later in this chapter.
- Functionally based marketing within the company is replaced by cross-functionally based marketing focused on customer needs.
- Quality, customer service and marketing are closely related, but they are frequently managed separately. A relationship marketing strategy makes these elements much more integrated.

Box 3.1

Transaction versus relationship marketing

Transaction focus	Relationship focus
Orientation to single sales	Orientation to customer retention
Discontinuous customer contact	Continuous customer contact
Focus on product features	Focus on customer value
Short time scale	Long time scale
Little emphasis on customer service	High customer service emphasis
Limited commitment to meeting customer expectations	High commitment to meeting customer expectations
Quality is the concern of production staff	Quality is the concern of all staff

Implementing relationship marketing strategies requires managers to go beyond their traditional functional roles. They need to take a broader perspective and develop stronger cross-functional capabilities in order to develop much closer relationships between suppliers, internal staff, customers and other relevant markets. Reorienting thinking and actions towards building a more relationship-oriented and customer-focused organization represents a significant challenge for senior managers.

The role of multiple stakeholders

Some companies adopt a strong integrated relationship approach to managing their stakeholders, but they are in the minority. However, we will start to see growing numbers of companies applying relationship marketing to non-customer stakeholders as the decade unfolds.

Philip Kotler (1992) has proposed a new view of organizational performance and success, based on relationships, whereby the traditional marketing approach – based on the marketing mix – is not replaced, but is 'repositioned as the toolbox for understanding and responding to all the significant players in the company's environment'. He outlines the importance of the relationship approach to stakeholders:

> The consensus in American business is growing: if US companies are to compete successfully in domestic and global markets, they must engineer stronger bonds with their stakeholders, including customers, distributors, suppliers, employees, unions, governments, and other critical players in the environment. Common practices such as whipsawing suppliers for better prices, dictating terms to distributors, and treating employees as a cost rather than an asset, must end. Companies must move from a short-term *transaction-orientated* goal to a long-term *relationship-building* goal. (Kotler, 1992)

Kotler's comments underscore the need for an integrated framework for understanding these relationships. In many large industrial organizations, marketing is still viewed as a set of related but compartmentalized activities that are separate from the rest of the company. Relationship marketing seeks to change this perspective by managing the competing interests of customers, staff, shareholders and other stakeholders. It redefines the concept of 'a market' more broadly as being one in which the competing interests are made visible and therefore more likely to be managed. (For an excellent example of how one company manages its relationships with its stakeholder markets, turn to the interview with Mike Hodgkinson, CEO of BAA, at the end of this chapter.)

Relationship marketing emphasizes building stronger relationships between the organization and all its stakeholder markets.

The six markets framework

Relationship marketing emphasizes building stronger relationships between the organization and all its stakeholder markets. In this new millennium, organizations need to place greater emphasis on fundamental issues such as understanding the dynamics of these markets and identifying the critical features which not only influence and drive a company's strategy but also affect its competitive position. The six markets framework, shown in Figure 3.3, illustrates the key stakeholder 'markets' or market domains where business leaders need to review their companies' performance.

Fig. 3.3   The six markets framework

While these market domains are interdependent, they vary in importance. For most organizations, three groups – customers, employees (internal markets) and shareholders (the dominant group within the influence market) – are especially critical. We will address the importance of shareholders later in this chapter and again in Chapter 9. Let us now look at these six markets in more detail.

Customer markets

There is no doubt that the customer is and should be the primary focus of marketing. But organizations need to work harder at marketing to existing customers. Those companies focusing their marketing activities on new customers often experience the 'leaking bucket' effect, where existing customers defect because too little marketing activity generally, and customer service specifically, is directed at them.

Too often organizations assume that long-term customers stay with them because they like them and are loyal to them, when in fact those customers are disaffected but stay because of inertia. Too many companies, once they have secured a customer's order, turn their attention to seeking new customers without understanding the importance of maintaining and enhancing the relationships with their existing customers. New customers are vital, of course, but a balance needs to be struck between the effort directed towards existing and new customers. We shall discuss this issue in greater detail in Chapter 9.

Internal markets

Many organizations overlook the important collaborative role marketing can play, in conjunction with operations and HR, in improving the internal exchange processes.

In reviewing internal markets we need to consider two aspects. First, every employee and every department in an organization is both an internal customer and/or an internal supplier. So organizations need to work as effectively as possible to ensure that every department and individual provides and receives high standards of internal service.

Second, all staff must work together in a way that is aligned to the organization's mission, strategy and goals. Here internal marketing should ensure that all staff 'live the brand' by representing the organization as well as possible, whether face to face, over the phone, by mail or electronically.

The structure of the organization can severely impede the development of customer relationships. Traditional vertical organizations with a hierarchical structure and functional orientation often favour individual functions at the expense of the whole business and the customer. Relationship marketing, with its emphasis on cross-functional marketing, focuses on the processes that deliver value for the customer. These processes cut across functions, and in customer-facing organizations key players are drawn together in multidisciplinary teams which marshal resources to achieve customer-based objectives. Managing an organization that is focused on the customer involves a strong emphasis on internal marketing.

The fundamental aims of internal marketing are to develop awareness among employees of both internal and external customers, and to remove functional barriers to organizational effectiveness. Because internal marketing is increasingly being recognized as an important activity in developing a customer-focused organization, we provide two short examples here: Woolworths and Virgin Atlantic.

How Woolworths sold its strategy to staff

High street retailer Woolworths recognized a long time ago the need to engage its employees in building the Woolworths brand, and has invested in a number of internal marketing programmes to this end over the past four years. These include a communications cascade, involving all UK employees, to promote the organization's mission and core values, and a brand development programme which, together with customer research, used many of the company's front-line employees to formulate the new brand proposition.

Woolworths recently embarked on a 'brand engagement' programme to communicate the new brand proposition and promote a deeper understanding of customer needs among key members of staff. The first challenge was to express the brand proposition in a way that non-marketing people could understand and use. The company achieved this by explaining the Woolworths brand promises in the context of what customers need and how they choose between different retailers to fulfil those needs. Answering the simple questions 'how can we be better?' and 'how can we be different?' lies at the heart of most successful brand engagement programmes.

The next step was to ensure that everyone understood the implications of the Woolworths brand promise, both for their own role and for all aspects of managing the customer's experience, including range, price, presentation, service and store environment.

While it is important that key messages are clearly understood, Woolworths recognized that you cannot rely purely on rationally presenting the facts to motivate and enthuse people. To win its employees' emotional engagement, Woolworths tried to communicate key messages in as direct and personal a way as possible. This involved using informal feedback to allow customers to express their perceptions of Woolworths and its competitors directly to the audience, and a series of interactive activities designed to encourage staff to find their own personal connection with the Woolworths brand vision.

To help embed the brand message and ensure that the brand strategy evolves consistently over time, Woolworths has produced a 'brand growth toolkit' which it has distributed via a range of media, including CD-Rom and the company's intranet.

How Virgin Atlantic bucked the airline trend

Virgin Atlantic Airways remains the biggest and most profitable part of the Virgin Group. One of the secrets of Virgin Atlantic's success has been enthusiastic, empowered, motivated employees. Richard Branson has said: 'I want employees in the airline to feel that it is *they* who can make the difference, and influence what passengers get.' So successful was Branson's strategy towards employees that the airline has attracted quality staff despite paying relatively low salaries. In management's eyes, the ideal employee was 'informal but caring' – young, vibrant, interested, courteous and willing to go out of his or her way to help customers. Branson explained:

> We aren't interested in having just happy employees. We want employees who feel involved and prepared to express dissatisfaction when necessary. In fact, we think that the constructively dissatisfied employee is an asset we should encourage and we need an organization that allows us to do this – and that encourages employees to take responsibility, since I don't believe it is enough for us simply to give it.

Virgin Atlantic's philosophy has been to stimulate the individual, to encourage staff to take initiatives and to empower them to do so. Staff often provide insights into what customers want or need – sometimes anticipating their expectations.

And Branson and his executives are open to suggestions from staff and to innovation, talking and listening and being inquisitive about all aspects of the business. Staff find Branson's constant presence motivating, seeing it as testimony to his interest and involvement in the business.

Referral markets

There are two broad types of referral market – existing customers and other referral sources. Perhaps the best form of marketing is where the customers do the marketing on the organization's behalf. Referrals from existing customers are an effective source of new business and creating referrals through strong word-of-mouth marketing is an important way of developing relationships with new customers.

In addition to existing customers, there are other sources of referral. An accounting firm, for example, can significantly boost its business from new customers introduced by banks, law firms and accounting firms operating in other geographic areas. Marketing to such referral markets represents a powerful way to build the business.

Organizations need to start by recognizing their key referral sources. They should then identify the present and likely future importance of these sources and develop a specific plan to determine the appropriate levels of marketing resources that should be devoted to each of them. But the benefits of such marketing activity may take some time to come to fruition.

Supplier markets

Supplier markets include both traditional suppliers and alliance partners. The historic approach by many organizations has been to try to get the best price from suppliers. This has often proved false economy, as both supply and quality often suffer as a consequence. But organizations' relationships with their suppliers seem to be undergoing a sea change. The old adversarial relationship, where a company tried to squeeze its suppliers to its own advantage, is giving way to one based more on partnership and collaboration. This approach fosters close long-term relationships and a 'win-win' philosophy rather than the 'win-lose' philosophy inherent in adversarial relationships.

> **Organizations need to start by recognizing their key referral sources.**

In a sense, alliance partners are suppliers too. The difference is that typically they supply capabilities and competencies which are usually knowledge rather than product based. They may also provide services. These alliances often arise in response to companies' perceived need to outsource an activity within its value chain.

Partnership and collaboration makes good commercial sense for most organizations. Long-term commitment to a supplier, based upon a mutually profitable relationship, brings a number of benefits. These include: enhanced product and service quality and a focus on continuous improvement; a greater likelihood of supplier-driven product and process innovation; lower total costs through supply chain integration; and higher levels of responsiveness.

Some companies now talk of the 'extended enterprise' in which very close relationships are developed with a much smaller supplier base, encouraging greater competition in the marketplace. As companies forge these closer relationships and alliances, the concept of companies competing is being replaced by the concept of 'supply chains' competing. We will discuss this in greater detail in Chapter 5.

Recruitment markets

Organizations increasingly are recognizing their people as being the most crucial resource in business. In order to attract and retain the highest quality recruits – those who share the organization's values and will make a major contribution to its future success – firms have to market themselves to potential employees, or the recruitment market. This involves creating an appropriate organizational climate, and then communicating the benefits of that organization. Where staff represent a key element of competitive advantage, such as in many service businesses, effective marketing to recruitment markets is essential to secure a constant supply of high-quality recruits.

A number of studies have highlighted the impact of recruitment practices on company performance. Many companies have learned to their cost that the shortage of skilled people is a bigger impediment to success than shortage of other resources such as capital or raw materials. Where there is a dearth of high-calibre recruits, some firms are turning to their own staff to suggest potential applicants, offering substantial payments as inducements. Andersen Consulting and Cisco, for example, both successfully use staff recommendations as part of their recruitment process.

Organizations need to market themselves in a way that attracts the calibre of person that matches the image of the firm they want to project to customers. More and more companies are now identifying a psychometric profile of the type of employee most likely to be successful in achieving customer-driven goals. The recruitment process itself is also an opportunity for the company to build a positive image with new recruits.

Influence markets

Influence markets include individuals and organizations which may have a positive or negative impact on the activities of the company. The most critical of these for any listed company is shareholders. This group, together with other members of the financial community – brokers, analysts, financial journalists and so on – is of special interest to the CEO. Analysts, in particular, have a major impact on shareholder value because of their influence on the investment community.

There is a whole range of potential sources of influence, including local and national government, standards bodies, consumer associations, environmentalists, environmental control authorities, user groups, industry bodies, regulatory authorities and the local community.

Companies need to market themselves to all relevant influence markets, but the relative importance of different groups within the influence market domain will vary from time to time. For example, a bank faced with fraud or insider dealing may suddenly find the press, regulatory bodies and central bank at the top of its influence market agenda. Barings found itself in this position a few years ago following the Nick

Leeson affair in Singapore. Similarly, actions by Greenpeace and other environmentalists over the Brent Spar offshore drilling platform brought environmentalists to the top of Shell's agenda.

Companies have tended to view public relations as a separate activity from mainstream marketing, but under the relationship marketing approach, the influence market – which is essentially public relations (PR) – is an integral component of the relationship-building process.

> *When companies do not manage their customer market properly, the likely outcome is obvious – falling sales and profits.*

Influence markets are a diverse group that need to be managed carefully in order to either maximize their positive value or minimize the negative impact they can have on an organization's activities. Every organization can benefit, and lose, as a result of the considerable influence these sources may wield. A business leader needs to identify the main influence markets for his or her organization and develop an appropriate market plan for them.

Failing to manage the six markets

When companies do not manage their customer market properly, the likely outcome is obvious – falling sales and profits. The impact of failing to manage other key markets may be less obvious, or at least slower to manifest itself. Some organizations may fail to manage just one of the six market domains, as the Ratners case study demonstrates. Others may neglect to manage their relationships within several of the six market domains, as the Fisons case study illustrates.

How Ratners lost its lustre

During the 1980s Ratner Group grew to become one of the world's leading jewellers. It developed a highly distinctive, volume-oriented approach to marketing jewellery and embarked on an ambitious acquisition-led growth programme. In 1991 chairman Gerald Ratner achieved notoriety when part of a speech he made at the Institute of Directors, in which he described one of his products as 'total crap', appeared on the front page of the *Sun* newspaper. Ratner was also reported as saying his products had 'very little to do with quality', and that one – an imitation book – was in 'the worst possible taste'. This episode contributed to a rapid downturn in Ratner Group's fortunes, and Gerald Ratner resigned. The new chairman, James McAdam, faced major difficulties in trying to turn the company around in the face of hostile shareholders and former customers.

This example represents one of the most visible mistakes a company chairman has made in recent years. By describing his product as 'total crap' Ratner alienated many constituents within the referral and influence market domains. The coverage of Gerald Ratner's negative comments about his own company were widely reported throughout the media. Inevitably this also created negative word-of-mouth publicity among previously loyal customers.

How Fisons fell from grace

Fisons, a mini-conglomerate operating in a range of sectors including agri-chemicals, pharmaceuticals, scientific equipment and horticulture, was once regarded as a superbly managed company.

In the early 1990s Fisons encountered problems in its horticultural business. Concern among members of its influence market that it was exploiting its large peat deposits led to the formation of the Peatlands Campaign. This involved ten highly influential conservation groups and was led by the Prince of Wales who called on gardeners to boycott some of Fisons' products. The campaign mounted: 34 local authorities publicly supported a boycott of peat products and B&Q, Britain's largest DIY and gardening chain, announced that on conservation grounds it had decided to ban all peat cut from Sites of Special Scientific Interest.

Further problems then occurred within Fisons' pharmaceuticals division, including delayed approval of drugs from the US Federal Drugs Administration.

Two years later institutions were questioning the board's failure to manage effectively both its business and its investor relations, and share prices plummeted.

This example provides a good insight into how a company's relationships with a wide range of markets broke down. These included shareholders, the business press, the financial press, the popular press, city analysts, environmentalists, and local and central government. Fisons also failed to manage its internal affairs in terms of the quality of new product development, thus losing face with the Federal Drugs Administration – a critical influence market which had to approve Fisons' drugs.

These two case studies illustrate the penalties in managing stakeholder markets badly. In the Ratners case, failing to manage strategic credibility before and after the debacle, together with an inappropriate and incomplete recovery programme, led to a massive decline in the group's fortunes. And Fisons destroyed relationships within a large number of key stakeholder markets: it upset shareholders, the financial press, environmentalists and regulatory bodies, and disenfranchized customers and even its own staff.

Assess your own performance in managing the six markets

As we have explained, relationship marketing involves not just establishing better relationships with customers but also developing and enhancing relationships with other key market domains. All businesses should aim to build a strong position in each of these six markets, but the precise emphasis they give to each should reflect their relative importance. The appropriate level of attention and resources can be determined through the following steps.

1   Identify key participants, or 'market' segments, in each of the markets.
2   Undertake research to identify the expectations and requirements of key participants.
3   Review the current and proposed level of emphasis in each market.
4   Formulate a desired relationship strategy and determine whether a formal market plan is necessary.

Box 3.2 shows an analysis of the key participants in each of the six markets for the property division of BAA.

Box 3.2

BAA: a review of key market participants

Customer markets
Existing
- airlines;
- utility services;
- freight forwarders;
- cargo handlers;
- hotels.

New
- off market airlines;
- new airlines;
- international airports;
- logistics/integrators;
- development around airports.

Internal markets
- marketing 'property' to BAA group.

Referral markets
- existing satisfied BAA customers;
- other airport people;
- business advisers/surveyors;
- property consultants/surveyors.

▶

Supplier markets
- framework suppliers;
- consultants;
- contractors;
- international suppliers.

Recruitment markets
- employment agencies;
- headhunters/search firms;
- graduates;
- internal transfers.

Influence markets
- shareholders;
- city analysts/stockbrokers;
- business press;
- general press and media;
- regulator;
- government;
- local authorities.

The relationship marketing network diagram, or 'spidergram' framework, shown in Figure 3.4, enables an analysis to be made of the current and desired emphasis on each of the six markets. Companies need to divide customers into new and existing categories to avoid placing all their emphasis on getting new customers at the expense of keeping existing ones.

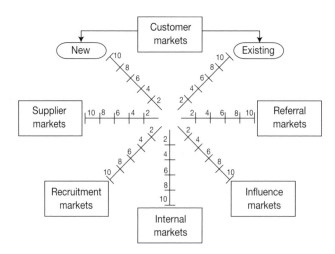

Fig. 3.4   Current and desired emphasis on six relationship markets

The following case study of British Airways illustrates how this framework can be used to review the existing and proposed relationships within each of the six markets.

British Airways puts its customers first – again!

In the mid-1970s British Airways was in poor shape. Its financial position was terrible and it lacked market focus. Following the appointment of Lord King and (now Sir) Colin Marshall, as chairman and chief executive respectively, in the 1980s, a revolution took place in BA. The new management placed considerable emphasis on the internal market and all staff went through a series of customer care programmes with names like 'Putting the customer first'. Towards the end of the 1980s, BA recognized the importance of retaining customers and this led to a number of initiatives aimed at retention, including the 'Latitudes' and 'Airmiles' programmes. Marketing to existing and new customers, travel agents and other referral markets improved greatly. The advertising agency Saatchi & Saatchi developed a series of outstanding global television commercials aimed at many of the relationship markets.

Between 1987 and 1995 profits rose from £173 million to £618 million. An external review using the six markets framework, based on the views of a number of people including former executives in BA, is shown in Figure 3.5. It represents a view of developments in BA in the mid-1990s.

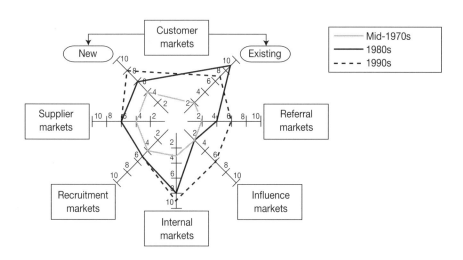

Fig. 3.5   BA and its relationship markets

At the time BA might have considered a number of issues in its relationship markets, as shown in '1990s' in the diagram. These included:

- paying greater attention to gaining new customers (BA had placed much emphasis on customer retention. Should more attention now be directed at new customers?);
- paying greater attention to 'influence markets' – especially government. (Around this time several US carriers had been granted rights to Heathrow slots, Margaret Thatcher, with whom Lord King had a close relationship, had been replaced as Prime Minister, and BA had failed to fully integrate with its North American airline partners. This raises the obvious question: could BA have forged stronger influence relationships in the past with governments, US regulators and so on?);
- reinforcing customer care and service quality issues with internal staff.

By the end of the 1990s, BA faced difficulties, including declining profits. The company sought to address its problems with a number of initiatives in 1999 and 2000, including a cost reduction programme, upgrading business-class seats to provide horizontal bedding and a major new internal marketing programme – 'Putting the customer first – again' – for all employees.

This review of relationships for the six market domains represents the first level of the diagnostic process that a business leader needs to make an initial judgement about the existing and desired emphasis for each market. The second level of analysis explores each market domain in much greater detail, right down to the existing and desired emphasis for each group or segment within each of the market domains.

Further spidergrams can then be developed for each of the six market domains. This is especially important for influence markets, in which, as we noted above, shareholders are often a critically important group, to the extent that their impact usually needs to be considered separately.

Figure 3.6 shows a spidergram for one market domain – the referral market – of one of the top accounting firms. It illustrates five key referral markets identified by the firm: existing satisfied clients, the firm's audit practice, banks, joint venture candidates and offices of its international practice. The firm concluded that although it was doing a satisfactory job for its audit practice and banks, it could improve referrals by putting more emphasis on the other three areas.

The two levels of analysis described above identify the key groups or segments in each market domain and provide an initial view on the existing and potential levels of marketing emphasis within them. The final two steps involve researching the expectations and needs of the key segments and then determining appropriate market strategies for each of them, including whether or not they need a detailed marketing plan. The organization can then decide whether it needs to develop a formal marketing plan for each market domain and/or for specific groups within the domains.

The marketing planning process for customers, which we discussed in Chapter 2, can also be applied to each of the other five markets. Not all six market domains – customer, referral, supplier, recruitment, influence and internal – necessarily need

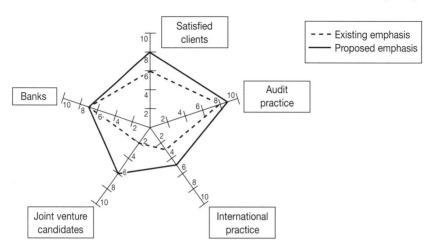

Fig. 3.6   Referral market review for a top accounting firm

their own formal written marketing plan, though some organizations may find it useful to develop them. But companies need to develop some form of market strategy to address each of them.

Relationship value management

Much of what has been written about determining, creating and delivering value has focused on the customer. But as we have pointed out, to maximize both customer and shareholder value organizations also need to address relationships with other relevant stakeholders.

The stakeholders described in the six markets framework are highly interdependent. The 'relationship management value model', shown in Figure 3.7, demonstrates how the value-creation process has linkages with specific stakeholders.

Every stakeholder in the six markets model plays a potential role in creating value. But as we said earlier, for most organizations three groups are especially important: customers, employees and external stakeholders – of whom shareholders are a key group in public companies and whom we discuss in greater detail in Chapter 9.

The relationship management value model provides a structure for business leaders to consider the value process within their organizations. The first stage is *to determine the value proposition*. This is likely to involve talking to customers and employees about what customers value in the organization's offering. New products may be the result of innovation that has not involved the customer, but it is increasingly being argued that even new products should involve the customer at each stage of development. Innovation plays a critical role in the delivery of value, and we discuss it in greater detail in Chapter 4.

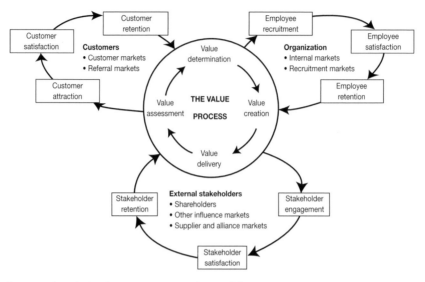

Fig. 3.7   The relationship management value model

The next stage is *to create the value offer*. This is likely to involve employees and other stakeholders, such as suppliers, and will take fully into account the value proposition determined by the customer. Next, *delivering the value* will involve engaging employees and external stakeholders and deciding how best to meet the customer's requirements in terms of maximizing value to them. These stages are likely to involve changes and improvements in both the organization's processes and service.

Finally, there is a *value assessment* stage. Many companies already monitor customer satisfaction and service quality but, while they should continue to do this, knowledge gained from these processes should be combined with knowledge gained during the value determination stage to ensure received value matches the value that was expected.

The linkage model

We have advocated above that business leaders adopt an integrated approach to creating value in their organizations and have shown how three key markets, employees, customers, and shareholders, are especially important in this process. But how are they related? Figure 3.8 shows the employee-customer-profit chain, or 'linkage model', which depicts the sequential roles employees and customers play in creating shareholder value. This reflects the practice of many leading service organizations. For example, Bill Marriott Jnr, chairman of Marriott Hotels, is a strong exponent of the need for the business to satisfy the three key groups of customers, employees and shareholders.

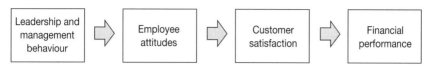

Fig. 3.8   The linkage model

Many service experts believe that employee satisfaction should be ranked first among these, because employee satisfaction drives customer and ultimately shareholder satisfaction. Frederick Reichheld, a partner in US consulting firm Bain and Company, and the author of the book *The Loyalty Effect* (Reichheld, 1996), argues that these three key stakeholders – employees, customers and shareholders – are the 'forces of loyalty'. So while other stakeholders can have a major role to play, these three are central to achieving success.

> *Adopting a relationship philosophy is just as important as developing a written strategy or plan.*

The logic in Figure 3.8 argues that an improvement in leadership and management behaviour has a positive impact on employee attitudes and employee satisfaction. The more satisfied and motivated an employee, the longer they are likely to stay with an organization and the better they will do their job. This will have a positive effect on customer satisfaction, so customers will stay longer and generate higher sales for the company. The result is strong profitability and increasing shareholder value.

> *A formal marketing plan for an internal market is of little value if customer contact staff are not motivated and empowered to deliver the level of service quality required.*

But it is not clear, for any given organization, how much one variable needs to improve to achieve a given level of improvement in another variable. For example, if employee attitudes and satisfaction increase by a measurable amount, what impact will this have on customer satisfaction and resulting profitability? We shall return to this issue in Chapter 9 which examines the value creation process in greater detail.

Summary

This chapter has focused on how the business leader should manage the relationship with his or her organization's stakeholders – an approach we have called 'relationship marketing'.

Relationship marketing extends the management of stakeholders beyond customers, and involves developing a cross-functional approach to managing relationships in six key market domains.

Companies need to give high priority to managing relationships with these stakeholders to create enhanced value. The most critical of these are employee value, customer value and shareholder value and there is a direct linkage between them. We shall examine value creation in greater detail in Chapter 9.

Adopting a relationship philosophy is just as important as developing a written strategy or plan. A formal marketing plan for an internal market is of little value if customer contact staff are not motivated and empowered to deliver the level of service quality required. The needs of members of all these markets need to be addressed in exactly the same way as those of customer markets.

> *The needs of members of all ... markets need to be addressed in exactly the same way as those of customer markets.*

We have used the six markets model in over 50 different organizations to develop plans for the six market domains and for segments within them. From this work it is clear that organizations must understand that their relationship-building activities directed at customers are necessary but not sufficient on their own. The organization also needs to identify the other relevant market domains and the groups or segments within them, and to develop strategies for all of them.

Checklist for CEOs

The CEO needs to ask him/herself the following questions.

Customer markets

- Do we achieve the right balance in our marketing efforts between existing and new customers?
- Do our marketing efforts in terms of money and executive time reflect this balance?

Internal markets

- Is every individual and unit within the organization seen as both a supplier and a customer?
- Are our internal staff oriented to the firm's mission?
- Do all our staff understand the importance of our customers?

Referral markets

- To what extent do we get referrals from existing customers?
- Do we market to all other prospective referral sources and third party intermediaries?

Influence markets

- How well are we creating shareholder value and communicating this to our shareholders?
- Do we market to financial analysts, journalists and the media?
- What about professional bodies, government, environmentalists and other relevant groups?

Recruitment markets

- Do we attract people of the right quality?
- Do we make our company the organization of first choice for prospective staff?

Supplier markets

- Do we develop 'a co-makership' relationship with our suppliers?
- What is our policy with respect to alliance partners?

Interview: Mike Hodgkinson, CEO, BAA

How BAA balances its commitments to its stakeholders

BAA is the world's largest commercial operator of airports. It owns and operates seven UK airports, including Heathrow, Gatwick and Stansted, and manages eight other airports around the world, serving 178 million passengers worldwide. BAA is also the world's leading travel retail specialist, with several hundred shops and other retail concessions in airports across the globe. Privatized in 1987 it is poised to significantly expand its international operations. Mike Hodgkinson took over as CEO from Sir John Egan in 1999.

We have to manage a complex web of relationships with our stakeholders. We are a public company, with all the City and shareholder issues that implies, but we also have major and very important relationships with national and local government and the local community, together with a raft of safety and security issues. And that's in addition to our relationships with our customers and suppliers. So we have to balance profit, quality and customer service with very important safety, security and environmental factors. All these different markets are of varying levels of importance to us, so we put different amounts of effort into maintaining them. Relationships with different stakeholder groups need to be co-ordinated in order to maximize customer and shareholder value, but managing all those competing interests is not easy.

We run most of our relationships using two methodologies: the balanced scorecard and the mission statement. Our commitment to our various stakeholder groups goes very deep into the company – for example, management bonuses are based on the balanced scorecard. The mission statement is a more formal testimony to our commitment. It is as follows:

> Our mission is to make BAA the most successful airport group in the world. This means: always focusing on our customers' needs and safety; achieving continuous improvements in the profitability, costs and quality of all our processes and services; enabling us all to give of our best; growing with the support and trust of our neighbours.

Our relationship strategies are such a fundamental part of the way we do business that they are written up in the business plan. We also use the annual budgeting process to try to reconcile those competing interests, setting physical targets for quality, safety, security and so on, as well as financial targets.

To a greater or lesser extent BAA has always recognized and tried to manage its different stakeholder groups. But as the world has grown more complex our approach has become more complicated and sophisticated. There were two pivotal points for us. One was privatization in 1987, which brought a new commercial imperative, and resulted in developments such as airport shopping. The other was opening Stansted airport in 1991. Until we had to market Stansted we thought our customer was the travelling public – we were a public sector organization, after all. But it soon became apparent that people cannot fly and use the airport without an airline. So we had to market ourselves heavily to our existing airline customers in order to persuade them to expand their operations with us, and to attract them and new airlines to Stansted.

For us, winning customers is just as important as retaining them: you have to work hard at both. We are selling ourselves to 150 airlines. And we sell shopping to 120 million passengers every year in the UK, but they might only travel once every five years.

Over the past nine years the biggest change in the way we do business has been in the nature of our relationships with our customers and suppliers. For example, what used to be a traditional arm's-length, even adversarial, approach with the airlines has moved towards a relationship based on partnership and collaboration. We put a massive amount of effort into forging and maintaining such partnerships.

The same goes for our relationships with suppliers. In the past we would put every job out to tender. But we realized that we could transfer what we learned from one job to another, so these days we tend to stick with the suppliers we know and can trust to do a good job. For example, runway maintenance work needs to be carried out in the six or seven hours that the runway is free of planes. So the critical skill is getting the people and equipment on to and off the runway, rather than the actual work itself. Using a different supplier every time is counter-productive: they have to learn how to mobilize their people and equipment before they can get on with the job. We have translated that policy to all our construction sites.

The particular nature of our business means we probably put more effort into our influence markets than many companies. In particular, we devote a fantastic amount of effort to our relationships with the local community, and local and national government. These three markets are as key to us as our employees, customers and shareholders. And the country is also an important stakeholder for us: we are critical to Britain's economic development.

We work hard at engaging with the local community, making local people aware of the benefits the airport brings them, so that we can work together towards common goals. For example, the wealth generated by the airport benefits the local community. Getting buy-in from the community to the controlled development of an airport helps all interested parties avoid the kind of protracted negotiations and public enquiries that have marked the development of Terminal 5 at Heathrow. Attitudes take five or six years to build up, and we embarked on Terminal 5 during the old adversarial days.

Implementing the kind of relationship marketing activities that are so important for us now requires managers to go beyond their traditional functional roles in order to develop closer ties with suppliers, staff, customers and other relevant markets. As well as the formal methodologies of the balanced scorecard and mission statement, we work very hard at internal marketing – getting employees behind what we are trying to do. I will present to the entire workforce annually, and each airport director presents to his employees quarterly. We want everyone – not just the management – to be aware of and involved in quality and safety and community issues, for example. You can't have the kind of involvement we have in the community with just two people. So at Gatwick airport, for instance, a large number of our 1800 employees are involved, and they find it very interesting and rewarding.

We don't invest a lot of time or effort in developing our referral or recruitment markets, as they tend to flourish on the back of everything else we do. If you get all the other things right you don't lose people. Our labour turnover is 2 per cent compared with the average of around 10 per cent. So we rarely have to advertise for new recruits, and when we do people queue up.

The same applies to our referral markets. By definition, our whole strategy should lead to referrals because people talk about their experience. It's an important aspect of marketing, but we don't target referral markets specifically: they grow by default if you are doing a good job elsewhere.

We have a core philosophy that runs through everything we do: get the process right and higher quality and lower costs will follow. It's a view that came out of the Japanese car industry, and was in marked contrast to the prevailing British view that you have to pay for higher quality. It's a much more accepted approach now than it was 15 years ago.

I have always held the broad view that if you manage yourself as a quality company, more money goes to the shareholders. In the short term you may find yourself spending more money on something than you might really want to, but in the medium term it will pay off by providing a better return for shareholders. In a sense it is easier for us to make that call than it is for other organizations, because much of our profit is influenced by the regulator, the Civil Aviation Authority (CAA). If we are seen to be running a quality business in the public interest the CAA will give us a better return.

But in general, organizations need to balance the short-term paper profit with the longer-term impact of spending more today. People talk about short-termism among investors, but I think you have to take a philosophical view. There's no mileage in running a low-quality business – everyone hates you. You're better running a high-quality business – at least that gives you a chance of making a profit. Not many low-quality businesses survive. A high-quality business can charge premium prices and customers still keep coming back for more. The shareholders reap the benefits of that.

References and further reading

Christopher, M. G., Payne, A. F. and Ballantyne, D. (1991) *Relationship Marketing: Bringing Quality, Customer Service and Marketing Together.* Oxford: Butterworth-Heinemann.

Denoyelle, P. 'Virgin Atlantic Airways – ten years after', INSEAD case study.

Heskett, J. L., Jones, T. O., Loveman, G. W., Sasser, E. W. Jr and Schlesinger, L. A., 'Putting the service-profit chain to work', *Harvard Business Review*, March–April, 164–74.

Kotler, P. (1992) 'Total marketing', *Business Week Advance, Executive Brief*, 2.

Mosley, R. (2000) 'The people behind the brand', *Market Leader*, Spring.

Payne, A. F. (1998) 'Relationship Marketing: The Six Markets Framework', draft working paper, Cranfield School of Management. (This chapter is based on a shortened version of this working paper and is used with permission.)

Payne, A. F. and Holt, S. (1999) 'A review of the "value" literature and implications for relationship marketing', *Australasian Journal of Marketing*.

Peck, H., Payne, A. F., Christopher, M. G. and Clark, M. (1999) *Relationship Marketing: Strategy and Implementation.* Oxford: Butterworth-Heinemann.

Reichheld, F. F. (1996) *The Loyalty Effect.* Boston, MA: Harvard Business Press.

4

Customer solutions, not product features: the innovation process

The role of the business leader is to nurture and embed the distinctive behaviours and organizational capabilities which deliver innovative solutions ahead of rivals.

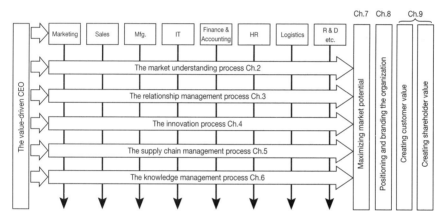

Fig. 4.1   Model of the value-creating process and relevant chapters in this book

We are all familiar with the sort of customer-focused slogans to which most firms nowadays pay lip service. For example: 'If it's not customer-driven our cars won't be either' (Ford Motor Company) and 'The customer is at the top of the organization chart' (Scandinavian Airlines Systems).

These are useful reminders and rallying points in speeches, but they rarely pervade or motivate the organization. The deeper meaning of being customer focused is the ability to create superior customer value. 'Superior' implies that our abilities are judged by reference to the 'best in class' competitor, and customer value is about being obsessive over the things customers value most highly and seeking to find better solutions.

The role of the business leader is to nurture and embed the distinctive behaviours and organizational capabilities which deliver these innovative solutions ahead of rivals. According to US marketing expert Peter Drucker (1998): 'The business has two

– and only these two – basic functions: marketing and innovation. Marketing and innovation produce results; all the rest are costs.' But there is no single simple recipe to follow. The contribution of the many elements which characterize the innovative organization depend on how well they interact and reinforce each other.

There are broadly four aspects that sustain the innovative organization: culture and climate, assets and capabilities management, organizational structure and controls, and new product and process development. In a sense, the CEO must sit above these four elements and exercise leadership by intervening to restore balance when they become out of kilter. He or she does this by encouraging his or her senior management team to continuously foster the market-driven approach, and by empowering employees to think innovatively about meeting customer needs each and every day.

But the business leader has to create the right climate in which innovation can thrive. He or she must set themselves the task of leading a high-profile and unremitting search for unique customer insights on which to build the innovation programme. The better CEOs are unwilling to delegate this entirely to the marketing department and seek to involve everyone in the organization.

> *There are broadly four aspects that sustain the innovative organization: culture and climate, assets and capabilities management, organizational structure and controls, and new product and process development.*

Thereafter the task is to nurture and balance. To achieve this balance, the business leader needs a deep understanding of the nature of successful innovation. Many emphasize process, technology, first-mover advantage or speed. But over-reliance on any single aspect sows the seeds of future disaster.

This chapter is devoted to a balanced consideration of each element of innovation, but underpinning everything is understanding – of the customer's purchasing environment, the way they perceive value and how they will respond to the proposed innovation.

The traditional view of innovation

Business leaders often confuse invention and innovation. Invention is about bringing new products and technologies to market, while innovation is about providing new solutions that offer value to customers. Peter Drucker (1998) defines innovation as 'exploiting change as an opportunity' – and such opportunities are legion in the rapidly changing environment in which all businesses now compete.

Drucker (in Doyle and Bridgewater, 1998) also made the famous distinction between efficiency – 'doing things right' – and effectiveness – 'doing the right things'. The distinction is crucial since efficiency is essentially about reducing costs, while effectiveness is about innovation. Faced with competition that is highly innovative, the business leader cannot hope to build viable strategies based simply on cutting costs. Indeed the penalties for so doing are corporate decline and demise, as we showed in Chapter 1. The past few years have seen large-scale acquisitions and mergers in practically every industry – financial services, telephony, pharmaceuticals, computing, food and drink – instigated by CEOs in pursuit of growth and shareholder value. Most will undoubtedly lead to short-term performance improvements, but up to four out of five will fail to generate long-term shareholder value.

Research shows resoundingly that acquisitions rarely provide the answer for companies that lack innovation skills. The financial focus of reducing costs and disposing of assets provides short-term benefits, but this strategy is essentially a reaction to the symptoms of change in the marketplace. Successful innovation, on the other hand, is a response to the causes of change and requires a longer-term, customer-led strategy.

> *Research shows resoundingly that acquisitions rarely provide the answer for companies that lack innovation skills.*

There are no short cuts to renewing an organization. Sustainable growth generated by continuous innovation is based upon the capabilities and attitudes of the people within the company, and depends on a culture that encourages entrepreneurship and processes which enable individual and team-based creativity to surface and flourish. At 3M, which invests over 7 per cent of its turnover in research and development, the link between its astonishing growth in sales and shareholder value is very clearly based on a vision that identifies innovation as a core company process. Some 30 per cent of 3M's current sales are from products launched in the past four years, and 10 per cent of sales come from products less than a year old (Figure 4.2). (For a fascinating insight into how 3M has developed and nurtured an innovative culture turn to the interview with its UK technical director John Howells at the end of this chapter.)

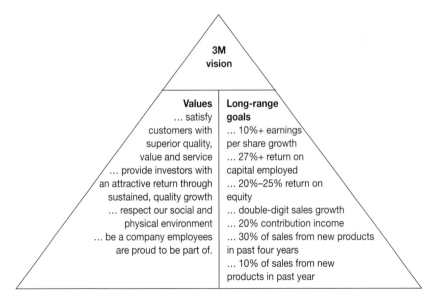

Fig. 4.2   The 3M vision: values and goals

When most people think of innovation they think of new products or services. Unquestionably, R & D investment in product development and new product launches is necessary to sustain growth markets, and companies such as 3M set themselves such product innovation targets as long-term strategic goals.

But as most business leaders would acknowledge, developing genuinely new products is a high-risk activity: industrial products have only a 50:50 chance of being successful, while consumer goods fare even worse, with a one in ten chance of succeeding. Given that it can cost as much to launch a packaged goods product as it does to open a new superstore, the CEO has to ensure that the new product development process is sufficiently robust to keep the risk of failure to a minimum and to avoid spiralling costs in the lead-up to market launch. This is usually done by adopting a multistaged review procedure during the development process, as Figure 4.3 illustrates.

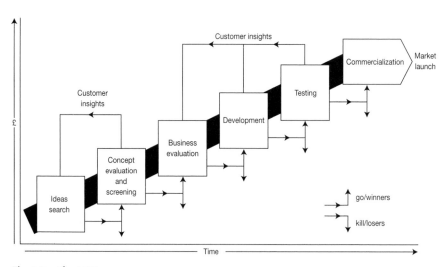

Fig. 4.3   The NPD process

The NPD process is characterized by go/kill decisions designed to weed out poor projects and to focus resources on the best bets. More new product projects are killed at the ideas search and screening gateposts than at any subsequent point; ideas and concepts are cheap, whereas capital expenditure on test plants and commercialization should only be agreed once the business case is pretty solid. Customer insights, developed through market research and with their direct collaboration, are a prerequisite to market understanding and product innovation. Clearly, the invention-led strategies which characterize the pharmaceutical and technology industries can produce marketplace breakthroughs that are notoriously difficult to market test. In these circumstances, customer insights may sometimes be misleading, so project management teams need to be both extremely cautious and highly tenacious.

Ringing the changes

On 10 March 1875, Alexander Graham Bell called to his assistant: 'Mr Watson, come here, I want you.' Nothing unusual about that – except that the exchange was the world's first telephone conversation. Excited by their discovery, Bell and Watson demonstrated their invention to senior executives at Western Union. The executives' written reply a few days later said: 'After careful consideration of your invention, which is a very interesting novelty, we have come to the conclusion that it has no commercial possibilities. We see no future for an electrical toy.' Bell went on to found AT&T, which grew over the next 20 years to become the largest corporation in the USA.

Successful inventions may offer genuine value to customers and be highly desirable. But the problem with inventions is that, even when they are patented, their value may not be sustainable. EMI discovered this in the 1970s when it launched the revolutionary body scanner into the medical market. Within two years, both General Electric and Siemens had launched competitive products, despite the risk of being sued for patent infringement. Direct Line revolutionized the UK car insurance market during the early 1990s. But though it offered superior value to customers, the low-price insurance product proved unsustainable for two reasons. First, competitors could quickly emulate the telephone sales approach pioneered by Direct Line, and within two years every insurance company was offering a comparable service. Second, Direct Line's innovation appealed to price-sensitive customers who were attracted by the discounts, but price-sensitive customers tend not to be loyal and switch when other companies offer lower prices.

But new product development does not have to be about introducing blockbuster innovations to the marketplace every time.

What's new about a new product?

There are many different types of new product innovations. You can consider 'newness' in two ways:

- new to the company, in the sense that the organization has never made or sold the type of product before, although other firms might have;
- new to customers – the product or service is the first of its kind and is new to market.

There are six different categories of new product innovation, as shown on the two-dimensional matrix in Figure 4.4.

Most companies feature a mixed portfolio of new product developments over time. The 'step-out' products and services (new-to-the-world inventions and new-to-company

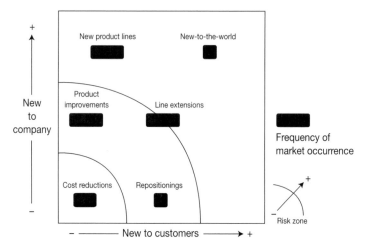

Fig. 4.4   Categorizing new product innovation
Source: Adapted from Booz, Allen and Hamilton, New York

lines) are in the highest risk zone. Many firms steer clear of these two categories, particularly in low-technology industries; they constitute about one-third of introductions to the market but represent almost two-thirds of the most successful product innovations. Examples include inventions such as the Xerox copier, the ubiquitous Post-It Notes from 3M and Sir Clive Sinclair's C5 electric car which failed dramatically.

> *In consumer markets ... business leaders have to contend with a further risk factor: how to brand the innovations considered to be in the high-risk category ...*

Product improvements and line extensions are lower risk and represent over half of all new product development activity. Usually, the strategy is to improve customer value by increasing performance and choice respectively. Nokia keeps adding new functions to its line of mobile phones, and the mobile communication network operator Orange adds new services to inspire more customers to use it. In the 1980s Procter and Gamble dramatically increased consumer choice and its share of the detergent market when it introduced liquid detergents to its line in addition to its existing powder brands.

The lowest risk developments are cost reduction and repositionings, or a combination of the two. During the 1980s, the R & D team of a multinational food company was working on a programme to reduce the cost of ingredients in four varieties of its best-selling instant soup, when the brand manager had the creative idea of repositioning the range as a slimming instant soup. With the unique selling point of having half the calories of the original and twice the gross margin, the range became an instant success as a niche subbrand and a strong cash generator for the company.

New brand development

In consumer markets, the traditional bastion of branded goods, business leaders have to contend with a further risk factor: how to brand the innovations considered to be in the high-risk category discussed above. In the past companies have tended to launch such products and services using stand-alone brand names – for example, Pringles rippled potato chips (Procter and Gamble) and First Direct Bank (HSBC Group) – to build brand values in their own right. The argument is that positioning the brand separately helps reduce the risk to the company should it have to withdraw from the market or recall the product for any reason. But in today's networked world, the public can get to know everything about a company – every mistake, policy and practice – so the CEO can no longer expect to control risk simply by adopting a stand-alone branding policy. Living with this degree of transparency means that boards need to regularly challenge the relationship between the company's reputation and the way product and service innovations are branded and developed.

How Persil Power got washed out

In April 1994, the Anglo-Dutch firm Unilever launched its revolutionary new washing powder 'Persil Power' across Europe. It was heralded as the first major innovation in detergents for 15 years, and had taken ten years and cost more than £100 million to develop. The product contained a magnesium catalyst, the 'accelerator', which Unilever claimed washed whiter at lower temperatures. The company believed it had developed a winning formulation and protected the magnesium catalyst with 35 patents. Unilever management had test marketed the new product in some 60 000 homes and more than 3 million washes by the time it was launched.

But in a matter of weeks, reports by Procter and Gamble, Unilever's main rival, and subsequent tests by the British Consumers' Association found that under certain conditions Persil Power significantly damaged clothes. After a very fierce public relations battle, Unilever was forced to withdraw the product after only ten months and to write off some £300 million in development and market launch costs. The debacle also cost the company dearly in terms of brand share, as the equity of the brand and consumer confidence in the company were quickly eroded.

What went wrong? With the benefit of hindsight, two main reasons stand out. One factor was the way market testing and segmentation had been carried out. Unilever had conducted most of its tests in Dutch households. Typically, northern Europeans separate their whites from their coloured wash and they tend to read product instructions. By contrast, consumers in southern Europe are more likely to wash whites and dyed fabrics together in a hot wash, regardless of any instructions to the contrary. The magnesium catalyst was fine at low temperatures with whites only but reacted with certain dyes at higher temperatures.

The second problem was that the product positioning was inappropriate. Persil Power was launched as a broad-based detergent suitable for all fabrics. In practice, it was only a niche product effective for whites at low temperatures.

This story exemplifies how companies emphasize process, technology and first-mover advantage at the expense of understanding customers. Unilever's senior management learned a great deal from this product launch and has since radically reorganized its NPD process to improve communications between research, development and marketing.

New geographic development

There are some outstanding examples of products that have been successfully intro-duced country by country on a rapid-fire succession basis, but there are as many others where the outcome has been quite different. In these situations, for example, sales never matched expectations, economies of scale failed to materialize, higher shares and greater margins proved elusive, and frustrated local managers could be heard to mutter 'I told you so' in 20 different languages.

The challenge of managing product innovation across a number of countries is to find a solution that avoids the extremes of total 'hands off' and destructive intervention. In the major national subsidiaries of its European opera-tions, Procter and Gamble has created 'category managers' who have the manufacturing, sales and marketing of specific product categories – such as hair care – under their wing. These category man-agement teams are responsible for developing and optimizing the product portfolios of particular cate-gories for their retail customers across Europe. This requires team skills in new product development, supply chain management (see Chapter 5) and cus-tomer relationship management (see Chapter 3). Because P & G regards these category management teams as core, it resources them centrally. Heinz, on the other hand, follows a decentral-ized approach in its core food business, with country CEOs responsible for the NPD process and customer relationships managed on a country basis.

> *The challenge of managing product innovation across a number of different countries is to find a solution that avoids the extremes of total 'hands off' and destructive intervention.*

There is no single way to develop new products for different geographical markets, nor are there any guarantees of success. But it is undoubtedly true that the trend is away from national endeavours – with a gradual roll-out of an adapted product across other borders – to global reach through a combination of centralized product devel-opment and manufacturing with local adaptations made during the final stages of manufacturing and service delivery.

The limitations of product innovation

The traditional approach to product and service innovation tends to be sequential and functionally driven, with marketing and sales acting as the arbiters of customer needs. The very simplified feedback loop illustrated in Figure 4.5 shows the 'hands off' that can occur when developing new products.

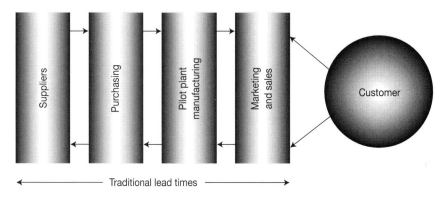

Fig. 4.5   Sequential processing

The flow of information from marketing and sales about what customers want is interpreted by a research and development function which produces test products. Developing and pilot-producing these samples for market testing is likely to involve briefing those in charge of purchasing, who in turn instruct suppliers. On the way back, the information about customer needs is handled through the same chain of events. The functional divisions between each stage of the process militate against rapid and active processing of information and problem-solving. Figure 4.5 could be expanded by separating marketing and sales and by including several suppliers, each with their own functional hierarchies and 'hands offs'. These all add more filters to how customer information is interpreted.

Business leaders who map the information flows across the transformation stages involved in NPD are shocked by their complexity, frustrated by the time they take and appalled by how far removed customers become. For example, during the 1980s Chrysler's 5500 engineers and technicians could only develop four new vehicles. The company used to spend between 12 and 18 months of its new product development process just sending out bids and negotiating with suppliers.

Further study of this process map should lead the business leader to two stark conclusions.

1   The traditional sequential procedures for moving ideas through to final products and services are no longer sustainable in today's business environment.
2   Developing new products and services is a blinkered approach to creating customer value.

We will now deal with both these issues in more detail.

Customer value and innovation

Truly innovative ideas that represent real breakthroughs in customer value are rarely produced in a sequential (or even concurrent) fashion when the end goal is purely to develop better products and services.

Customer value is created when an organization's offer is better, cheaper and faster than the competition. To achieve these goals in the context of new products and services, the company has to be closer to its customers. This calls for innovative thinking at all levels in the organization and for the organization itself to be innovative. Critical to creating this synergy between innovative thinking and the process of innovation is a shift to multifunctional teams, process measures and a broader definition of innovation.

Multifunctional teams and process measures

Using multifunctional teams in the innovation process has the effect of collapsing the traditional 'hands off' between functions shown in Figure 4.5, and introducing concurrency in tasks, as illustrated in Figure 4.6.

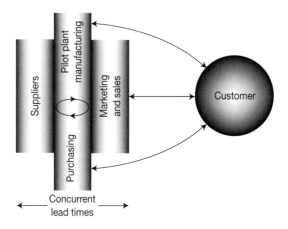

Fig. 4.6   Concurrent processing

Multifunctional teams can reduce the time to market for product innovation by as much as 75 per cent. It used to take the automobile industry between eight and ten years to take an idea from concept to the dealer's showroom. Now, companies like Land Rover can introduce new models in under two years as a result of concurrent engineering.

By introducing a process measure of value-added time versus non-value-added time, the innovation team can work together to identify the total time involved in value-adding activities and to eliminate time wasted in 'hands off' during the process. This leads to parallel activities across the multifunctional team, better internal communications and a clearer interpretation of customer needs and insights within the team.

A broader definition of innovation

Innovation is about new solutions that offer better value to customers. Clearly, new product development fulfils these requirements, but so can the renewal of the innovation process discussed in the last section if it brings new products and services to market more quickly. Truly innovative ideas that represent real breakthroughs in customer value are rarely produced in a sequential (or even concurrent) fashion when the end goal is purely to develop better products and services. Though organizations might recognize the importance of NPD in generating growth, managing the political process often gets more priority than managing the real outcome: we do things right instead of doing the right things.

> **The critical question the business leader must ask him or herself is: besides introducing better products and services, how else do customers experience our innovative capabilities day to day?**

The critical question the business leader must ask him or herself is: besides introducing better products and services, how else do customers experience our innovative capabilities day to day?

The answer, of course, is that the most effective way to build a reputation as an innovative company is through a comprehensive market-led approach. This focuses on building value-generating relationships with customers through the core processes by committed people within the organization – as well as introducing new products and services.

Customer focus

Since today's markets are changing so rapidly, innovation has to be multifaceted and seek to provide customers with solutions, not just products. To do this, companies need expert knowledge of the customer's entire value chain. This means listening to customers with a mindset that emphasizes change and renewal over stability.

Core processes: an effective organization

Unless companies have the systems to deliver high-quality products and services through efficient supply chains, they can do no more than aspire to a customer orientation. Effective marketing depends upon the means as much as the goals. Without building up its core processes (the five discussed in this book – market understanding, relationship management, innovation, supply chain management and knowledge management) the organization is unlikely to be agile enough to provide fast, high-quality solutions for the customer's emerging problems.

Building these core processes requires the organization to develop effective internal and external partnerships. Internal effectiveness is team based while external partnerships are created through relationships with suppliers and other businesses to generate a level of expertise which gives competitive edge. Increasingly, it is the organization's ability to put together this constellation of partnerships – in e-commerce and IT, manufacturing, sales and marketing, for example – which determines its effectiveness at delivering customer value.

People: commitment and capabilities

Ultimately, the organization's effectiveness in developing its systems and implementing strategy relies upon the commitment and skills of its employees. Creating these capabilities depends, in the first instance, on the CEO's ability to communicate an inspiring vision of the innovative organization and commitment to customers. But it also means selecting and training people who share their vision and are committed to implementing it. This is a subject we explored in Chapter 3 and will go on to develop further in Chapter 9.

> *Ultimately, the organization's effectiveness in developing its systems and implementing strategy relies upon the commitment and skills of its employees.*

In today's organization, the contribution that the marketing department can make is to take the lead in identifying opportunities for innovation created by the changing environment. Developing superior products and services is simply not enough – in fact, you could argue that it is 'putting the cart before the horse'. The marketing department's challenge is to break free of the product-constraining silos around which corporate assets and capabilities have traditionally been deployed, and to consider the opportunities it has to add value at the corporate level, rather than in the context of revenues, costs and returns associated with a particular product grouping or business unit. It is largely the intangible assets – know-how, methodologies, brand equity, patents and people – which represent the stock of the organization's capabilities. When both assets and capabilities are accounted for on a pan-company basis, many new ways of creating customer value unfold.

Asset- and capabilities-based innovation

In our experience, cost rather than value considerations typically drive the management of corporate assets. The problem with the cost-driven approach is that it fails to develop the real capabilities within the organization that will enable it to differentiate itself from the competition over the long term. Let us look at how two companies have gone beyond using the twin measures of asset utilization and functional capabilities towards a value-driven approach to managing their business.

Motorola's metamorphosis

In the 1970s Motorola faced enormous difficulties competing with Japanese consumer electronics firms in its core business of radios and televisions. In common with many other American companies at the time, it suffered from the apparently unbeatable Japanese ability to combine quality, innovation, design and low prices. Motorola decided to shift its marketplace strategy away from selling consumer electronics towards newer, high-tech markets, such as mobile phones and semiconductors, where it felt it could re-create competitive advantage.

This shift to higher technology and more sophisticated products had practical implications for a company used to making low-cost radios. Early on, the board realized that its workforce lacked both the necessary skills to run more sophisticated manufacturing processes and the ability to commit to continuously upgrading their skills commensurate with the new strategy.

So the company set up the Motorola University (MU) to meet the need for retraining and developing the skills of its workforce. The MU became an important enabler of the new marketplace strategy and developed world-class teaching skills in total quality management, process control and other aspects of what became known as 'Six Sigma quality', an efficiency programme designed to cut product costs year on year. Motorola is now regarded as a leading exponent of quality manufacturing, innovation and skills development, and has transformed itself into a high-tech company supporting a cellular infrastructure and manufacturing semiconductors, mobile phones and computers.

Without the astute management of the university, would the company have succeeded?

Motorola is not alone in having a corporate university. But it is distinctive in the extent to which it uses the university throughout the business rather than simply as a training and development vehicle.

For example, when Motorola recently negotiated an alliance with Siemens, part of its offer was the undertaking to provide training in quality manufacturing. Siemens is a vital partner for Motorola in Germany but it also competes with Motorola across some product categories. Offering this training was a bold move by Motorola. The university transcends individual business units, even those in competition with Siemens, and Motorola's strategy clearly demonstrates the power of this corporate asset to develop the customer value proposition. Motorola's 'Six Sigma' efficiency programme has been adopted by a number of companies, including General Electric and Invensys.

Quality is an important component of Motorola's capabilities, which it has now made available to its business customers, and the MU is a key contributor to its reputation and brand equity.

Tesco's turnaround

In 1995 Tesco became the market leader in UK grocery retailing. Its arch-rival Sainsbury's had led the field since before supermarkets were introduced in the 1950s. Arguably, Sainsbury's was still the equal of Tesco in the 4Ps of Price, Product quality and range, Promotion and Place. Yet consumers now considered Tesco's performance to be stronger, perceiving it to be the more progressive grocer of the two in its efforts to be genuinely innovative in meeting customer needs.

In the early 1990s, under the leadership of Sir Ian (now Lord) MacLaurin, Tesco's senior management team began to concentrate on aspects of performance measurement beyond the 4Ps. Thus Tesco was the first to introduce value-added services, including loyalty cards, financial services, free Internet access and guaranteed shorter queues at the checkout. Until then the corporate strategy had focused on margins and management efforts were directed at extracting higher returns in a nationwide cost-efficiency drive. Under the new value-based regime, the strategic goal was changed to 'delivering the best shopping trip to each and every customer'. In 1993 Tesco embarked on a series of initiatives designed to offer better value, improved stores and a higher level of customer service.

In order to manage the changes required to deliver better customer service throughout the shopping experience, Tesco broke down its customer service strategy into three areas.

1 *Culture*. Culture is the most difficult and intangible element of service delivery to manage effectively. With the launch of 'First class service' things began to change fast as each of the 130 000 staff was given responsibility to look after customers in the way they thought best. Staff now perceive every customer as valuable and understand that, over a lifetime, each individual has the potential to spend an average of £90 000 with the company.
2 *Standards*. By setting, measuring and managing service performance in store, such as the pledge to a 'One in front' policy at the checkout, the company was able to elevate service delivery from a level that individual store management deemed appropriate.
3 *Facilities*. Facilities were upgraded with the launch of the 'New look' initiative in 1993. The initiative was about introducing a series of tangible innovations, such as removing barriers at the entrance to the store and setting up more customer service desks, designed to improve the shopping experience.

The culture and climate created by these value-based initiatives was seen by the management as 'pure alchemy' which has allowed each individual store to develop stronger alliances with its own customers.

Tesco's success in satisfying customers has not gone unnoticed in other quarters. In 1997, the company's operating profits overtook Sainsbury's for the first time in its history and the directors of Britain's 250 largest companies unanimously voted it their 'Most admired company'.

Breaking down barriers to innovation

It is currently fashionable to aspire to become 'market driven'. Chief executive officers exhort their employees to get closer to customers and make decisions from the market back. In 1996, Percy Barnevik, chairman of Asea Brown Boveri, was asked to comment on leadership and innovation at the World Economic Forum in Davos, Switzerland. He highlighted three principal items for the boardroom agenda.

1 Create a customer focus and ensure that this is present from top to bottom.
2 Make the organization see innovation and continuous change as a way of life – not an exception.
3 Exercise leadership through deep understanding, coaching and empowerment, and a willingness to intervene when necessary.

Despite the fact that Asea Brown Boveri is a decentralized, engineering-driven maker of heavy industrial equipment, it is undoubtedly committed to being innovative and market orientated.

Most firms adopt other less successful orientations which can create barriers to innovation. According to George Day (1998), these orientations can be broadly grouped into three types of organizational myopia.

1 *Inside out, not outside in.* Successful firms are especially susceptible to this pitfall. These are organizations which may once have been market driven but do not realize until they encounter trouble that they have lost their focus. IBM fell into this trap in the 1980s. Profits and revenues almost tripled during the decade, but this performance masked a loss of focus as Big Blue became progressively more distant and unresponsive. The emphasis was on pushing hardware – often not the best and rarely competitively priced – rather than meeting customer needs. This internal orientation encouraged a reluctance within the organization to migrate customers from mainframes to distributed processing, where its smaller competitors were seeking to innovate by stealth.
2 *The customer compulsives.* 'We've never met a market we didn't like' is the slogan of companies that are customer compelled. Each function feels empowered to get its own inputs and insights from customers and to act autonomously on what it has learned, which means that few common themes emerge in their responses. While each initiative may be innovative in its own way, the totality is often incoherent, which leads to unfocused product and service initiatives, lengthening response times and organizational conflict. Customer-compulsive companies lack the leadership they need to set priorities about which markets to serve and to align the innovation process across different functions.
3 *Technology push over market pull.* A curious backlash is forming against giving customers primacy in decisions. Instead, a growing number of influential voices believe that in some contexts it is better to ignore the customers. Strategy experts Hamel and Prahalad (1994), in *Competing for the Future*, assert that customers are unable to envision breakthrough products and services. The companies that slavishly follow their customers, they say, 'may be able to protect their share of

existing markets but won't be able to lead customers where they want to go but don't know it yet'. To justify this position, Hamel and Prahalad resort to the valid but misleading observation that customers seldom ask for new products they eventually come to value. It is true that 15 years ago most customers were not clamouring for books and CDs over the Internet, cars with on-board navigation systems or home shopping. Yet they had a recurring problem, a deep-seated need to be satisfied by these offerings – otherwise the innovations would not have succeeded.

Technology-driven firms are the most resistant to a market-led orientation. Are they right to put their emphasis on technological leadership and on performance superiority grounded in best science?

The evidence suggests that high-tech firms are most successful when they adopt a balanced approach which reconciles the market-driven versus technology-led dichotomy. A study by Glen Bacon *et al.* (1994) of six such high-tech companies, including Hewlett-Packard and General Electric, revealed that successful innovations exploited the organization's capabilities, were closely aligned to market strategy and were continually exposed to timely, reliable information about customers and user preferences.

> **The evidence suggests that high-tech firms are most successful when they adopt a balanced approach which reconciles the market-driven versus technology-led dichotomy.**

It may be that as a CEO or board member yourself, you can readily identify with the sentiments expressed by Percy Barnevik but, in practice, see elements of these organizational myopias creating barriers to innovation in your own organization.

But you can inspire your employees to innovate and commit to customers by nurturing and embedding the distinctive behaviours and organizational capabilities that deliver innovative solutions ahead of rivals, as we said at the beginning of this chapter.

The four broad aspects that sustain the innovative organization are shown in Figure 4.7. These are the foundation elements that set innovative firms apart. The business leader will recognize that they do not simply add together; instead they are multiplicative, which means that one element drags the rest down (Figure 4.8). For instance, a rigid organizational structure with functional skills and hierarchies that guard their own areas will thwart the sharing of market understanding and undermine the participative culture and innovation process.

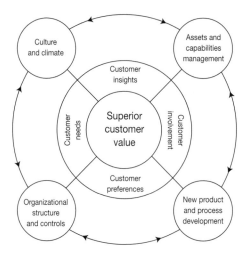

Fig. 4.7   The innovative organization

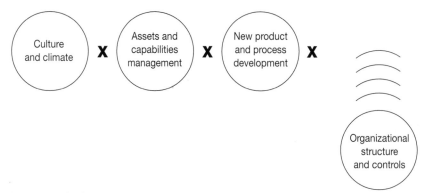

Fig. 4.8   Multiplicative foundation elements

Summary

Invention is about bringing new products and technologies to market, while innovation is about developing new solutions that offer value to customers. In competitive markets, the business leader cannot hope to sustain market advantage by simply lowering costs through improving performance. Organizations generate sustainable growth by continuous innovation, which is a response to the causes of change in the business environment rather than to change itself. Continuous innovation requires a long-term, customer-focused strategy.

Most managers consider innovation to be the introduction of new products and services to the marketplace. This activity undoubtedly contributes significantly to company growth, but it is not enough on its own. Today, innovation needs to be more broadly defined so that the assets and capabilities of the organization can be managed to create customer value at a corporate level, rather than in the context of the revenues, costs and returns associated with a particular product group.

The CEO should be trying to remove any barriers which may prevent these corporate assets and capabilities being utilized in this way. The marketing department, together with other corporate functions, may be too focused on product and service innovations, with the result that customers' needs are being neglected.

Innovation is multifaceted, and has to provide customers with solutions as well as products. It is the business leader's job to keep a balance between the four foundation elements of innovation identified in this chapter so that innovation in their organization helps create and sustain superior customer value.

Checklist for CEOs

CEOs and their board colleagues should ask themselves the following questions.

- Do I understand the nature of successful innovation?
- Do we see innovation and continuous change as a way of life rather than an exception?
- Are there any barriers to innovation in our organization?
- Does our organization confuse invention or new product development with innovation?
- Do our organizational culture and climate foster innovation?

- Does our assets and capabilities management encourage innovation?
- Do our organizational structure and controls inhibit innovation?
- Does our new product and process development lead to timely innovation?
- How do customers experience our innovative capabilities day to day?
- Does our innovation create new solutions that provide real added value to the customer?

Interview: John Howells, technical director, 3M, UK and Ireland

How 3M evolves through innovation

Ever since it was founded in 1902 the Minnesota Mining and Manufacturing Company has demonstrated an enlightened understanding of where the world and its customers are going. In 1921 it developed the world's first waterproof sandpaper, in 1925 it invented masking tape to ease the messy task of paint spraying, in 1939 it invented the first reflective road sign, in 1947 Scotch Magnetic audio tape, and in 1980 the ubiquitous Post-It Note. Today 3M is one of the world's premier manufacturing companies with operations in over 60 countries. Continuous innovation based on an intimate understanding of its customers has been the key to its success. John Howells is technical director of 3M in the UK and Ireland.

If creativity is thinking of novel and appropriate ideas, innovation is successfully implementing those ideas within an organization. Creativity is the concept; innovation the process.

You can't compartmentalize innovation. It's not something that happens just in the lab. It must run throughout the organization, from the lab, through the accounting and marketing departments, to the factory floor and the executives' offices.

Innovation needs to be a corporate character trait, something that is built up over time, a tradition. Dr William Coyne, senior vice-president of R & D at 3M, calls innovation the soul of 3M. He says: 'It is the reason we are here today and it will be the reason that we continue to evolve and grow.'

But innovation is difficult and risky. It is slippery, treacherous ground. It's not easy for us, and we have to constantly work at it. You can never afford to be arrogant or complacent. Once you've achieved something is the time to start worrying.

The innovation success that 3M has enjoyed has not depended on miracles, eurekas or accidental scientific discoveries. It has been based on a deliberate and rigorous commitment to the technological development of our unique product range within a culture that is focused on customer needs and that encourages personal creativity. We don't claim to get it right all the time, and there is no magic formula for success. But we have spotted three essential ingredients which make success more likely: an intimate knowledge of the customer, an imaginative exploitation of technologies, and a culture that encourages risk taking and thereby supports a flow of creative ideas.

We work hard at nurturing these business operations to protect the process of innovation.

We have identified six steps towards building a tradition in innovation. The first is to declare the importance of innovation and create the vision. The second is foresight and insight. You have to understand your customers' needs, industry trends, what changes are coming and when. Getting customers to convey their problems is not simple; their needs can be as much a mystery to themselves as to their suppliers. The best products are those that people don't know they need. Discovering these secrets is as crucial to our success as discovering the secrets of nature in our labs.

The next step is to push the organization to go beyond incremental improvements. It has to set itself goals that will stretch it, forcing it to make quantum improvements. We have invested over $6 billion of our turnover over the past five years in R & D, which we believe is considerably more than the competition in most of our markets.

In recession R & D expenditure actually increased as a deliberate strategy to win competitive advantage. In such a fertile creative environment a thousand flowers will bloom. But hand in hand with this goes tight financial control and quantitative measures for innovation.

The financial goals of the company provide a framework to measure innovation. These include the commitment to shareholders that over 30 per cent of our sales will come from products less than four years old. Recognizing that product life cycles are becoming shorter, we recently set ourselves the new goal that 10 per cent of our sales must come from products less than a year old.

The fourth stage in creating a culture of innovation is to empower people to be innovative. As an early CEO, William McKnight, stated over 70 years ago, 'Put fences around people and you get sheep'. The fifth stage is open and extensive communication. And the last – but not least – step is acknowledging the need for and establishing the right system of reward and recognition.

All employees are encouraged to use 15 per cent of their working time to pursue their own ideas. The actual figure is somewhat meaningless – people often spend a lot more than 15 per cent of their time pursuing their own ideas. What's important is that the system has some slack in it and that people are expected and encouraged to be creative. The results speak for themselves. Some of our best loved and most successful innovations, including the Post-It Note, have been generated this way.

Innovation brings risks and is synonymous with change. You can only encourage a risk-taking environment if you tolerate failure. Approximately 90 per cent of the ideas put forward at 3M fail at one of the various gateposts before reaching the status of a formal project. The key is to spot losers early enough to minimize both financial and organizational risk.

One secret of continuous innovation is to keep a company feeling new by capturing the excitement generated by a new venture. As our businesses have grown they have tended to divide and spin off into new markets – usually through the application of existing technologies. This means that we are contin-uously looking to create new small businesses within our large corporation. A classic example of this was the way we extended our experience in manufac-turing adhesive tapes for industrial use to the manufacture of medical tapes for use in hospitals. Today, 3M has a $3 billion healthcare business embracing dental, pharmaceutical and medical markets. It is this constant generation of start-up business units and teams which has helped us stay focused and fast – a benefit normally only enjoyed by companies in the first months and years of their existence.

Pace is by far the biggest issue facing companies like ours today. Innovation is time sensitive and to get the most from innovations you need to move quickly. This is vital in a world where product life cycles are measured in months, not years.

As a result, we demand more cross-functional team-working and a more rigorous approach to risk management and prioritization. While we pursue many product developments at once, we place our biggest bets on products that change the basis of competition and redefine what the customer expects.

3M also exploits knowledge very well. Technology transfer continues to drive our business growth forward and works best when employees actively exchange ideas and information. In many ways, 3M has been practising good knowledge management since long before it became fashionable.

As well as long-term corporate development work in the US, we have a large number of divisional laboratories around the world which develop existing or new products to support 3M businesses, manufacturing plants and customers.

3M has always thought of itself as an innovative company looking for creative customers. Indeed, many of our innovations are the direct result of close collaboration with imaginative partners. Over recent years we have extended that principle and are now building a system of interconnecting networks of people from companies large and small, independent research institutions, universities and government. Creating alliances that blur traditional organizational boundaries comes naturally to 3M. Our diverse portfolio of products – over 50 000 at the last count – means that many of our competitors and suppliers are customers too. Our very complexity creates skills in employees that, in turn, have a direct bearing on managing partnerships successfully.

Finally, it is worth pointing out that innovation is anything but orderly. It is, after all, an intensely human activity. And managing in chaos is often the right way to operate if you want innovation to flourish. The competition never knows what we are going to come up with next – and neither do we.

References and further reading

Bacon, G., Beckman, S., Mowery, D. and Wiben, E. (1994) 'Managing product definition in high-technology industries', *California Management Review*, 36, Spring.

Cooper, R. (1993) *Winning at New Products: Accelerating the Process from Idea to Launch*. Reading, MA: Addison-Wesley.

Day, G. (1998) 'What does it mean to be market-driven?', *Business Strategy Review*, 9 (1), 1–4.

Doyle, P. and Bridgewater, S. (1998) *Innovation in Marketing*. Oxford: Butterworth-Heinemann.

Drucker, P. (1998) 'The discipline of innovation', *Harvard Business Review*, November–December.

Hamel, G. and Prahalad, C. K. (1994) *Competing for the Future*. Boston: Harvard Business School Press.

Knox, S. D. and Maklan, S. (1998) *Competing on Value: Bridging the Gap between Brand and Customer Value*. London: Financial Times Pitman Publishing.

Mitchell, H. and Peck, H. (1997) 'Does Tesco hold all the cards?', European Case Clearing House, Cranfield University, ref. no. 598-032-1.

5

Breaking down the boundaries: the supply chain management process

Only those organizations that have strong and innovative brands supported by agile supply chains capable of responding rapidly to volatile demand will survive and prosper in tomorrow's markets.

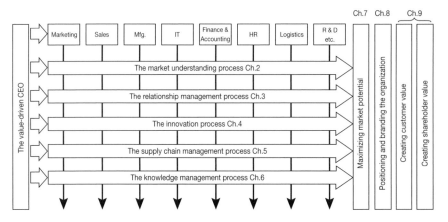

Fig. 5.1 **Model of the value-creating process and relevant chapters in this book**

Logistics has traditionally been regarded as a collection of necessary, but not strategic, activities, often referred to disparagingly as 'trucks and sheds'. In many companies the only time questions were raised about inbound and outbound logistics was during cost-cutting exercises. But logistics and wider supply chain issues are a major potential source of competitive advantage, and leading organizations are starting to recognize them as such. Indeed, increasingly we are finding supply chains competing rather than individual companies.

Supply chain issues are now emerging as key priority areas in many companies. But the CEO and his or her board need to be actively involved if their organization is to realize the full potential of the supply chain as a competitive force. Logistics cuts across conventional organizational and functional boundaries, so unless the business leader provides strategic guidance and political support, any initiative for change is doomed to fail. It is difficult enough trying to effect change within the business; trying to forge closer working relationships with other organizations in the supply chain is in another league entirely.

One of the drivers behind business leaders' new-found interest in the supply chain is the growing recognition of the impact logistics and supply chain strategies can have on shareholder value. Several of the major determinants of shareholder value are directly affected by logistics and supply chain decisions. For example, the way the logistics 'pipeline' is structured and managed significantly affects the level of both fixed and working capital. And the quality of logistics service is directly connected to sales revenue in most markets. So both the balance sheet and the profit and loss account are influenced directly and indirectly by logistics and supply chain management. Figures 5.2, 5.3 and 5.4 highlight the key linkages.

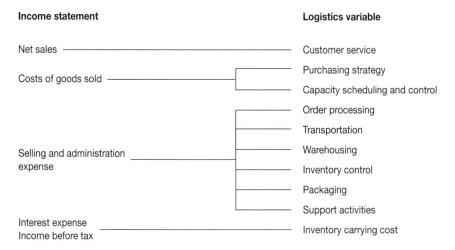

Fig. 5.2   Logistics impact on the profit and loss account

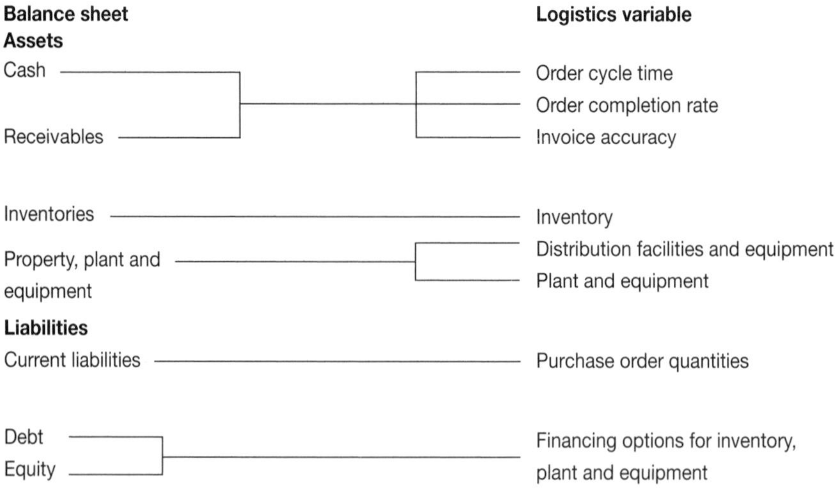

Fig. 5.3   Logistics impact on the balance sheet

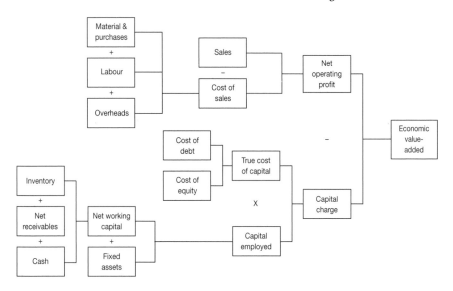

Fig. 5.4 Logistics and economic value-added

Marketing success has always depended on having the right product in the right place at the right time, but over recent years this mantra has taken on a new urgency as companies struggle with new sources of global competition. Strong brands and innovative technologies are no longer enough; important though they are, even the strongest brands and ground-breaking products need to be supported by a supply chain. The rules of competition are changing and those businesses that fail to recognize that will find marketplace success becoming ever more elusive.

Marketing success has always depended on having the right product in the right place at the right time ...

There are many tough new rules of competition, but the following are the most significant for supply chain management.

1 Companies compete through capabilities or 'the way they do things'.
2 As markets become increasingly 'commoditized' companies must find new ways of differentiation.
3 Mergers, acquisitions and organic growth are consolidating customer buying power.
4 To cope with these new challenges, suppliers need to leverage the strengths of their upstream and downstream partners in the 'extended enterprise'.

Strong brands and innovative technologies are no longer enough; important though they are, even the strongest brands and ground-breaking products need to be supported by a supply chain.

Before we go on to examine what each of these challenges means in practice for the successful business of tomorrow, let us look at how Dell Computer in the USA has used the supply chain to gain an advantage over its rivals to become the world's second-biggest PC-maker.

How Dell competes through its supply chain

The personal computer sector was in its infancy when, in 1983, medical student Michael Dell began buying up remainder stocks of outdated IBM PCs from local retailers, upgrading them in his college dorm and selling them on at bargain prices to eager consumers. Dell soon abandoned his studies to concentrate on his growing computer business, and by 1985 Dell Computer was building its own machines. The machines themselves were technologically unremarkable: it was the way they were sold – directly to the customer – that gave Dell a unique advantage over established, product-focused PC-makers.

The industry leaders jostled to produce increasingly technologically sophisticated machines, but paid scant attention to the mundane business of supply chain management. These computers were invariably made-to-forecast and, because they were sold through shops, resellers and systems integrators, languished for months in warehouses or on shop shelves before the customer bought them.

Dell, meanwhile, remained focused on the end-user, so avoiding the pitfalls of falling component value (the price of processors, for instance, drops by an average 30 per cent a year) and rapid obsolescence which cost its competitors dear. By selling directly to the customer Dell could configure and assemble every PC to order, so avoiding the risks associated with carrying finished inventory. This enabled it to maintain its cost advantage over its rivals. Dell's low-priced machines with their bespoke configuration became an attractive alternative for those customers confident enough to buy direct.

For years Dell was judged a successful niche player, but the industry believed most customers would always prefer to purchase their equipment through traditional channels, where help was on hand and they could see and touch the products before they bought them.

In a bid to break out of its perceived niche, Dell embarked on an ill-judged flirtation with conventional retail distribution channels. Retail sales plummeted as soon as Dell offered a new PC through its direct channels. Dell had to compensate the retailers for their losses, and in 1993 posted its first ever loss.

Dell pulled out of the retail market in 1994 and retrenched with a vengeance, rebounding immediately with profits of $149 million. It concentrated on finding ways to leverage the strengths of its original direct sales strategy, focusing on minimizing inventory and increasing return on capital employed. Leanness, flexibility and, above all, time compression were the keys. Over the next three years Dell closely re-examined its operations and squeezed every moment of non-value adding time out of its procurement and assembly processes. By 1997 the company was not only a model of just-in-time manufacturing, but had applied its own exacting time standards to the rest of its supply chain.

The majority of components are warehoused within minutes of Dell's four factories (in Texas, Ireland, Penang, Malaysia and China), and many components are ordered from a supplier only when Dell receives a customer order. Dell reduced the number of suppliers in 1992 from 204 to 47 in order to achieve this co-operation and integration, and prefers to source from suppliers close to its plants rather than from more distant offshore suppliers, despite higher local manufacturing costs.

Suppliers bill Dell for components only when they leave their warehouse in response to a customer order. The components themselves spend only half a day as Dell's own inventory.

Dell has forged ahead with Internet sales as an even more cost-effective version of its direct sales approach. Within six months of going online, Dell was making Internet sales of $1 million a day.

Customers can monitor prices on screen as they configure their PC, and receive confirmation of their order within five minutes of tapping in their payment details. No more than 36 hours later their bespoke PCs are trundling off the production lines and on to delivery trucks. Most of this time is spent testing the machines and loading software. Dell is paid for most sales within 24 hours of an order being placed, while rivals wait around 35 days for payment through primary dealers.

By the end of 1997, Dell was growing three times faster than the industry average and had become the world's second biggest PC-maker (by unit sales) after Compaq. Dell's growth and return on investment are the envy of the industry and are reflected in the staggering rise of its share price. An investment of a few thousand dollars at the start of the 1990s would have made the owner a multimillionaire by the end of the decade. Other established industry players have tried to emulate Dell's direct sales formula, but have retreated after encountering the same channel conflicts as Dell did in 1993.

In the company's 1997 annual report, Michael Dell listed the reasons behind the firm's phenomenal success:

- First, we bypass computer dealers and avoid related price mark-ups. This became a dramatic advantage as competition in the indirect channel drove up the cost of dealer incentives.
- Second, we build our systems to a specific customer order, which eliminates inventories of finished goods to resellers and enables us to move new technologies and lower-cost components into our product lines faster.
- Third, our direct contacts with thousands of customers every day enable us to tailor our support offerings to target markets and to control the consistency of customer service around the world.
- Fourth, we leverage our relationships with key technology partners and with our customers to incorporate the most relevant new technologies into our products rapidly.
- Finally, our low inventory and low fixed-asset model gives us one of the highest returns on invested capital in our industry.

Source: Christopher (1998)

Competing through capabilities

Having the largest plants producing products at low cost supported by the biggest advertising budgets used to be a guarantee of market success. But economies of scale no longer apply as more agile competitors leapfrog technologies and find new routes to market. These days fast-moving niche players can capitalize on what may be short-lived market opportunities through focusing on skills and competencies that allow them to meet customer requirements more closely and more rapidly than their bigger, more established competitors. The Dell example clearly illustrates this.

> *Economies of scale no longer apply as more agile competitors leapfrog technologies and find new routes to market.*

In today's turbulent and uncertain marketplace the key to survival is agility. Agility is an organization's capacity for rapidly adapting its strategy and operations to large-scale, unpredictable changes in the business environment. An agile business focuses on eliminating barriers to quick response, be they organizational or technical, from one end of the supply chain to the other.

Agility shouldn't be confused with 'leanness'. Being lean is about doing more with less. Lean is often used in connection with manufacturing to imply a 'just-in-time' approach. But many companies which have adopted lean manufacturing are anything but agile in their supply chain. The car industry provides a good example of this paradox.

Most western car assembly companies have adopted the so-called Toyota Production System. This has made their manufacturing processes much more efficient, but finished inventories are often extremely high and customers may still have to wait months for the precise model and options that they want. This is an inevitable result of focusing on lean manufacturing rather than agility across the supply chain as a whole. While 'lean thinking' focuses on eliminating waste, agility implies a very flexible organizational structure, closely connected to the marketplace, with a network of supply chain partners working in a highly synchronized way.

Differentiation in a commodity world

The growing trend towards 'commoditization' in many markets represents a major change in the rules of competition. A commodity market is one where customers perceive little difference between products, as a consequence of which they will happily switch between makes. Research suggests that consumers are increasingly less loyal to specific brands and will choose from a portfolio of brands within a category. In these situations the availability of the product becomes a major determinant of demand. More and more consumers are making buying decisions at the point of purchase, and if there is a gap on the shelf where Brand X should be they will probably buy Brand Y instead.

The trend towards commodity status is also occurring in business-to-business and industrial markets. Technology improvements, the emergence of more and more 'clones' and more uniform product quality make it increasingly difficult to differentiate physical products. In many markets today product features and excellence are taken for granted by customers, who choose instead on the basis of service.

Organizations which focus on creating more responsive supply chains can become 'time-based competitors'. In other words, they differentiate themselves by the way they react to customers' specific service needs in ever shorter time frames. The success of RS Components, the UK-based distributor of electrical and electronic components, is a testament to how superior service can result in a price premium for standard products.

RS Components has created a market leadership position in the distribution of electrical, electronic and other replacement items across a range of industrial sectors. The cornerstone of its success is a carefully managed supply chain based upon very close co-operation with key suppliers, underpinned by shared information and vendor-managed inventory. This allows it to provide same-day delivery from a product range of over 100 000 items, and because it can respond so rapidly customers are prepared to pay top prices for the service. (In Chapter 7 we look at how RS Components has successfully added a new electronic distribution channel, and in Chapter 9 go on to examine how its web site has enabled it to individualize its approach to customers.)

The growth of customer buying power

A major phenomenon of recent years has been the concentration of buying power in many markets. Market concentration occurs as organizations get taken over, merge or grow organically at the expense of their competitors. In Western Europe the Single Market has accelerated this process. In the past countries tended to develop their own industrial base independently of their neighbours, but now that trade barriers have virtually disappeared most industries suffer from significant overcapacity. The populations of the USA and the European Union are roughly similar, but there tend to be more players in any given industry in Europe than there are in the USA. This overcapacity is compounded by the emergence of global competition in newly developing countries. Mergers and acquisitions will inevitably continue, to the point where a handful of companies will dominate an industry on a world-wide basis.

This has profound implications. Greater buying power by fewer customers will place more pressure on suppliers. Customers will demand even higher levels of service at lower prices. At the same time these more powerful customers will be actively seeking to reduce their supplier base.

So what does a company have to do to become a preferred supplier in this new environment? The answer, it seems, is to create and deliver more customer value than its competitors. Winning organizations will be those which recognize that a significant element of enhanced customer value is superior logistics service. Suppliers need to concentrate their efforts on their most valuable customers, using the principles of key account management, as we outline in Chapter 7.

Leveraging the 'extended enterprise'

Management's task is complicated by the fact that they are now operating in a deflationary rather than inflationary environment. In market after market global overcapacity, growing competition and more powerful customers are combining to exert a fierce downward pressure on prices. Falling prices in the marketplace makes reducing costs a priority for most organizations. But because the real cost of making things is at an all-time low in most industries as a result of automation, new technology and new thinking, the opportunities for cutting manufacturing costs further are limited. Consequently the pressure for cutting costs falls on the supply chain.

In the new marketplace individual companies arguably no longer compete with other stand-alone companies; rather, supply chain competes against supply chain.

In the new marketplace individual companies arguably no longer compete with other stand-alone companies; rather, supply chain competes against supply chain. When organizations work independently of their upstream suppliers and downstream customers, costs and inefficiencies tend to build up at the interfaces.

Instead of the traditional arm's-length, even adversarial, relationship between buyers and suppliers, in the 'extended enterprise' there should be no discernible boundaries in a seamless end-to-end supply chain.

As the 'network organization' becomes more common, partners in the supply chain need to co-operate and co-ordinate their efforts. The network organization comprises a complex web of linkages between focused partners, each of which adds value through specializing in an activity where it can provide a differential advantage.

The challenge for the business leader is to leverage the full capabilities of his or her organization's supply chain partners by managing the chain as a value chain. In other words, the more firms focus on their core competencies and outsource those activities they believe can best be performed by others, the more they need to see the supply chain as a confederation of closely linked partners co-operating to create a highly differentiated value chain.

Clearly, to make such an idea reality requires a totally different way of dealing with suppliers and customers. In particular it means complete transparency of information on demand and supply. Already we are seeing how the packaged goods and grocery industry is being transformed through the value-added exchange of electronic point of sale (EPOS) information. This has enabled suppliers to respond directly to true demand rather than forecast demand. As a result retailers are less likely to run out of stock, and there is significantly less inventory in the supply chain as a whole.

Time compression holds the key

The supply chain can be compared with an oil pipeline. Long pipelines have more oil in them than shorter ones. So if demand at the far end changes – say, a different grade of oil is required – it will take longer to respond to that changed demand the longer the pipeline. Agility is all about the ability to change rapidly, so the total 'end-to-end' time in the supply chain has a direct impact on responsiveness.

Few organizations know the true length of their end-to-end pipeline. One useful measure is the cash-to-cash cycle time. This cycle begins with commitments for sourcing and procuring materials and components, continues through manufacturing and assembly to final distribution, and finishes with the customer paying the supplier.

The total pipeline time, often measured in months rather than weeks, is represented by the number of days of inventory in the pipeline. These might include raw materials, work in progress, goods in transit, time taken to process orders or issue replenishment orders, as well as time spent in manufacturing, queues or bottlenecks and so on. Companies must control this total pipeline in order to be agile. Figure 5.5 illustrates how cumulative lead time builds up from procurement through to payment.

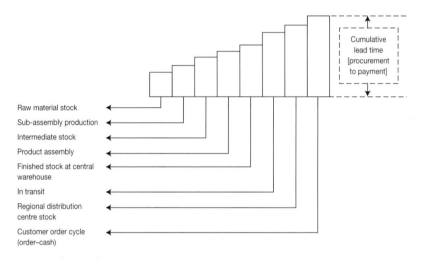

Fig. 5.5   Cash-to-cash cycle time

Most organizations face a fundamental problem. It takes longer to procure, make and deliver the finished product to a customer than the customer is prepared to wait for it. This mismatch of expectations is referred to as the lead-time gap. Figure 5.6 highlights the problem.

In the conventional organization the only way to close the gap between the logistics lead time (the time it takes to complete the process from goods inwards to delivered product) and the customer's order cycle (the period they are prepared to wait for delivery) is by carrying inventory.

A company typically bases the amount of inventory it carries on its forecast of what the market will require. But no matter how sophisticated the forecasting technique, its accuracy normally leaves something to be desired. While companies should continuously strive to improve the accuracy of their forecasting, the real answer to the problem lies in reducing the lead-time gap.

The company that achieves a perfect match between the logistics lead time and the customer's required delivery time needs neither forecasts nor inventory. Not only is such a company more responsive to customer demand, and hence more agile, it can also reduce the cost of financing the pipeline. But how do you close the gap?

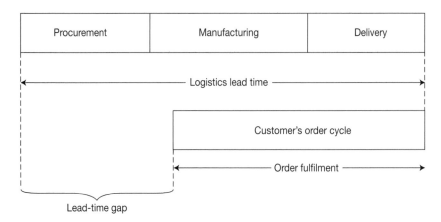

Fig. 5.6   The lead-time gap

There are three elements of total pipeline time which can often be significantly reduced: inbound logistics, internal operations and outbound logistics. Figure 5.7 highlights the areas where companies should do a detailed analysis of existing processes: the interface with suppliers, internal processes and the interface with customers. Let us briefly consider each of these in turn.

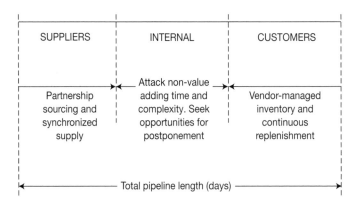

Fig. 5.7   Achieving agility in the supply chain

The supplier interface

One of the biggest barriers to greater agility is the long lead times suppliers seem to need to replenish their stocks. It is not unusual for inbound lead times to stretch into months. Where products are complex and comprise many components or raw materials, the slowest moving element will determine the length of the pipeline. So even if 99 out of 100 components are available within days, if the hundredth is on a three-month lead time that single item will dictate overall response time.

So how do you cut time out of this critical interface? The key word here is 'partnership' – currently one of the most overworked words in the management lexicon. Partnership with suppliers is critical to developing more responsive supply chains. One of the early lessons that companies as diverse as Nokia and Nissan have drawn is that to partner successfully you need to significantly rationalize your supplier base. You cannot have closely integrated supply chain arrangements with thousands of suppliers. Instead you need to develop closer relationships with a smaller number of strategic suppliers. British high street retailer BhS has reduced the number of its clothing suppliers from hundreds to a handful. The relationship it has with its remaining suppliers is based on transparent information and synchronized operations.

Working more closely with suppliers enables processes to be integrated, allowing a 'seamless' information system and physical pipeline to be established. A continuous flow of information and products leads to reduced paper and stock.

There are clearly many implications for both customer and supplier in this new world of transparency and openness. For example, each side becomes more dependent on the other, but this drawback is outweighed by the benefits which come from moving in step with each other – not least enhanced agility.

Internal processes

An organization's internal processes are a major barrier to agility in the supply chain. Many of these processes will have been in place for years and, while there may once have been good reasons for them, such procedures may be harder to justify today. In the same way, historical internal processes often militate against creating a climate of innovation, as we discussed in Chapter 4, and of knowledge management, as we go on to discuss in Chapter 6. So it is important to take a long hard look at the way we do things, with a view to reengineering them to achieve greater agility. A critical concept here is 'value-adding time' as opposed to 'non-value adding time'.

> **It is important to take a long hard look at the way we do things, with a view to reengineering them to achieve greater agility.**

Value-adding time is time spent doing something that creates a benefit for which the customer is prepared to pay. So manufacturing is a value-adding activity as well as the physical movement of the product and the means of creating the exchange. The old adage 'the right product in the right place at the right time' summarizes the idea of customer value-adding activities. Any activity that contributes to achieving that goal could be classified as value-adding.

On the other hand, non-value adding time is time spent on an activity which, were it not done, would not deprive the customer of any benefit. Some non-value adding activities are inevitable because of the way our processes are currently designed. For example, if production is inflexible and manufacturing requires large batch sizes, then inventories are bound to rise, and since time spent as inventory in a warehouse is non-value adding time, then the organization should focus on ways to reduce the production batch size.

Flowcharting supply chain processes is the first step towards understanding what opportunities there are for improving productivity through engineering the logistics process.

Once processes have been flowcharted you can then start to debate which elements of the process really add value. The acid test of a value-adding activity is that eliminating it would deprive the customer of a real benefit.

Much of the non-value added time in the logistics pipeline is idle time – the product is standing still as inventory. Often inventory is finished too early. If the final finishing or configuration of the product could be postponed it would reduce the total amount of pipeline inventory while increasing flexibility. Companies such as Hewlett-Packard now design their products so that the final 'localization' can be delayed until the last possible moment. This means that inventory can be held in a generic form rather than as finished product.

The customer interface

A major problem for many organizations is that they do not have a clear view of the final marketplace. An upstream supplier of packaging materials selling to an original equipment manufacturer, for example, is unlikely to know the day-to-day level of demand for the final product at retail level. Even the manufacturer might not have a very good idea of final demand because its view of the marketplace is obscured by intervening inventories.

Being able to capture information on demand as close to the final point of consumption as possible helps agility enormously. We explore the importance of data in understanding and serving the market in Chapter 7. Companies which have access to their customers' sales or usage data are well placed to plan and schedule capacity and can often make to order. A real breakthrough of the past decade has been the linking of buyers' and suppliers' information systems through initiatives such as Efficient Consumer Response (ECR) and Quick Response. And electronic data interchange (EDI) and the Internet have enabled partners in the supply chain to act on the same data. Consequently they now have a much clearer picture of real demand rather than depending on the distorted and noisy picture that emerges when orders are transmitted from one step to another in an extended chain.

A close connection with the marketplace through shared information makes for a more responsive supply chain. For example, at Cisco Systems – the fast-growing provider of network routing and switching equipment – nearly three-quarters of customers place orders directly through the Internet.

Suppliers are immediately alerted to the need for components, and contract equipment manufacturers, who also directly monitor the company's orders, then build uniquely configured products on a just-in-time basis. At the same time the third party logistics service provider is informed of the impending shipment requirements. As a result customized products can be delivered and installed in much shorter time frames than previously. By linking suppliers and contract manufacturers through its 'digital value net' Cisco has been able to outsource 70 per cent of its production. This has allowed it to quadruple output without adding capacity and to shorten its time to market for new products by 66 per cent in just six months.

These information linkages do not have to be based on advanced technology, though IT and electronic commerce certainly help information to be shared. (We explore the significant benefits of e-commerce in creating customer preference in Chapter 7.) More important is the willingness of all parties in the supply chain to act as partners and to communicate openly. Some of the biggest improvements in supply chain agility have occurred through a change of attitude among the parties involved: the old adversarial approach has been ditched in favour of a relationship based on 'win-win' thinking.

Turning the supply chain into a demand chain

The traditional approach to supplying products to markets is fundamentally different from this new model which is emerging. The traditional approach is based on optimizing production and transportation through calculating 'economic batch quantities'. It is essentially a 'push' type of system where the product is produced ahead of demand, normally against a forecast, and is then held in the market-place awaiting orders.

... a supply chain tends to focus on making the flow of material from source to user as efficient as possible ... a demand chain focuses more on effectiveness ...

Under the new model the supply chain should effectively become a 'demand chain' – everything that is moved, handled or produced should ideally be in response to a known customer requirement. By its very nature a supply chain tends to focus on making the flow of material from source to user as efficient as possible. By contrast, a demand chain focuses more on effectiveness: it seeks to be market driven by responding to the needs of the market more rapidly. The key to the transformation from supply chain to demand chain is agility.

Table 5.1 summarizes the major differences between the traditional model and the new approach.

Table 5.1   Agile supply chain management versus traditional approach

Traditional approach	Agile approach
• Stock is held at multiple echelons, often based on organizational and legal ownership considerations.	• Stock is held at the fewest echelons, if at all, with finished goods sometimes being delivered direct from factory to customer.
• Replenishment is driven sequentially by transfers from one stocking echelon to another.	• Replenishment of all echelons is driven from actual sales/usage data collected at the customer interface.
• Production is planned by discrete organizational units with batch feeds between discrete systems.	• Production is planned across functional boundaries from vendor to customer, through highly integrated systems, with minimum lead times.
• Majority of stock is fully finished goods, dispersed geographically, waiting to be sold.	• Majority of stock is held as 'work in progress' awaiting build/configuration instructions.

Going global

A dominant feature of today's supply chain landscape is the increasing globalization of sourcing, manufacturing and markets. Only a short time ago markets were primarily domestic and were supported by 'local-for-local' manufacturing and sourcing. Now, as barriers to trade continue to fall, the globalization of supply chains continues apace. If it is properly managed the global supply chain can give a company a significant platform to reach a wider market at lower cost. But there are a number of pitfalls.

For example, many companies have moved their sourcing and/or manufacturing offshore in order to cut acquisition costs. But in doing so they may have increased their exposure to supply chain risk.

Take the case of Marks & Spencer. In 1990, when many rated the company as Britain's best run and most profitable retailer, it sourced virtually 100 per cent of its clothing products in the British Isles. Ten years later, its market capitalization slashed by half and facing the biggest crisis of its life, only 50 per cent of its clothing range is sourced in the UK and Ireland, the remainder coming from 'low-cost' sources such as Sri Lanka, China and the Far East.

Moving sourcing offshore is not intrinsically a bad thing to do, but if a company wants to compete successfully in a fast-changing volatile market, that procurement strategy must be supported by an agile and highly responsive supply chain. In Marks & Spencer's case, its global supply chain capability was limited: the order-to-delivery times on many of its lines were over six months long. As a result M & S had to mark down prices and hold frequent sales as it tried to clear the pipeline.

By contrast, companies like The Limited in the USA have invested heavily in information technology and systems to enable them to respond rapidly to changing fashions and to minimize their exposure to risk. Each of The Limited's several thousand stores tracks consumer preferences daily using the organization's point-of-sale data. Based on this, orders are sent by satellite links to suppliers around the world. Four times a week goods are flown back on a chartered Boeing 747 from The Limited's consolidation centre in Hong Kong to its distribution centre in Columbus, Ohio. At the distribution centre the goods are price-marked and re-sorted for immediate shipment by truck and plane to the retail stores. The whole cycle from reorder to in-store display can be achieved in six weeks. Conventional systems take more like six months.

As the trend towards globalization continues, the need for global pipeline management becomes even more crucial. Only those organizations that have strong and innovative brands supported by agile supply chains capable of responding rapidly to volatile demand will survive and prosper in tomorrow's markets. (For a highly informed view of the critical importance of sophisticated supply chains to successful organizations, turn to the interview with John Allan, CEO of Exel, at the end of this chapter.)

Summary

It is the responsibility of the CEO and his or her board to ensure that the supply chain strategy within the business is aligned with the overall corporate strategy. If an organization is to be truly market driven all its core processes must be managed against the same underpinning strategic goals.

But many organizations still lack a clearly articulated and defined supply chain strategy. This should view the supply chain as a value chain, specifying where customer and consumer value is to be created. This might involve recognizing that it is more appropriate for some elements of value to be created by other partners in the supply chain. The trend towards outsourcing and the emergence of 'virtual' companies suggests that organizations are increasingly accepting this concept. Supply chain strategies need to be externally focused and embrace the concept of the 'extended enterprise' which incorporates both upstream and downstream partners in the value chain.

The challenge for the value-driven business leader is to put aside the conventional wisdom of the past in which the focus has been on enhancing the position of the individual firm and instead to think on a much wider scale to create a business that is truly 'boundary-less'.

Checklist for CEOs

CEOs and their boards need to ask themselves the following questions about their organizations' supply chain strategies.

- Do we understand the impact logistics and supply chain strategies have on our balance sheet, profit and loss account and, ultimately, shareholder value?
- Do we have a clearly articulated and defined supply chain strategy?
- Does this strategy view the supply chain as a value chain, specifying where customer and consumer value is to be created?
- Do we understand the difference between 'agility' and 'leanness'?
- Are we working more closely with our supply chain partners than we did in the past?

- Do we know the true length of our supply chain, and the number of days of inventory it contains?
- Are we working to cut time out of the interface with our suppliers?
- How many of our supply chain processes are value-adding activities, as opposed to non-value adding activities?
- Do we have access to data on our final marketplace from our customers?
- Do we share information on our marketplace with our own suppliers?

Interview: John Allan, CEO, Exel

How Exel gets the right product in the right place at the right time

John Allan was CEO of Ocean Group plc, a leading provider of global logistics services, for six years before the company merged with logistics company Exel earlier this year. He is now CEO of the combined organization, which provides logistics services to around 70 per cent of the world's top 250 companies. As the head of an international business, as well as being a supplier of logistics services to other leading organizations, Allan is well placed to comment on the growing importance of supply chain issues to successful companies.

Supply chain issues haven't traditionally figured very high on board-room agendas. But that is changing. Competition is intensifying, product life cycles are shortening and customers are becoming more discriminating. As such, having the right product in the right place at the right time has become not just vitally important, but a necessary condition of doing business. The supply chain now represents a big and important set of issues – which is a complete change from five years ago. And it's not just a big company issue either. With increasing globalization even modest-sized organizations need a good supply chain strategy.

And it is customers who are driving improvements in the supply chain. Customers are becoming more powerful, as buying power concentrates, and even end-consumers are growing increasingly demanding. Many markets are becoming commoditized, and where there is little to choose between products companies have to develop service criteria which, in their customers' eyes, differentiate them from competitors. Clearly, in such an environment an efficient, agile, flexible and responsive supply chain, which can deliver the products to the people faster and more cheaply than the competition, is becoming a powerful competitive weapon.

Increasingly, particularly in commoditized markets, customers are looking not just for innovative products and excellent service from their supplier but for added value too. That means suppliers who want to keep their customers' business have to be ruthless in cutting non-value adding activities out of their operations and encouraging a climate of innovation. This is normally achieved through a closer relationship between the two parties, and often involves the customer cutting the number of suppliers it works with. It is much easier to have the sort of close and open relationship that encourages innovation and value creation if a business is dealing with tens rather than hundreds of suppliers.

But I am reluctant to use the word 'partnership' when describing the relationship between customer and supplier. At Ocean Group, for example, we saw ourselves as suppliers of logistics services. We had over 20 major global accounts, but only a handful of true partnerships.

Paradoxically, though, the trend is for companies to work with fewer suppliers, and despite growth in direct selling via the Internet, supply chains are actually getting longer as companies become more international. Developments in electronic commerce mean that customers can access a wide range of suppliers and source products from all over the world at the touch of a button or the click of a mouse. And a company that decides to work with an organization like Ocean Group/Exel, for example, gets immediate access to a whole raft of new product suppliers through the link we provide.

So a CEO needs to manage both the close relationships and the extended supply chain, and an absolutely critical element of supply chain management these days is information. The supply chain used to be driven by the physical movement of goods; today it is much more about information management. A flexible and agile supply chain certainly requires a change of culture from an arm's-length, even hostile, relationship between customers and suppliers, to one based on 'win-win' thinking, but technological capability is equally vital.

Increasingly we are finding that the dialogue between Ocean Group/Exel and our customers focuses on IT and information management rather than the physical movement of boxes. It's a question of adding value again. Customers tend to think that anyone is capable of doing the physical job: the key differentiator in this business is managing data. And developments in e-commerce mean that managing data has become much more sophisticated, much easier to do and much more economic.

Companies recognize that in many cases it is supply chain that competes with supply chain, rather than company with company, and as such that other partners in the supply chain may be better able than they are to add value in a particular area, to the end of overall supply chain efficiency. Some companies –

notably in the electronics and technology industries – are getting out of manufacturing altogether and we're seeing a huge growth in contract manufacturing.

But one of the things we have learned is that in a fast-changing world you need to build in flexibility to your supply chain, because you can guarantee that what's optimal today won't be tomorrow.

Being part of a more concentrated 'extended enterprise' rather than the looser, more traditional customer/supplier relationship takes some managing. Greater mutual dependency can be a problem, for example. How do you manage that? One way is to become bigger, as we have. Our expanded business allows us to provide more to a larger number of big customers, and reduces the risk that we will become over-dependent on one or two major customers.

But we work very hard at the relationship with those bigger customers. We have changed the structure of our organization from geographic to customer defined, and now have dedicated account managers for each of our 20-odd major global accounts. As such we have a deep understanding of their businesses, their markets and their needs, and are committed to tailor-making services for them, so fulfilling their expectation that we will create more value for them.

It is increasingly the case that the supply chain is becoming a 'demand chain'. More and more customers want customized products, which is driving suppliers increasingly to make to order.

The traditional functional silo structure in many organizations has conspired against optimizing value in the supply chain. But more and more companies are now organizing themselves around processes or product groups. In the organizations we work with logistics is moving from being a big operational department to a strategic supply chain function.

And at Ocean Group/Exel we have reorganized our business to try to get as many people as possible to focus on industry sectors and individual customers rather than their traditional 'function'. We believe this is the way to unleash innovative ideas about improving service to our customers, rather than having lots of generalists. To do that they need lots of contact with customers – and while technology facilitates quick and easy communications, people need to know who they are doing business with, and there is no substitute for a face-to-face meeting. I participate in these relationships. The CEO has to lead from the front and ensure the company's supply chain strategy is aligned with the overall corporate strategy. But in so doing you also learn a huge amount about how customer needs are changing.

References and further reading

Christopher, M. (1998) *Logistics and Supply Chain Management.* London: Financial Times Pitman.

6

Competing through information: the knowledge management process

The way organizations manage their knowledge has become a key source of competitive advantage.

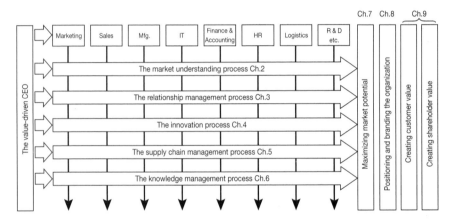

Fig. 6.1   Model of the value-creating process and relevant chapters in this book

Knowledge has overtaken capital, labour and natural resources to become *the* basic economic resource. In modern industrial nations knowledge-intensive industries are responsible for a steadily increasing proportion of the national net product. Knowledge is the only resource that increases with use. Consequently, the way organizations manage their knowledge has become a key source of competitive advantage.

The emergence of the knowledge networked economy, where those with the best information wield the most power, has been a catalyst for positive change in the way organizations perceive and pursue knowledge. This sea change is summed up by George Shaheen, former managing partner and CEO of global consulting firm Andersen Consulting. He says: 'Knowledge capital is our most valuable asset and it drives our organization. It's what we sell, and what we must continue to protect and perfect. Our people should diligently find new ways to share and reuse information and deploy it around the world.'

Shaheen makes it sound simple. But creating a knowledge management culture represents a radical shift in thinking and operating for most organizations, and is far from easy to achieve. As such it *has* to be led from the top. Migrating the attitudes and operations inside the organization towards a knowledge-based approach to value-creation calls for the firm but sensitive hand of the CEO. United States management expert Peter Drucker recently summed up the management challenge: 'In the knowledge economy all staff are volunteers, but our managers are trained to manage conscripts.'

Understanding that knowledge is volunteered, and cannot be conscripted, is key to successfully inculcating a knowledge management culture. Consequently trust is an absolute prerequisite for change. But people's willingness to contribute and communicate knowledge must be encouraged and supported by robust organizational systems and ongoing opportunities to learn.

> *... creating a knowledge management culture represents a radical shift in thinking and operating for most organizations, and is far from easy to achieve. As such it **has** to be led from the top.*

Advanced technologies and enhanced capabilities, epitomized by the Internet, now allow information and ideas to be exchanged across the globe 24 hours a day, seven days a week, at the touch of a button or the click of a mouse. This opening up of communication media and channels has been accompanied by the traditional domains of knowledge being unlocked. Growing collaboration, both within and between companies, is breaking down the barriers long guarded by 'knowledge gatekeepers', and reinvigorating the flow of knowledge around the organization and throughout the value chain.

In the 'Information Age' acquiring or creating relevant and useful knowledge and using it effectively to benefit the business is the crux of successful knowledge management. But while the value-driven business leader must recognize that knowledge is an asset that can and should be shared, they should also understand that you cannot treat all knowledge the same. There is a spectrum of knowledge ranging from *tacit knowledge* to *explicit knowledge*. Tacit knowledge refers to what we know, but find difficult to articulate. Human beings, individually and collectively, are the repositories of tacit knowledge, so it can only be liberated and used in a climate of trust. Explicit knowledge is more tangible: it can be captured in written or process form and easily reused. As David Snowden, director of the knowledge and differentiation programme within IBM Global Services, points out: 'The act of sharing tacit knowledge always creates something new. Explicit knowledge can be purchased, stolen or reinvented; tacit knowledge is unique, the engine of innovation and capable of real-time reactivity in decision-making.'

> *Understanding that knowledge is volunteered, and cannot be conscripted, is key to successfully inculcating a knowledge management culture.*

But knowledge *per se* has no intrinsic value: its value comes from exercising it. Which begs the all-important question: what do we need to know? If we discover knowledge in the process of using it, how do we find out what we need to know in order to extract and exploit its value?

Intellectual capital and knowledge management

As we said earlier, knowledge and the way it is applied is now a key source of competitive advantage. This is evident in the significant discrepancy between many organizations' stock market value and their book value. For instance, how does a company such as Microsoft command a market capitalization almost 20 times its balance sheet valuation? Or, equally, why does the stock market place such a high value on some of the new Internet stocks, despite the fact that many of them have yet to make a profit? It may be due to their growth potential or market dominance, but the biggest factor is invariably the *intellectual capital* they have created. The process of creating and leveraging this capital is *knowledge management.*

Knowledge **per se** *has no intrinsic value: its value comes from exercising it.*

One performance measure that is now being taken seriously by many organizations is 'market value-added' or MVA. At its simplest MVA is the difference between what the market says a business is worth and the asset value of that business as represented in its balance sheet. It can be defined as: MVA = current market value of the business – total capital employed. The greater the MVA, the more value that has been created for shareholders. Conversely, the smaller the MVA (even, in some cases, a negative value), the smaller the value created for shareholders.

In the past, competitive advantage derived from physical size and capabilities. Today it is more likely to flow from the people skills, databases and competencies which combine to create 'intellectual capital'.

In the past, competitive advantage derived from physical size and capabilities. Today it is more likely to flow from the people skills, databases and competencies which combine to create 'intellectual capital'. There are various ways of measuring intellectual capital. In a supplement on intellectual capital to Skandia's 1997 interim report, it was suggested that:

> Intellectual capital (IC) can be described as a company's intangible resources and can be assessed as the difference between its market value and its book value, expressed as adjusted shareholders' equity. Another value model is Tobins Q, where IC is assessed as the difference between the market value of a company and the replacement cost of its fixed assets. Still another one is calculated intangible value (CIV), where IC is assessed as the discounted present value of the company's excess profitability in comparison with its business competitors.

> Intellectual capital may be defined as an organization's 'intangible resources', but it is largely derived from human faculties, including the ability to think, reason, under-

stand, learn and be creative. Dave Ulrich, a professor in the School of Business at the University of Michigan, offered a simple formula for representing and calculating intellectual capital: Intellectual capital = competence x commitment. Ulrich (1998) wrote:

> Firms with high competence but low commitment have talented employees who can't get things done. Firms with high commitment but low competence have less talented employees who get things done quickly. Both are dangerous. Intellectual capital requires both competence and commitment. Because the equation multiplies rather than adds, a low score on either competence or commitment significantly reduces overall intellectual capital.

The fact that competence and commitment can be both created and destroyed points to the practical potential of intellectual capital: it can be manipulated and managed. But to extract and exploit intellectual capital, the CEO and his team must first recognize that it exists in the organization.

United Kingdom academics Hope and Hope (1997) identify three types of intellectual assets:

- *human capital or competencies* – these include the experience, skills and capabilities of people;
- *structural or internal capital* – these include patents, trademarks and copyrights; knowledge stored in databases and customer lists; and the design and capability of information systems;
- *market-based or external capital* – these include the profitability and loyalty of customers and the strength of brands, licences and franchises.

The challenge for CEOs and their boards is how best to realize, utilize and organize these intellectual assets so that their value is self-evident and self-perpetuating. The solution lies in knowledge management (Figure 6.2).

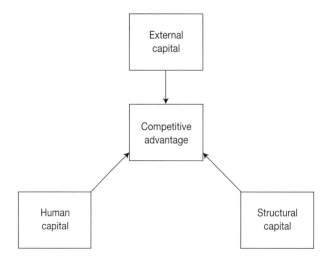

Fig. 6.2   Using knowledge management to leverage intellectual capital

As Probst, Raub and Romhardt (1999) wrote:

> The knowledge environment in which companies must function today is structurally much more complex than that which existed several centuries ago. From a quantitative point of view, human knowledge has grown exponentially. Following Guttenberg's invention of the printing press, it took more than 300 years for the worldwide volume of information to double for the first time. Since then, it has doubled virtually every five years.

It is important to distinguish between information and knowledge. IBM's David Snowden makes the distinction using the metaphor of a map and a human guide:

> A map is a set of data organized into a coherent and reusable form – it is information. The guide, on the other hand, is knowledgeable. She does not need to consult a map, takes into account recent experience and has the ability to relate my ability to her knowledge of the terrain. The guide is the fastest way to achieve my objective, provided that I trust her. If I do not have that trust, and am not prepared to take the risk of experimentation, then I will fall back on information – the map.

While some would represent the relationship between data, information and knowledge as a linear progression, Snowden advocates an alternative perspective. He believes that such linear models are not only misleading but false, as they do not take into account the symbiotic relationship between knowledge and information. 'Knowledge is the means by which we make sense of data, not some meta level of information,' he says. In other words, 'Sense-making is the purpose of knowledge and the only valid objective of knowledge management.'

The view that the role of knowledge is to create information reflects the current climate of uncertainty, and the need, as a consequence, to be more sensitive and responsive to change in order to remain competitive.

Leveraging intellectual capital for competitive advantage

The strategic importance of knowledge is inextricably linked to the company's capabilities and network of relationships. Put simply, it is a measure of the company's competitive strength and sustainability, as depicted in Figure 6.3.

The question is not why knowledge is strategically important, but how. Within the global marketplace there is a constant commotion of market activity: markets reaching maturity, markets fragmenting, markets disintegrating and new competitors entering the fray. In such a turbulent and fast-moving environment the need for relevant knowledge has become more acute if business leaders are to assess and target markets successfully.

The question is not why knowledge is strategically important, but how.

The problem for many CEOs wanting to identify and establish the right knowledge management strategy is the dearth of guidance. Because knowledge management is a relatively young discipline, there are few successful models to choose from, and these

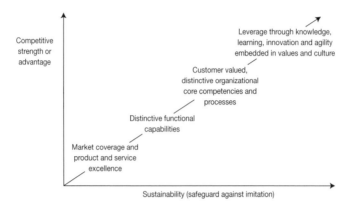

Sustainable advantage is based on building mutually reinforcing relationships between customer capital, organizational capital and human capital:

Competitive strength or advantage

Leverage through knowledge, learning, innovation and agility embedded in values and culture

Customer valued, distinctive organizational core competencies and processes

Distinctive functional capabilities

Market coverage and product and service excellence

Sustainability (safeguard against imitation)

Fig. 6.3   The strategic importance of knowledge
Source: Robert Davies, Strategic Performance Group

would need to be adapted anyway according to the unique situation of the company concerned. To help fill this gap, Harvard Business School and Bain and Company carried out some research into the knowledge management practices of management consulting firms. As knowledge is the core asset of consultancies, it was thought their experience would provide insights which had universal relevance.

The study revealed that consultancies employ two distinct knowledge management strategies – 'codification' and 'personalization' – as shown in Figure 6.4.

- The *codification strategy* focuses on codifying and storing knowledge in databases where it can be easily accessed and used by everyone in the company. This knowledge can be reused, and 'reuse economics' allows the business to grow.
- The *personalization strategy* emphasizes the transfer of knowledge from person to person, using computers purely to communicate rather than to store knowledge. Problems are resolved and valuable insights are gained through dialogue and discussion.

It seems that the strategy an organization chooses is determined by the way it interacts with clients and employees, and by the economics of its business. For example, companies pursuing a standardized product strategy benefit more from a knowledge management strategy based on knowledge reuse ('codification'). On the other hand, those using a customized product approach gain from a knowledge management strategy capable of handling unique needs through innovation ('personalization').

Crucially, the study found that successful companies favour one or other of the contrasting strategies. As Harvard professors Morten Hansen and Nitin Noria, and world-wide managing director of Bain and Co, Thomas Tierney (1999), wrote: 'Executives who try to excel at both risk failing at both.' The reason is that each strategy attracts a certain kind of person – broadly either 'implementer' or 'inventor', and a mix of both can be 'unwieldy and deadly'.

CODIFICATION	Competitive	PERSONALIZATION
Provide high-quality, reliable, and fast information systems implementation, by reusing codified knowledge.	strategy	Provide creative, analytically rigorous advice on high-level strategic problems by channelling individual expertise.

REUSE ECONOMICS:		EXPERT ECONOMICS:
Invest once in a knowledge asset; reuse it many times.	Economic model	Charge high fees for highly customized solutions to unique problems.
Use large teams with a high ratio of associates to partners.		Use small teams with a low ratio of associates to partners.
Focus on generating large overall revenues.		Focus on maintaining high profit margins.

PEOPLE-TO-DOCUMENTS:	Knowledge management strategy	PERSON-TO-PERSON:
Develop an electronic document system that codifies, stores, disseminates, and allows reuse of knowledge.		Develop networks for linking people so that tacit knowledge can be shared.
Invest heavily in IT; the goal is to connect people with reusable codified knowledge.	Information technology	Invest moderately in IT; the goal is to facilitate conversations and the exchange of tacit knowledge.
Hire new college graduates who are well suited to the reuse of knowledge and the implementation of solutions.	Human resources	Hire MBAs who like problem-solving and can tolerate ambiguity.
Train people in groups and through computer-based distance learning.		Train people through one-on-one mentoring.
Reward people for using and contributing to document databases.		Reward people for directly sharing knowledge with others.
Andersen Consulting, Ernst & Young	Examples	McKinsey & Company, Bain and Company

Fig. 6.4   How consulting firms manage their knowledge
Source: Harvard Business Review, March–April 1999

For example, each strategy dictates a different incentive system to stimulate knowledge-sharing. The codification strategy relies on getting people to write down what they know in order to build up a common repository of knowledge. The level and quality of employees' contributions is taken into account in their performance reviews. By contrast, the personalization strategy encourages people to share knowledge directly with others, rewarding them according to the direct help they have given to colleagues.

The knowledge management strategy an organization adopts both reflects the nature of the existing workforce and is reflected in the kind of people it attracts. If the CEO wants to alter the strategy, he or she may well have to change the people too – in more ways than one.

Before we go on to examine how an organization can develop a knowledge culture, let us take a look at how an organization can use knowledge management to gain a competitive edge.

Sharing best practice at GKN

GKN, the UK engineering group, is planning to use the Internet to disseminate information among its workers around the world about how to optimize manufacturing practices. It hopes this strategy will cut its capital spending bill by tens of millions of pounds a year.

The initiative is an innovative attempt to use modern electronic technologies to capture the kind of knowledge about production methods that is rarely written down, let alone communicated to other groups of workers. Such knowledge includes traditionally informal techniques such as 'learning from Nellie', where a new recruit learns from studying the actions of an experienced employee.

The project intends to capture, from the 19 000 workers in the automotive drivelines division, ideas for improving the manufacturing processes involved in making constant velocity joints. These best practices will then be shared via a GKN intranet site, being translated into other languages where appropriate. This project, designed to share tacit knowledge, will augment existing schemes to communicate explicit knowledge, thus offering further scope for both enhancing performance and cutting costs.

Source: *Financial Times*, 7 February 2000

Developing a knowledge culture

Developing and nurturing a knowledge culture depends not only on recognizing the value of knowledge and pursuing a defined knowledge management strategy, but on creating a climate which encourages the acquisition and sharing of knowledge in all its various forms. According to USA academic James Brian Quinn, who originated the concept of the 'intelligent organization', the business leader needs to consider four levels of knowledge:

- 'know-what', i.e., cognitive knowledge;
- 'know-how', i.e., advanced skills;
- 'know-why', i.e., systems understanding and trained intuition;
- 'care-why', i.e., self-motivated creativity.

'Moreover,' says Quinn, 'the value of a company's intelligence increases markedly as one moves up the intelligence scale from cognitive knowledge towards self-motivated creativity.'

A knowledge-oriented organizational culture encourages both group and individual contributions: it is very 'social'. Openness, trust, communication and collaboration are key characteristics. The emphasis is on human action and interaction in all areas of the business, so that experience, expertise and experimentation are employed appropriately to maximum effect. Electronic tools have their place in helping understanding and boosting efficiency, but they must be counterbalanced by a degree of personal interface and human judgement. In addition to actively sourcing knowledge internally and externally, the CEO must ensure that employees are given the tools, techniques, training and trust to use it.

Inertia or feelings of superiority or vulnerability often work against new knowledge being taken up or existing knowledge being shared and grown. 'Organizational blindness' is a condition where individuals' knowledge becomes so set through routine that people will not believe it can be improved. Good leadership is vital to encourage employees to be alert to alternatives and to question the status quo. It is up to the CEO to instil confidence and strengthen morale, as innovation and progress are only achieved by open-minded, questioning employees. The visible commitment and enthusiasm of senior management underpins any organizational change. Employees only take notice of what managers and supervisors do, not what they say. Values and trust go hand in hand. Such a climate creates happier employees, and happier employees create happier customers.

> *A knowledge-oriented organizational culture encourages both group and individual contributions … openness, trust, communication and collaboration are key characteristics.*

Promoting trust and the values that work to create better stakeholder value requires knowledge to be liberated. In essence, improving the value of the 'sum of the parts' means improving the value of the parts themselves. A knowledge culture should seek to spread 'ownership' of knowledge assets throughout the organization, so that knowledge input and output increase and feed off each other.

But there are limits to the extent to which knowledge can and should be disseminated. People only need to be able to access the knowledge they need to do their jobs. Distributing knowledge indiscriminately and 'knowledge overkill' can be self-defeating. It can, for example, defeat the efficient division of labour, overwhelm the human capacity to absorb, assimilate and act on knowledge usefully, or breach codes of secrecy. For knowledge to have a value and to be valued, it must be treated as valuable.

Everyone should be engaged in gathering and applying intelligence, as responsibility for knowledge is increasingly integrated into many functions. But some companies have even gone as far as creating new positions, such as chief knowledge officer (CKO), in response to intensified competition where better management of intellectual assets can generate critical advantage.

The CKO's principal task is to design and deliver a knowledge management programme. The CKO, who is usually appointed directly by the CEO, normally does this by identifying internal knowledge 'champions' – employees who are keen to implement knowledge initiatives and will enthuse and win the commitment of others. Since knowledge is all about people, inspiring a 'contagion' of knowledge awareness and value is the surest way of embedding a knowledge culture.

Dialogue is essential for knowledge to be produced, promoted and preserved, so establishing a common language is crucial to any knowledge management system.

Knowledge management goals will never be achieved unless everyone agrees on definitions of basic terms like 'data', 'information', 'skills', 'competencies' and 'knowledge'. Other management disciplines, such as finance and logistics, can call on a well-established and detailed vocabulary. So the objectives for an investment project, for example, can be described unambiguously in financial terminology. But because knowledge management is a relatively new discipline, its language, which stems in part from the organization's behaviour and operations – its culture – has yet to fully evolve.

Formal systems for sharing knowledge

One of the first things the CEO must do when seeking to implement a knowledge management culture is to look at the way people in his or her organization work. Working lives and habits have changed, and these changes need to be reflected in new policies and practices. Advances in technology and communications have given workers greater flexibility and mobility, to the point where many employees are no longer anchored to an office but work wholly or partly from home or in transit out in the field. Mobile telephony, with its lightning speeds of voice and data transfer, the Internet and wider use of videoconferencing enable 'virtual offices' to operate in ways previously unimaginable.

Barriers to knowledge sharing include high staff turnover, high-rise hierarchical structures and incentive schemes based on individual rather than team performance. Such barriers need to be broken down ...

But while the opportunities to share and enhance knowledge are expanding all the time, there remain threats. Barriers to knowledge sharing include high staff turnover, high-rise hierarchical structures and incentive schemes based on individual rather than team performance. Such barriers need to be broken down if employees are to want, as well as be able, to share knowledge. Not everyone is a born communicator, so organizations need to offer a range of tools and techniques to accommodate different styles of communication and creativity. Chief executive officers also need to allow employees the time to share knowledge or purely for productive personal reflection.

Transferring knowledge is a multifaceted, multidimensional and multilateral process. But there are three key steps (Figure 6.5).

1   Knowledge must be invited or enticed to flow from the minds of employees. As mentioned earlier, a conducive culture has to be accompanied by facilitative practices. Activities such as mentoring, shadowing, team-working, brainstorming and even periods of job swapping/rotation can encourage knowledge sharing and help to obtain valuable insights that would otherwise remain hidden.

2   The second step is to make that knowledge available, accessible and usable. Information technology allows the computerized acquisition, synthesis and distribution of knowledge. Centralized knowledge bases constructed of integrated

feeds and networked communication systems (intranets and extranets) allow more open and direct access to the company's library of knowledge, whether that is contained in a database or in e-mail correspondence and online discussion groups. Information technology also enables huge volumes of data to be stored, developed, retrieved and examined in a very sophisticated way. But technology needs to be backed up by training and in-company support in order for knowledge to be exchanged and integrated.

3　The third step is to encourage staff to share knowledge, whether it stems from a personal or collective experience, and whether it was gained within or outside the organization. The value the company attaches to knowledge creation and the contribution of knowledge to the enterprise should be reflected in appraisal and reward systems and reporting systems. The CEO and his or her team should make it clear that knowledge is not the responsibility of the R & D or IT departments, but of the entire organization. Management style and the way the organization functions day to day has a tremendous influence on the extent to which employees feel comfortable offering insights, expressing ideas or exchanging and using information. For example, is the organization recruiting the right people and fully realizing their potential and value? Are plant and equipment properly allocated, fully operable and adequate? Is everyone recognized for their achievements and given sufficient support if they run into trouble while performing their duties? Are expectations realistic and reasonable? If the answer to such questions is 'no', are the policies, decision-making processes and resources in place to effectively redress the situation?

Fig. 6.5　Exploiting the power of knowledge

As IBM's Snowden says: 'In the future we will manage the ecology of the company and its environment to allow the most effective deployment of its intellectual assets. This is a style of management which is more about enablement than it is about direction.'

The key word when it comes to knowledge management is 'partnership'. Drucker asserts that 'partnership with the responsible worker is the *only* way to improve productivity. Nothing else works at all'. The growing use of process teams and networked organizations highlights how successful partnership can be. Reorganizing around core processes, rather than functions, tends to reduce the number of people involved, consequently lowering costs and decreasing susceptibility to the ills of hierarchies. Problem-solving and much of the decision-making can be done at source, which frees up senior personnel to concentrate on more strategic issues and allows those at the customer interface to demonstrate their understanding of customers' concerns. Empowered employees make better workers and company ambassadors.

Organizations and individuals need to be more flexible in order to cope with increasing knowledge. Chief executive officers can encourage organizational learning practically through incorporating social spaces in both the work environment and work schedule. Informal gatherings of employees in cafeterias, lounges and on the Internet produce rich sources of information and knowledge, and they play an important part in the circulation and volunteering of knowledge. What is more, they are the natural theatre for storytelling, the most powerful tool we possess for communicating knowledge.

Knowledge should be sourced from and shared among a host of players, including colleagues, customers, competitors and suppliers. The advent of 'knowledge communities' and learning networks to collectively address problems that individual member organizations are unable to tackle alone is further testament to the benefits of liberating and leveraging knowledge through learning together.

The movement towards lifelong learning reflects the expanding role and remit of knowledge. Lifelong learning devolves responsibility for creating and disseminating knowledge and equips people with a broader range of capabilities and understanding. Companies should encourage continuous personal and professional development alongside traditional programmes of training and education, because individual growth contributes to organizational growth.

Linking knowledge to marketing strategy

Wharton professor George Day, a leading authority on marketing strategy, summarized the value of knowledge and its application to market-driven businesses. He wrote:

> The knowledge base of a market-driven organization is arguably its most valuable asset. Some of the knowledge is the raw material the firm processes and sells – think especially of the work of consultants and employees in financial services or software firms. More knowledge is deeply embedded in the core processes. What distinguishes a market-driven firm is the depth and timeliness of market knowledge that enables it to anticipate market opportunities and respond faster than its rivals. When this knowledge is widely shared,

it is a common reference point and assumption set that ensures the strategy is coherent rather than a disconnected set of activities. (Day, 1999)

There are two interrelated points to raise here. One is the importance of *selectivity* – identifying and focusing on core competencies, rather than trying to be the best at everything. The other is the importance of *husbandry* – tapping into, harvesting and cultivating the expertise and experience of those involved in the core processes. The implication is that the knowledge management strategy of the business should reflect its marketing and corporate strategy.

In order to manage knowledge effectively, we must know where knowledge is located, and how to develop and deploy it most productively. There are numerous types of knowledge – trends, future convergence, supply, the workforce, the work context, politics, public attitudes, media and so on. Marketing, however, is predominantly concerned with four types of knowledge, as outlined in Table 6.1. Each has its own unique value that will vary according to the particular context.

Table 6.1   Marketing knowledge

Knowledge type	*Business value*
Customer knowledge	Matching the organization's competencies to the target customers' needs requires in-depth knowledge of customer requirements and behaviour. The creation and delivery of customer value forms the basis upon which long-term, profitable relationships are built.
Competitor knowledge	An awareness and understanding of competitor activity and aspirations can help clarify one's own market position, illuminate new opportunities and improvements, and prevent similar mistakes being repeated. Competitors can be good teachers, as well as good motivators.
Process knowledge	Greater efficiency and efficacy can be obtained through organizing activities in ways that align input, throughput and output with the operations of the wider value chain. Processes deliver productivity and contribute profitability.
Technology knowledge	The intelligent use of technology, and information technology in particular, can greatly enhance processes and improve performance. However, the choice of technology and its appropriate application and use is vital.

The four types of knowledge in Table 6.1 provide a solid foundation on which to construct a market knowledge base. A deeper and more accurate understanding of the forces driving the customer and the market, and the pressures facing them, help make the business more customer focused.

United States academic and marketing expert Roger Blackwell's conceptualization of the way knowledge moves from 'mind to market' is depicted in Figure 6.6. This progression involves the following steps:

- gathering and analyzing knowledge about consumers, their problems and their unmet needs;
- identifying partners to perform the functions needed in the demand chain;
- sharing knowledge about consumers and customers, technology and logistics with demand chain partners;
- developing products and services that solve customers' problems in conjunction with other firms in the demand chain;
- shifting the functions that need to be performed by the channel to the organization that can perform them most efficiently and effectively;
- developing the best logistics transportation and distribution methods to deliver products and services to consumers in the marketplace.

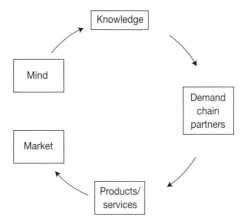

Fig. 6.6   'Mind to market'
Source: Blackwell (1997)

We need to move away from a simplistic notion of customer orientation. It is no longer sufficient to be market led. In a world of continuous change customers cannot be expected to anticipate step changes in things such as technology, lifestyles or fashion. Instead the organization needs to be ideas driven and market-informed.

As the workplace and marketplace have been transformed, so too has the character of business goals. Hope and Hope (1997) pin this change on an apparent shift in work objectives, from 'lowest unit cost' to 'highest value-adding' work. The difference in approach is portrayed in Figure 6.7.

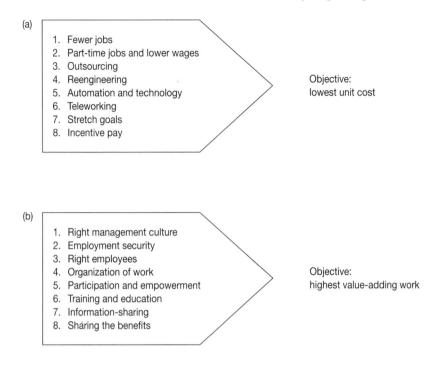

(a)

1. Fewer jobs
2. Part-time jobs and lower wages
3. Outsourcing
4. Reengineering
5. Automation and technology
6. Teleworking
7. Stretch goals
8. Incentive pay

Objective:
lowest unit cost

(b)

1. Right management culture
2. Employment security
3. Right employees
4. Organization of work
5. Participation and empowerment
6. Training and education
7. Information-sharing
8. Sharing the benefits

Objective:
highest value-adding work

Fig. 6.7   **(a) Eight steps to the lowest unit cost approach;**
(b) eight steps to the highest value-adding work
Source: Hope and Hope (1997)

Productivity in the knowledge-oriented firm will be defined in terms of innovation, quality and relevance, or the generation of value through maximizing intellectual capital. Because investment in knowledge does not immediately or visibly translate into financial results, as do traditional, tangible outputs (return on investment or number of sales per employee, for instance), an organization needs new methods to measure and monitor performance. As Hope and Hope (1997) write, these measures will be 'less concerned with the volume of output (such as the number of orders processed) and more concerned with the value-adding content of work (whether orders are processed correctly the first time and without delay)'. The evaluation of performance therefore centres on customer service and satisfaction rather than on operational efficiency.

We need to move away from a simplistic notion of customer orientation. It is no longer sufficient to be market led.

Summary

Knowledge is fast becoming *the* key economic resource, and the extent to which organizations manage it will increasingly determine their success in an ever more competitive and chaotic business environment. The CEO has to spearhead any knowledge management programme, as it involves a radical departure from traditional organizational thinking and requires a fundamental change in culture.

Business leaders should adopt a three-stage approach to developing and nurturing a knowledge culture: recognizing the value of knowledge, pursuing a defined knowledge management strategy, and creating a climate which encourages the acquisition and sharing of knowledge. Trust is an absolute prerequisite for any knowledge management initiative to succeed, but employees must also be given the tools, techniques and training to share and utilize knowledge effectively.

Being market led is no longer enough. Today's organizations need to be ideas driven and market-informed. Such organizations will be increasingly concerned with adding value rather than reducing unit costs, and new performance and monitoring measures, which centre on customer service and satisfaction rather than on operational efficiency, need to be developed accordingly.

 Checklist for CEOs

Business leaders need to ask themselves the following questions about their organizations' knowledge management strategy.

- Do we understand the relationship between data, information and knowledge?
- Does our organization follow a *codification* or a *personalization* knowledge management strategy?
- Do our recruitment practices and incentive systems reflect and support our organization's knowledge management approach?
- Do we work to create a climate within our organization which encourages the acquisition and sharing of knowledge?

- Do the values and day-to-day business practices in our organization support a climate of openness, trust, communication and collaboration in which knowledge management can flourish?
- Are employees given the tools, techniques and training to use knowledge?
- Do we know where, both within our own organization and in the value chain, knowledge resides?

Interview: John Neill, CEO, Unipart Group of Companies

How Unipart uses knowledge to create its future

Unipart was created in 1987 as the result of a management buyout from British Leyland (BL). The parts, service and components subsidiary of BL was lacklustre and, dogged by strikes, restrictive practices and poor product quality, epitomized all that was wrong with British industry. Today Unipart Group of Companies is one of Europe's leading logistics and parts organizations, with a diverse range of international businesses. One of Britain's brightest industrial stars, it is now held up as a model for others. Employees are shareholders, the company practises a stakeholder philosophy, and it believes in long-term 'shared destiny' relationships. Its visionary CEO, John Neill, who joined BL in the mid-1970s, has been the architect of the turnaround.

We began the process of transformation by focusing on quality and customer service. We believed that our future success in global markets lay in the knowledge and skills of the people in the company, which meant continuous learning and improvement in order that Unipart was always one step ahead of the competition. We also knew that relationships – with employees, customers and other stakeholders – would be the foundation of business success. Employees now own nearly 50 per cent of the group, and we work hard to develop and empower them to keep them committed to the company, to the customer and to continuous improvement. While individuals are important, we place a high value on teamwork, pooling resources and sharing knowledge and experience.

Before the buyout this organization was characterized by strikes, stress and underachievement. We had to change if we were to stay in business. Competition was aggressive, product life cycles were shortening, our skills base was shrinking, our costs were too high, our customers were becoming less loyal and more demanding, our time to market was too long, and so on.

We set ourselves the strategic challenge of learning from the best in the world, renewing our skills regularly, eliminating waste across the supply chain, leveraging the benefits of IT and improving continuously. Continuous improvement underpins everything we do; there is no end game.

To this end we needed to introduce a new approach that was both practical and philosophical. That involved developing lean processes, investing in new technology and inculcating radically different attitudes. We had to change our processes, our operations and our culture. Culture change was the most difficult to achieve, but we did it through creating, capturing and sharing knowledge.

You have to constantly renew your knowledge: it used to be every few years, but such is the pace of change that now it is every few months.

We gathered knowledge from the best companies in the world, like Toyota and Honda, and adapted, developed and used it to create competitive advantage. But we had a very definite process to do that, rather than leaving it to serendipity.

The first step was to create a base of knowledge and introduce learning as a key component of the business rather than as a bolt-on. We began by creating a shared vision and values, then demonstrated the high value we placed on learning by setting up an in-house university – the Unipart U. The U remains a very visible, very strong statement of our commitment to learning and knowledge management. All company directors are 'deans' and the learning is renewed continuously. There are over 200 courses taught by our employees and managers. Their contributions continually refresh the content of courses and enable the company to apply continuous learning principles and constantly adapt its working practices.

But learning is integrated into day-to-day work. What people learn in the morning they 'do' in the afternoon. Knowledge gained in the classroom can be transferred immediately to the shop floor to deliver a competitive edge to the business. Our Contribution Counts (OCC) circles are Unipart's team problem-solving programme. Everyone is trained to use simple techniques to make improvements at the sharp end of the business, and we track the results. People work unsupervised to solve problems and 75 per cent of the company is involved at any one time.

Our Contribution Counts circles have proved to be a very effective way of empowering people, and have been extended to include customers, suppliers and members of the community.

But our future success depends on our ability to reduce the cycle time for learning. Learning needs to be fast, relevant, customized, focused and just in time if it is to be effective and give the business a clear competitive edge.

We recently introduced a radical new concept called 'Faculty on the Floor'. This enables employees to work on production-related problems through direct access to computer-based problem-solving tools and best practice web sites in specially built learning centres on the shop floor. Once they've solved their problem they can apply the knowledge in their day-to-day work environment. The Faculty on the Floor allows employees to capture learning and share it throughout the organization very quickly. It is designed to give people on the shop floor the knowledge they need to continually improve the quality of our products and services while driving ever-increasing levels of efficiency.

While the Unipart U is about learning in the morning and doing in the afternoon, the Faculty on the Floor is about learning at 10 o'clock and doing at 11 o'clock – or 'learning at the speed of light'.

But we are accelerating learning even further. For example, some problem-solving circles now run live online. Teams can access the findings from other circles to help them, and once they have reached a conclusion share it immediately via the intranet. Creating and distributing such knowledge instantly has brought huge advantages: in the few months since we set up the intranet-based system we've recorded direct savings of nearly £3 million, and there are inestimable indirect benefits.

We've taken this one step further and created the Virtual U, offering online courses within a managed learning system on our intranet. Businesses, customers and suppliers across our eight industry sectors will be able to tap into the information and knowledge in the Virtual U whenever they choose. There are enormous benefits for both our employees and the organization as a whole.

Employees are at the centre of learning and can plan their own learning portfolio, while learning at their own pace. And the Virtual U provides us as a company with a database of where our learning capabilities are, which helps us manage our overall organizational capability. The Virtual U provides a very deep level of learning in a fraction of the time that traditional courses take, and as such provides great value to both employees and the company.

At Unipart we want to use learning to build strategic capability in order to meet our strategic goals. These include moving into new market sectors, producing higher quality at lower cost, and creating new products and services. We are now creating that capability, but we know that sustainability is key and, as the saying goes, 'the grass grows back' – it is human nature to revert to your comfort zone. You have to make the organization constantly receptive to and comfortable with change if you are going to achieve your goals quickly. And you do that by closing the gap between learning and doing.

You use learning and knowledge management as a basis for people to 'discover their way through change' – but people only become committed if they learn themselves rather than being taught.

A common misconception is that knowledge management is about IT. It isn't: it's about people, though IT facilitates the process. In a recent survey 300 CEOs rated knowledge management as their second highest priority, after globalization. But most of those CEOs saw it as an IT issue – fuelled by the KM (knowledge management) consultants. An IT-led approach to KM may fail to produce any useful business-focused know-how. Most KM initiatives fail because they don't recognize that the active participation of people is the key ingredient, and because they are poorly communicated. The most valuable knowledge in a company usually comes from large cross-company cross-functional networks. If we only learn from our own environment we might get short-term benefits but eventually we will suffer from the problem of learning myopia.

Knowledge management is a leadership issue. Leadership is about communicating with and listening to employees, customers and other stakeholders. Management systems often need to be adapted to support the learning organization goals. This means that, in most cases, traditional command and control structures are no longer effective ways of driving change. Employees at all levels need to be highly skilled and equipped with the tools and techniques to identify and deliver improvements in their day-to-day jobs. That requires the highest levels of employee involvement and a clear, shared vision.

Underpinning everything we do is a strong knowledge management system. The CEO has to create a vision for the future, but he or she must get early adopters and buy-in to create teams to help communicate this vision across the enterprise.

At Unipart we think of knowledge management as the systematic capture, codification and effective deployment, through coaching, of best practice ideas and ways of working.

We are forever in transition, looking for new ways of learning, understanding and creating, utilizing new technologies and providing a new future for all of us. Through valuing and investing in people's knowledge, skill and commitment, and strengthening relationships within and outside the company, any company should be able to propel itself wherever it needs to go.

References and further reading

Blackwell, R. (1997) *From Mind to Market.* HarperBusiness.

Day, G. (1999) *The Market Driven Organisation.* New York: Free Press.

Hansen, M. T., Noria, N. and Tierney, T. (1999) 'What's your strategy for managing knowledge?' *Harvard Business Review*, March–April.

Hope, J. and Hope, T. (1997) *Competing in the Third Wave.* Boston: Harvard Business School Press.

Probst, G., Raub, S. and Romhardt, K. (1999) *Managing Knowledge: Building Blocks for Success.* Chichester: John Wiley.

Quinn, J. B. (1992) *Intelligent Enterprise.* New York: Free Press.

Snowden, D. (1999) 'Knowledge flow not information flow'. *Market Leader.*

Ulrich, D. (1998) 'Intellectual Capital = Competence × Commitment', *Sloan Management Review*, Winter.

Part 3

Delivering customer value

Keeping customers satisfied: maximizing market potential

It is a hard truth that much of the blame for marketing plans failing can be laid at CEOs' doors

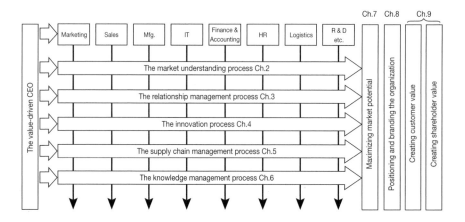

Fig. 7.1 Model of the value-creating process and relevant chapters in this book

Strategic marketing planning is very difficult, as we outlined in Chapter 2, but, done properly, pays real dividends. But careful strategic planning can be a matter of life or death for businesses operating in the brave new world of the twenty-first century, characterized as it is by growing consumer power, global account management and gathering momentum in the digital economy.

Once the really difficult part of strategic marketing planning has been done, especially determining the needs, or preferences, of the resulting segments, the company needs to prioritize its strategic marketing objectives and strategies.

This can easily be done by means of a structure like the one shown in Figure 7.2. This shows the segments classified on the vertical axis according to 'Market attractiveness' and on the horizontal axis according to 'Relative company competitiveness'. The criteria for the vertical axis usually include: market size, market profitability, market growth and market risk. This essentially classifies segments according to the

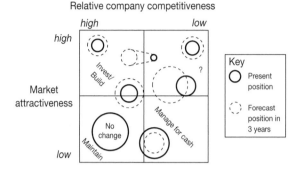

Fig. 7.2   Two-dimensional priority matrix

potential of each for growing the organization's profits over the planning period (often three to five years). The horizontal axis records how well the organization meets the needs of the different segments compared with competitors. The circle sizes relate to the current turnover in each segment. The lighter circles indicate projected sales (objectives) in three years' time.

From this graphical representation of the portfolio of segments, a number of marketing and business options present themselves.

1   In the top left box in Figure 7.2, where strengths are high and markets are attractive, the probable option would be to invest heavily in these markets and increase market share.
2   In the bottom left box, where strengths are high but markets are less attractive, a likely aim would be to maintain market share and manage for sustained earnings.
3   In the top right box, low strengths, combined with an attractive market, indicate a probable policy of selective investment to improve competitive position.
4   In the bottom right box, low strengths allied to poor market attractiveness points to a management for profits strategy, or even withdrawal.

This picture of the organization is a powerful summary of its current position and priorities for the next few years, as it shows:

- the current sales by segment;
- the potential for profit growth in each segment;
- the current competitiveness in each segment;
- the predicted sales (objectives) by segment in three years' time;
- the predicted competitiveness (objectives) by segment in three years' time.

The current and projected profit can also be shown either by putting a 'cheese' in each circle, or by repeating the matrix, but using profit to represent the circle sizes rather than sales. All that is missing are the strategies that will be adopted to achieve the sales and profit objectives.

Strategies to achieve the objectives

Strategies usually consist of a combination of the following:

- improved productivity;
- market penetration;
- new products;
- new markets;
- a combination of new products and markets;
- new strategies.

Each of the above has a number of components. For example, improved productivity can include price increases, a better product mix, a better customer/market mix, charging for deliveries and so on. Market penetration consists of market growth and increasing market share. New products or services can be developed for existing markets. Existing products or services can be sold into new markets. These last two strategies can be combined, of course, although clearly the risk is highest here. Finally, if the gap is still not filled, the only remaining option is new strategies, often in the form of acquisitions, joint ventures, licensing and so on.

The above strategies are based on the Ansoff matrix, depicted in Figure 7.3. All these different strategies are summarized in Figure 7.4, which is a valuable overview of the only actions that can be taken to achieve corporate objectives. These strategies should be included in the strategic marketing plan as appropriate.

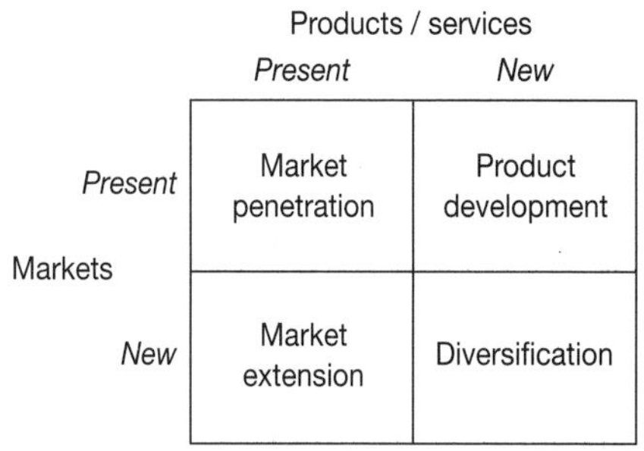

	Products / services	
	Present	*New*
Markets *Present*	Market penetration	Product development
Markets *New*	Market extension	Diversification

Fig. 7.3   Ansoff matrix
Source: Ansoff (1965)

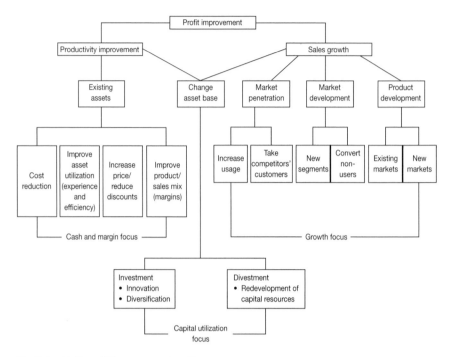

Fig. 7.4   Unit profit improvement options
Source: After Professor John Saunders, used with his permission

Strategic planning for key accounts

The growing concentration of power into the hands of fewer and fewer powerful global customers makes key account management (KAM) increasingly critical to corporate success. Pareto's 80/20 law, which stipulates that 80 per cent of any result is achieved by only 20 per cent of inputs, is now so important that all CEOs are beginning to take a much closer interest in the way their key accounts are managed.

> The growing concentration of power into the hands of fewer and fewer powerful global customers makes key account management increasingly critical to corporate success.

Time and effort invested by the CEO and his or her board in this growing area of commerce will have a multiplier effect in creating sustainable competitive advantage. (Turn to the interview with Ben Maddocks, global relationship director at international professional services firm PricewaterhouseCoopers, at the end of this chapter, to find out how one organization has reoriented itself around its key customers.)

Key account management is a natural development from customer focus and relationship marketing in business-to-business markets. It can enhance the efficiency and profits of both buyer and seller provided it is managed with integrity and imagination. But because the scope of KAM grows ever wider and more complex, those involved, both at a strategic and at an operational level, need to continuously update and develop their skills.

Key account management has evolved gradually, but stems from breakthroughs in fields such as industrial marketing, sales management, purchasing management, the psychology of customer behaviour and relationship marketing.

As the relationship develops, and the role of the customer evolves from anonymous buyer to something approaching a business partner, the level of involvement between the two parties becomes correspondingly more complex. There are some characteristic positions along the evolutionary path – exploratory KAM, basic KAM, co-operative KAM, interdependent KAM and integrated KAM. Each of these development stages is distinct because of the particular issues affecting the relationship at the time. These are shown in Figure 7.5.

This shows an ever upward, positively developing relationship, but no selling company should assume this will always be so. As with personal relationships, the business relationship can founder on a number of scores, ranging from a relatively minor misunderstanding to a massive breach of trust. Also, over time, the market position and priorities of both partners may change, obviating the strategic need for a close relationship. Figure 7.6 shows this range of relationships diagrammatically.

Exploratory KAM could be described as a 'scanning and attraction' stage: seller and buyer send out signals and exchange messages before deciding to get together.

At the *basic KAM* stage transactions have begun and the supplier's emphasis shifts to identifying opportunities for account penetration. This means the key account manager will need a greater understanding of the customer and the markets in which

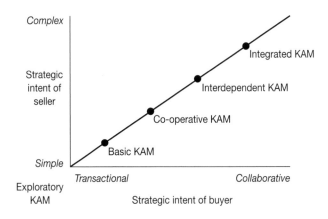

Fig. 7.5   Key account management development stages
Source: Adapted from a model by Millman and Wilson (1994)

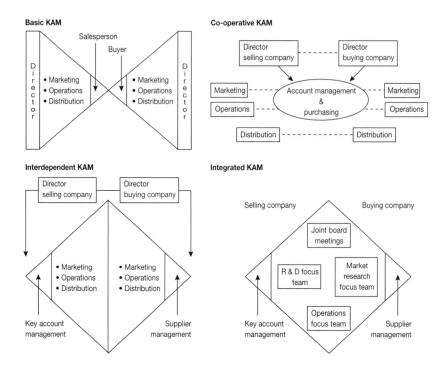

Fig. 7.6   Key account management relationships
Source: Adapted from *Key Account Management Report* (1996)

it competes. The buying company will still be market-testing other suppliers for price in its quest for value for money. So it is essential that the selling company concentrates on the core product and its surround, including all the intangibles, to tailor-make a customer-specific package. One of the early things the seller should do is simplify its systems to make them more customer-friendly.

By the *co-operative KAM* stage, trust has developed and the selling company may be a preferred supplier. But the buying company may not be prepared to use just one supplier, and will test the market to check alternative sources of supply.

By the time *interdependent KAM* is reached the buying company sees the selling company as a strategic external resource: the two will be sharing sensitive information and solving problems together. Both parties are so mature at this stage that each allows the other to profit from their relationship. Pricing will be long term, perhaps even fixed, and there is a tacit understanding that expertise will be shared. Much of this expertise will be directed into product improvement or simplifying the administrative systems which underpin all the commercial transactions. At this stage, the various functions of each partner communicate directly. The role of the key account manager and the main buyer is to oversee the interfaces and ensure that nothing happens to discredit the partnership.

The seller–buyer relationship can extend beyond partnership. *Integrated KAM* is where the two sides come together to create value in the marketplace greater than either could create individually. The two companies operate as an integrated whole, though they maintain their separate identities. The interfaces at all levels now function independently of the key account manager. The role is not redundant, but the incumbent can take a far more strategic approach. The borders between the buyer and seller are now blurred. Focus teams, made up of personnel from both companies, generate creative ideas and overcome problems. The key account manager and the main buyer contact merely co-ordinate their efforts. Nothing is allowed to get in the way of creative outcomes. Electronic data systems are integrated, information flow is streamlined, business plans are linked, and the once unthinkable is now willingly explored.

Companies need to decide which relationship is appropriate for any given customer, and personal relationships provide a guide. Most people have many passing acquaintances, where the relationship hardly extends beyond a nodding 'Good morning!'. At the other end of the scale are warm and intimate relationships with family and friends.

If we reversed our behaviour towards these two groups, we would be judged mad. Nor would we want the kind of intense relationship we have with our best friends with everybody we meet: not only would it be inappropriate, but we would lack the emotional resources to handle it.

Likewise, organizations lack the resources to run all their KAM relationships at the integrated level, even if it would be appropriate to do so. Like human beings, they have a spread of relationships and, like us, they can decide which relationships they would like to improve, keep the same or cool.

But unlike us, organizations should not be ruled entirely by their heart. All their relationship decisions should be guided by strategic considerations about the business potential to be gained, because the investment in time, people and resources made in the relationship must be justified.

However, these relationships tend to evolve, and the speed of progress is largely determined by the rate at which the buyer and seller can develop the necessary levels of trust. So companies may well have key accounts at a number of different levels.

Most business leaders ought to be able to recognize their own KAM relationships in these descriptions, because they all appear to go through these stages, even if they stick at one particular level for a long time. The evolutionary nature of development also means that a particular relationship can be in a transitional phase, somewhere between any two stages described above.

Identifying where relationships are now is a helpful indicator of what lies ahead and its implications for the organization and staffing. Here the role of the key account manager is critical to success.

Systems that classify key accounts into simple categories such as A, B and C are inadequate. Most companies are judged by profit, so key accounts should be classified according to the potential of each for growth in profits over, say, a three-year period.

Research carried out at Cranfield shows that four criteria are used to classify key accounts: available size of spend, margins available, growth rate, purchasing criteria and processes. Each of these is weighted and scored, so that each key account appears on a kind of thermometer, which ranges from low to high, according to each account's profit growth potential.

Figure 7.7 shows how to combine the different stages of KAM with these classification criteria so that objectives and strategies can be set for each account.

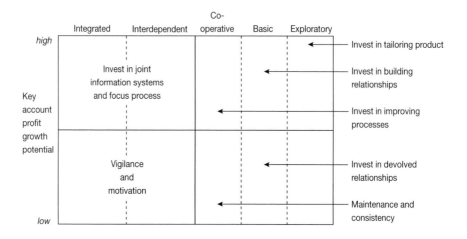

Fig. 7.7   Identification of objectives and strategies

Taking each box in Figure 7.7 in turn it is possible to work out sensible objectives and strategies for each key account. Starting with the bottom left-hand side boxes (low potential/high strengths), common sense would dictate retention strategies, as these accounts are likely to continue to deliver excellent revenues for some time, even though some of them may be in static or declining markets. This is especially possible because the company is already enjoying good relationships with the account, which should be preserved. So prudence, vigilance and motivation are essential here. Crucially, companies should be seeking a good return on their previous investments, and any financial investment should be mainly of the maintenance kind. This way, cash and resources will be available for investing in key accounts with greater growth potential.

The top left-hand boxes (high potential/high strengths) are where companies will derive most of their profit and sales growth. Here you need an aggressive investment approach, providing the returns justify it. It is probably appropriate to use net present value (NPV) calculations as a basis for evaluating these returns, using a discount rate higher than the cost of capital to reflect the additional risks involved. Any investment here will probably go on developing joint information systems and relationships.

The top right-hand box (high potential/low strengths) poses a problem, because few organizations have sufficient resources to invest in building better relationships with all accounts falling in these boxes. Therefore, for each account, a company needs to forecast net revenue streams for three years and discount them at the cost of capital (plus a considerable percentage to reflect the high risk involved) in order to evaluate which ones justify investment. Having done this, and selected those to invest in, under no circumstances should financial accounting measures such as NPV be used to control them – it would be like pulling up a new plant every few weeks to see if it had grown!

Instead, organizations need to set measures such as sales volume, value, 'share of wallet' and the quality of the relationship as objectives. As selected accounts move gradually towards partnerships it becomes more appropriate to measure profitability as a control procedure.

Accounts in the boxes on the bottom right-hand side (low potential/low strengths), and those not invested in from the top right-hand side, should not occupy too much of a company's time. Some can be handed over to distributors while some can be handled by an organization's own personnel, providing all transactions are profitable and deliver net free cash flow.

All other company functions and activities should be consistent with the goals set for key accounts according to this broad categorization. For example, some key account managers will be extremely good at managing accounts in the exploratory, basic and co-operative KAM stages, where selling and negotiating skills are paramount. Others may be better suited to managing the more complex business and managerial issues surrounding partnership and synergistic relationships.

All companies in the Cranfield research rated selling and negotiating skills as a prime requirement for key account managers, whereas all buying companies rated trust and the ability to make strategic decisions as most important. Indeed, many will not allow a salesperson to lead the key account team. The key task in key account management is matching the person to the key account. At the interdependent and integrated KAM stages the key account manager needs general management skills.

Key account managers need to produce strategic plans for all key accounts at the integrated and interdependent stages, and for each key account in the top right-hand box in Figure 7.7, which has been selected for building relationships beyond exploratory, basic or co-operative stages.

The content of such plans will be the same as for the strategic marketing plans described earlier in this chapter, but as Figure 7.8 shows, such plans frequently cover more than one market, or product, as many major global customers frequently deal with several different divisions of the supplying company. The Cranfield research indicates that such customers increasingly require an integrated plan for all their dealings with their global suppliers, which explains the growing interest in key account management as a major determinant of corporate success.

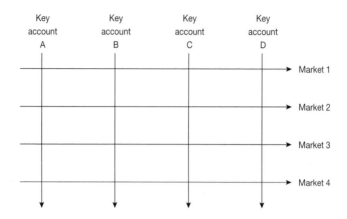

Fig. 7.8   Key account management in different markets

Where does strategic marketing planning fit?

There is some confusion as to how strategic marketing planning fits into general strategic planning. Strategic decisions are concerned with:

- the long-term direction of the organization, as opposed to day-to-day management issues;
- defining the scope of the organization's activities in terms of what it will and will not do;
- matching the activities of the organization to the environment in which it operates, so that it optimizes opportunities and minimizes threats;
- matching the organization's activities to its resources, be they finance, workforce, technology or skill levels.

Strategic management is typically dealing with an uncertain future and new initiatives, so it is often the harbinger of change. Organizations build their business strategies in a number of ways. There are six accepted strategy forming models.

1   *A planning model.* Strategic decisions are reached using a sequential, planned search for optimum solutions to defined problems. This process is highly rational and is fuelled by concrete data.

2   *An interpretative model.* The organization is regarded as a collection of associations, sharing similar values, beliefs and perceptions. These 'frames of reference' enable the stakeholders to interpret the organization and the environment in which it operates, cultivating an organizational culture particular to that company. So strategy becomes the product not of defined aims and objectives but of the prevailing values, attitudes and ideas in the organization.

3   *A political model.* Strategy is not chosen directly, but emerges through compromise, conflict and consensus-seeking among interested stakeholders.

Since the strategy is the outcome of negotiation, bargaining and confrontation, those with the most power have the greatest influence.

4   *A logical incremental model.* Strategies emerge from 'strategic subsystems', each concerned with a different type of strategic issue. Strategic goals are based on an awareness of needs, rather than the highly structured analytical process of the planning model. Owing to a lack of necessary information, such goals can often be vague, general and non-rigid in nature until such time that events unfold and more information becomes known.

5   *An ecological model.* The environment impinges on the organization in such a way that strategies are virtually proscribed and there is little or no free choice. In this model, the organization which adapts most successfully to its environment will survive in a way that mirrors Darwin's natural selection.

6   *A visionary leadership model.* Strategy emerges as the result of the leader's vision, enforced by his or her commitment to it, his or her personal credibility, and how he or she articulates it to others.

An organization is unlikely to use a pure version of any of these models, but rather a hybrid of some of them. One or two may predominate though, giving strategic decision-making a distinct flavour.

Academics cannot agree on a single, best approach, and company executives have to get on with formulating strategy as best they can, using a combination of experience, intuition and hope. The process broadly follows some sort of logical sequence leading to setting objectives and formulating strategies and tactics for achieving them, together with a consideration of the associated financial consequences. The formality of this process will depend on the degree of product and/or market complexity, the size of the organization and environmental turbulence – in other words, the degree of formality will be driven by the dominant decision-making model in the organization.

Strategic marketing planning has to be discussed in the context of strategic planning as described above, and an organization's marketing planning will normally be a microcosm of whichever overall strategic planning approach the organization adopts. Marketing planning is based on markets, customers and products, while business planning involves other corporate resources which will have a bearing on the identified markets. Corporate planning usually involves applying business planning to several different units of the business aggregate.

If marketing is a major activity in an organization, as in the case of consumer goods and service organizations, it is usual to have a separate strategic and tactical marketing plan. In other cases, the marketing elements are incorporated into the business plans of the other organizational functions, at the stage when marketing objectives and strategies are set. Often, these business plans are integrated into a corporate plan, which will contain long-range corporate objectives, strategies, plans, profit and loss accounts, and balance sheets.

One of the main purposes of a corporate plan is to provide a long-term vision of what the company is striving to become, taking account of shareholder expectations, environmental, resource market, and consumption market trends, and the distinctive competence of the company. In practice this means that the corporate plan will contain the following elements:

- desired level of profitability;
- business boundaries: which products will be sold to which markets (marketing); what facilities will be developed (production and distribution); the size and character of the labour force (personnel); funding (finance);
- other corporate objectives, such as social responsibility, corporate image, and so on.

Box 7.1

Why the CEO must lead marketing planning

Everyone in the organization must be aware of the marketing planning process as outlined in this chapter and Chapter 2 and be very clear about the role they are expected to play in it. But it is a hard truth that much of the blame for marketing plans failing can be laid at CEOs' doors. It is they who have to get the planning process accepted and, through their personal commitment and enthusiasm, maintain the energy and momentum of the initiative. But too often they are both unfamiliar with and uninterested in marketing planning.

In companies where CEOs have successfully effected change, they have actively intervened in:

- defining the organizational framework;
- ensuring that the strategic analysis covers critical factors;
- maintaining the balance between short- and long-term results;
- waging war on unnecessary bureaucracy;
- creating and maintaining the right level of motivation;
- encouraging marketing talent and skills to emerge;
- encouraging creativity and insights.

The marketing department cannot operate successfully if it is trapped inside a separation mentality. Instead of operating in isolation, it needs to be at the hub of the marketing planning information network. As such it can:

- advise on improved planning structures and systems;
- facilitate the transmission of relevant data;
- request inputs from managers, departments or operating divisions;
- act as a catalyst to break down interdepartmental/interfunctional rivalry or barriers;
- evaluate marketing plans against the overall corporate strategy;
- monitor ongoing plans and keep top management informed;
- support and advise line managers and staff;
- initiate special research on industries, markets, and so on.

Some weak CEOs try to abrogate responsibility and ask the marketing department to provide not only the plan but also the objectives and strategies. While this is technically feasible (assuming that the expertise is available), it is not desirable, because top management must set and lead corporate direction. What is their role, if not that?

Measuring marketing effectiveness

Accounts are measured because it is a legal requirement. But the marketing budget is a discretionary spend and historically has never been measured according to any universally accepted and systematic rules. Consequently, the marketing budget is often the first to be cut the moment profits come under pressure. This unprofessional approach, however, is changing rapidly as CEOs demand more accountability, hence measurability, from their marketing colleagues.

Chief executive officers should follow a number of principles when evaluating their organizations' marketing processes.

Objectivity

In marketing there are two basic kinds of data: hard data and judgemental data. Hard data measures outputs such as sales volume and value, market size, market share and profit margins. Judgemental data explains the reasons for the outputs. A SWOT analysis, for example, would normally seek to establish how well a particular organization meets the needs or requirements of a defined group of its customers. This presupposes that we actually know what these needs are, and herein lies perhaps the biggest problem of marketing – how to be sure.

Hard data is relatively easy to gather from external databases and most organizations have reasonably good measures of market size, total sales by product or service type and by application. Those which do not can commission such data relatively easily and cheaply from any good market research organization or consultancy. Figure 7.9 illustrates the types of data that all business leaders should ensure their organization has.

But marketing departments should not rely on their own internal database for such information, as this will typically hold data only on current and possibly lapsed customers.

The most important word missing from Figure 7.9 is 'why?'. Why do customers and consumers behave the way they do? What motivates them to buy what they buy in the particular way they buy it?

Nearly every independent survey over the past 50 years has indicated a substantial gap between the rational views of suppliers and the real reasons for their customers' actual behaviour. But organizations persist in relying on the views of their own

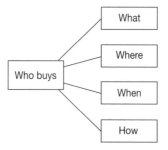

Fig. 7.9   Types of data all organizations should have

managers – the sales force in particular. And more recent evidence indicates that attitudes are not always linked to behaviour: many people approve of a product or an organization, but do not necessarily use it. For example, a recent survey of corporate good citizenship by the Consumers' Association in Britain showed that the three highest-rated companies were performing badly on profits, while the three lowest rated were exceptionally profitable. Another survey showed that Peugeot 106 drivers rated their cars far more highly than Ford Fiesta drivers, though the latter were far more likely to repeat purchase. So business leaders should be careful to ascertain how their marketers gather the motivational information they use and how current it is.

Marketing metrics

Business leaders need to measure the effectiveness of their organizations' marketing efforts. 'Marketing metrics' seeks to measure and evaluate customer relationships. The 1980s saw the desktop personal computer (PC) explosion, followed by database building. The 1990s saw the customer service movement, sales automation, brand valuation and the balanced scorecard. The end of the twentieth century saw the advent of marketing metrics, partly because of a realization that marketing had never been truly accountable, and partly because technology now allowed senior managers to measure and evaluate customer relationships in a way never previously possible.

The general rule on marketing metrics should be: 'If you can't measure it, think carefully about whether you should do it.' The general model to follow should be as shown in Figure 7.10.

In the case of the strategic and tactical marketing plans, the major items listed in Table 7.1 need to be measured.

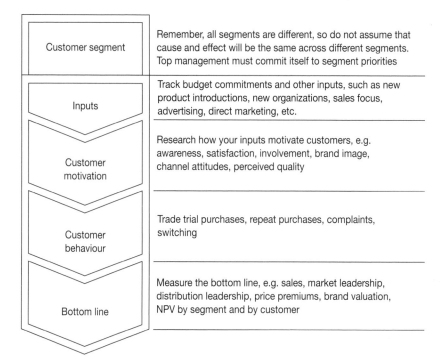

Fig. 7.10 Marketing metrics model

Table 7.1 Major marketing plan items to be measured

Marketing plans	Measurement
• Market segment attractiveness	Track the important factors that make markets more, or less, attractive
• SWOT analyses	Measure real strengths and weaknesses, against properly researched customer attitudes *and* behaviour. Also measure key external indicators
• Key issues to be addressed	Track whether key issues have been addressed
• Assumptions	Record and track what actually happens
• Strategic marketing objectives	Track key success indicators
• Strategies, programmes and budgets	Track progress on strategies, programmes and their outcomes

When selecting measures, check:

- alignment – do the measures reflect the objectives and strategy, or are they disconnected?
- actionable – are they directly actionable by someone?
- predictive – can the measures provide early warning signals?
- causal – do they indicate root causes, or are they merely symptoms?
- necessary – will other measures suffice?
- measurable – are they easy to measure and report?

Getting wired – the impact of e-commerce on the customer-focused company

A book on creating a company for customers would be incomplete without a few words of guidance for business leaders on the electronic revolution. This revolution is changing the strategies of all organizations, whether they like it or not. But for those prepared to embrace it, e-commerce can create significant competitive advantage.

E-commerce does three basic things.

1   It separates the processing of information about products from the products themselves, by helping people search for, find and evaluate products independently of those who have a vested interest in selling them.
2   It provides consumers with as much information about suppliers as suppliers traditionally have accumulated about consumers.
3   It creates a new dimension of competition between brands, based on who acts most effectively in the consumers' interests.

The Internet offers organizations the potential to establish a new interactive sales and communication channel with their customers. For example:

- e-commerce provides a direct link between organizations and their customers and suppliers;
- it lets others bypass the distribution chain (disintermediation), resulting in huge cost savings;
- it provides tools for delivering information-based products to customers (knowledge is the source of value itself – as in disease management, for example);
- it gives consumers what they want – speed, choice, control, comparability. This represents perhaps the biggest opportunity for open-minded companies.

But the Internet also poses a number of threats – not least from small start-up companies which are springing up like mushrooms. For example:

- you'd better act quickly – they're faster than you;
- they do not have as much to risk;
- you have to deal with your legacy bureaucracy;
- company size has little to do with it;
- geography has nothing to do with it;

- no one sleeps on the net. It is open 24 hours a day;
- price comparison makes it difficult to have different prices in different markets.

What is e-marketing?

Put simply, the Internet is just another medium for communicating with customers, along with the mail, the telephone and the field sales force.

But our research at Cranfield suggests that CEOs are still struggling with how to build the Internet into their marketing strategy. For the detail they can turn to resident experts or specialist reports, but what causes them anxiety is where to position it within the channel mix, and when they should consider using it.

Growing use of the buzzword 'e-business', rather than e-commerce, reflects the fact that the Internet can be used for any number of applications which involve communication between people or organizations. Our focus here is on marketing, ranging from communicating with prospects, through online sales, to product and service delivery.

... our research at Cranfield suggests that CEOs are still struggling with how to build the Internet into their marketing strategy.

The technical backbone of the Internet supports many different communications, including e-mail, discussion groups, electronic data interchange from computer to computer, online advertisements and web sites. For simplicity, we will concentrate on the role company web sites play in communicating with customers.

Even if an organization does not have a web site, its products or services are being discussed anyway in discussion groups and one-to-one e-mail conversations by customers exchanging views, by influencers such as journalists and consultants, and by prospective customers seeking information.

So the decision CEOs must take is not whether or not their company should be involved, but the appropriate level of involvement and the part the Internet should play in the channel mix.

The Six 'I's model

The Internet is an important new way of interacting with customers, but organizations should not consider it in isolation: it is just one communication channel.

... the Internet is an important new way of interacting with customers, but organizations shouldn't consider it in isolation: it is just one communication channel.

To assess its potential contribution, we need a model for the role of IT in marketing generally. Our Six 'I's model, shown in Figure 7.11, summarizes the ways in which IT can add value to the customer and hence improve the organization's marketing effectiveness. We will discuss the Internet under these six headings.

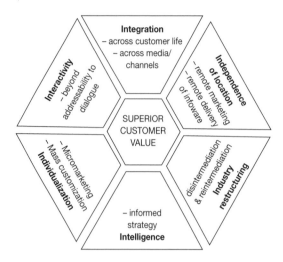

Fig. 7.11   The dimensions of IT-enabled marketing

Integration: know your customer

Companies these days are well aware of the need to build long-term customer relationships. A corner shop can achieve this through the information the owner keeps in his or her head about each customer's likes and dislikes. But larger organizations need customer relationship management systems which manage data throughout the customer life cycle, from initial contact, through information exchange and sales, to delivery and post-sales service.

The consumer wants to be able to reach the supplier through multiple channels, so this data must also be integrated across communication mechanisms. This allows a telephone salesperson to know about a service request that was sent yesterday by e-mail, for example, and sales representatives in the field can call on information about previous purchases and customer profitability to help them judge discount levels.

This integration is as important with the Internet as with any other communication medium. The fact is often lost on senior management, who delegate the web site to enthusiasts in an isolated corner of the organization, or outsource its development and operations with minimal provision for information transfer – hence repeating the mistakes made in the early days of the call centre.

Advertising your products on the World Wide Web (the web) is easy. More difficult, but absolutely crucial, is to gather vital customer information, obtain customer feedback, utilize existing knowledge about the customer and exploit the web's inter-active nature to add value through product configuration, online pricing and so on.

Interactivity: beyond addressability to dialogue

Knowing your customers means closing the loop between the messages you send them and the messages they send back. Developments in IT mean that interactive communication tools such as the telephone and the Internet are increasingly being used to complement less interactive mechanisms such as mail or media advertisements.

Growing use of carefully targeted direct mail as a means of communicating with individual customers has led some to call this 'the age of addressability'. Interactivity goes one step further – although in many cases the limited interactivity of the reply coupon will continue to be both sufficient and appropriate.

The best-known example of electronic commerce, book-selling, exemplifies how the Internet can be used for an interactive dialogue with a known customer.

The market structure is shown in Figure 7.12. Publishers have traditionally sold via high street retailers, complemented by a relatively tiny direct mail operation. They can now sell via Internet retailers such as Amazon.com, or via their own direct Internet service.

The high street retailers are naturally looking to protect their business by developing their own web channels, and electronic publishing, where the product is distributed as well as ordered electronically, poses an emerging threat to printed books.

Web sites such as Amazon.com exploit the web's interactive nature to allow the customer to search for books on particular topics, track the status of an order placed earlier, ask for recommendations of books similar to their favourites, read reviews placed by other customers, and so on.

The web site builds knowledge of the customer which allows it, for example, to notify them by e-mail if a new book appears on a topic of particular interest.

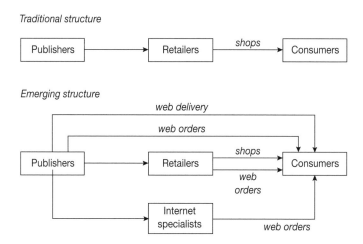

Fig. 7.12 The evolving book market

Individualization: information-enabled tailoring

Gathering integrated information about a customer gives an organization the basis to individualize its products or services. For a small premium, customers can order Levi's jeans, tailored to their own measurements, over the web. Likewise compact discs (CD)s can be 'cooked' to order, the customer selecting the tracks they want in the order they want.

How Dell's direct approach pays dividends

We looked at Dell Computer as an exemplar of supply chain management in Chapter 5, and refer to it again in Chapter 8 as being a good example of an organization which has aligned its brand positioning with its core processes. But Dell also pioneered the heavily IT-enabled direct marketing approach to computer sales, which makes it worthy of examination in this chapter too. Its direct approach is interesting in many ways, not least the manner in which it has individualized the product, price and surrounding services.

Dell's channel structure is summarized in Figure 7.13.

Dell began by selling personal computers 'off the page' in the computer press, using mail and telephone to dramatically undercut its rivals, with their expensive networks of field sales forces and shops. It has since added a small field sales force of its own to concentrate on senior relationships in its largest clients – a strategy we discussed earlier in this chapter.

Dell's experience in telephone selling gave it a natural head start in understanding how it could effectively add the Internet to the channel mix. The manager responsible for its web

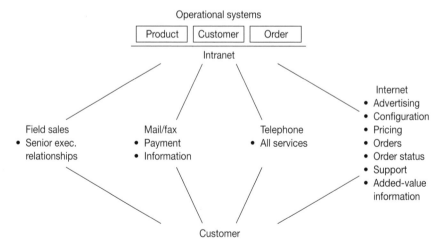

Fig. 7.13   Interactivity and individualization at Dell

site has even claimed that if a company knows nothing about telemarketing, it must learn about it before developing an Internet strategy.

Dell had been forced from an early stage to collect and distribute integrated information about its customers and their purchases, so that any telephone operator could deal effectively with any call. When a web site was added as an alternative route to purchase, it was linked into the same databases so it could share the same information on products, customers and orders.

Dell's web site provides all the services that are available by telephone, plus more. As well as the usual 'brochure-ware' of words and pictures describing what products are available, the site includes:

- a configuration service that helps the user to tailor the computer they want, and to calculate its price;
- a facility to order online; alternatively, the user can print out details and order by other means such as fax, post or telephone;
- information on the order's status, lead time and so on;
- automated customized pricing for its major 'platinum' customers;
- added-value services such as online support, information on future product releases and discussion forums for users to communicate with each other.

A high proportion of visitors to the site still ultimately place their order by other mechanisms such as the telephone. This highlights two important points: the impact of the Internet cannot be measured simply by measuring online sales; and, more generally, IT-enabled channels are often complementary.

Its web site has certainly helped Dell reduce its traditional operating costs. According to a spokesperson: 'We do not see Dell.com as a competing channel. We see it as a complementary channel. A lot of people visit Dell.com and then call us on the telephone and buy. Is that a bad thing? No, because it takes six to eight telephone calls to sell a computer, and we just made five of them go away, with a commensurate reduction in operating expenses.'

Independence of location: the death of distance

Individualization is closely linked to independence of location. What's the difference between shoes made to measure by the village cobbler and a kitchen made to order by an Internet design service?

Both achieve individualization, but the latter combines it with post-industrial revolution economies of scale. The design service serves a widely spread geographical population, using the data transport provided by the Internet and the physical transport of our twenty-first century infrastructure, along with a database-driven manufacturing facility.

> *Independence of location allows companies to achieve individualization economically.*

Independence of location allows companies to achieve individualization econom-ically. Niche products can serve their target markets even if those markets are spread globally.

To what extent can physical products become independent of location? The distri-bution channel has often been inseparable from the sales channel – think of car dealer-ships or supermarkets. Exploiting the Internet's potential means looking at whether the two are more effective together, separate, or in some new configuration. Consider Amazon again.

How Amazon and Barnes and Noble battle it out

The largest US bookseller, Barnes and Noble, has played 'me too' on its web site since its launch in March 1997, copying initiatives by Amazon as quickly as possible to neutralize Amazon's advantage. What differences remain between the two players?

Amazon relies on the physical proximity of its offices to the largest wholesaler of books in the USA, Ingram Book Company. Ingram stocks 400 000 titles and provides 59 per cent of Amazon's sales. The only stock Amazon carries itself are the 1000 top sellers (Figure 7.14).

Barnes and Noble, by contrast, has its own distribution network, designed for supplying its shops, with huge stocks, which means that it often gets books out faster than Amazon.

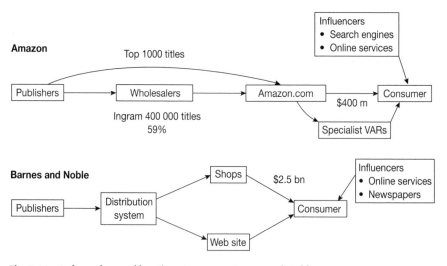

Fig. 7.14   Independence of location: Amazon v. Barnes and Noble

Amazon is also vulnerable to competition from other web-based retailers which draw on the same wholesalers, such as Bookstacks and Bookserve.

So physical distribution considerations are still key to both these market leaders. And as for the online fight for the sales order, Amazon has been forced to buy visibility expensively to combat the threat from Barnes and Noble and others.

Amazon struck deals with the search engine/directories such as Yahoo! and Excite in a bid to ensure that web users seeking books would find their way to its site.

Barnes and Noble, meanwhile, with profits then greater than Amazon's entire turnover, struck a deal with America Online (AOL), a service provider with 8.5 million subscribers, which gave it privileged access to much of AOL's potential market. Barnes and Noble also invested in advertising the site in papers such as the *New York Times.*

Amazon's aggressive strategy led to high growth, but at the expense of continuing losses. Its revenue of $16 million in 1996, representing 3 per cent of e-commerce in that year, grew to over $100 million in 1997, the year it went public, gaining $50 million in funding. But 1997 was still unprofitable, with losses of $10 million in the first six months alone. Amazon's continuing difficulty in making a profit in 1998, as its sales rose to around $400 million, did not stop the stock market valuing the company by the end of the year at $17 billion, compared with $2.9 billion for Barnes and Noble.

Amazon continues to innovate in an attempt to maintain its differentiation. It extended its 'top 20' listing of best-selling books to include every book listed on the web site, providing an endless source of depressing news for authors of niche items who might discover their masterpiece languishing at number 4503 in the bestseller list.

In a bid to compete with niche sellers such as Pandora's Books, which sells out-of-print science fiction, Amazon, with its wholesaler Ingram's assistance, set up an associates programme. So, for example, a business school web site can point its visitors to Amazon.com to buy books by its faculty, in exchange for 8 per cent of the resulting revenue. Amazon is now diversifying into sales of compact discs and videos, and recently launched an auction service where users can auction just about anything.

The details of this fight change every day – such is the fast-moving nature of the web – but whatever the outcome, the story disproves that all players in the online market have equal share of voice. On the web as elsewhere, the fight for visibility can be expensive.

Intelligence: informed strategy

Better customer data can improve decisions on marketing strategy, as we discussed earlier. A major computer manufacturer discovered in a marketing planning exercise that the market's buying criteria segmented according to the application for which the computer was used – accounting, stock control, marketing and so on. But the company had no data on this: all its records were by client company name and industry segment.

Rectifying this problem involved changing its order-taking procedures to track what the customer envisaged using the computer for when they bought it. This extra data had to be gathered whatever channel the order was placed through – distributors, direct sales force, telesales or the Internet – again illustrating the importance of data integration. The information could then be aggregated to enable more effective planning, and to support new initiatives to serve particular target segments more effectively.

> *Better customer data can improve decisions on marketing strategy ...*

A UK bank is using intelligence from an integrated marketing database to inform its channel mix. Customer lifetime value informs decisions such as whether the bank should propose a face-to-face meeting with a financial adviser, and the bank uses geodemographic data to profile customers of its Internet banking service in order to decide which of its other customers to contact about the service.

Industry restructuring: redrawing the market map

Some industries are already being restructured as organizations redefine themselves to take advantage of IT-enabled marketing, or are replaced by newcomers which operate according to the new rules. Retail financial services is a case in point.

Telephone bankers such as First Direct represent the first, comparatively modest, step towards the breakdown of the dominance of the 'one-stop-shop' local bank branch. We will examine First Direct's strategy in detail in Chapter 8. Other challenges to the traditional banks include competitors which are setting up banking services on the Internet, forcing the major clearers to respond with their own Internet services.

A North American study in 1997 calculated that a transaction conducted over the Internet cost 1 cent, compared with $1.07 for a branch transaction and 27 cents for an automated teller machine.

In addition to carrying out basic transactions, the Internet is being used to replace human advice in product specification. Web sites can be used to work out monthly mortgage payments, tax and so on: the user simply enters the required details into an online form. New electronic intermediaries will search for the best live quote from a range of life insurance companies.

When is it appropriate to use the Internet?

To recap, the Internet can be used as part of a strategy for IT-enabled marketing

- based on integration of customer data;
- providing interaction with the customer;
- allowing the product or surrounding services to be individualized;
- contributing to information needed for planning purposes;
- reducing the constraints of location.

Innovative organizations are using these features to restructure industries to their own and their customers' advantage. But do these examples form a model that will apply to another case?

To answer this question, you need to examine the nature of each customer interaction. Whether or not the Internet is an appropriate medium for a particular customer interaction varies according to circumstances – not least the characteristics of the segment.

Classic segmentation theory suggests that the channel may form a primary basis of segmentation, or that a single segment may be served by several channels. Individual customers will also have their own channel preferences, of course, and you may have to leave the choice to them. But in general you can determine where the Internet will be appropriate by considering whether its features match the needs of the interaction. Some of the main features are summarized below.

> *You should determine what proportion of your target segment has access to the Internet.*

When the connected subset is appropriate

You should determine what proportion of your target segment has access to the Internet. We have come a long way since the days of the 'nerd' stereotype, but there is still a bias towards more highly educated, more affluent consumers and, in the business-to-business sector, professionals using computers regularly, such as those in the IT industry (Figure 7.15).

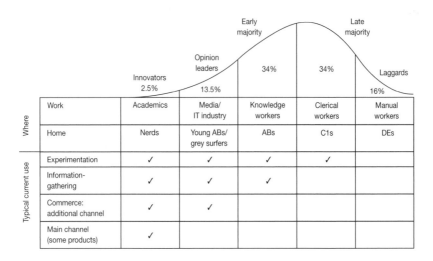

		Innovators 2.5%	Opinion leaders 13.5%	Early majority 34%	Late majority 34%	Laggards 16%
Where	Work	Academics	Media/ IT industry	Knowledge workers	Clerical workers	Manual workers
	Home	Nerds	Young ABs/ grey surfers	ABs	C1s	DEs
Typical current use	Experimentation	✓	✓	✓	✓	
	Information-gathering	✓	✓	✓		
	Commerce: additional channel	✓	✓			
	Main channel (some products)	✓				

Fig. 7.15   How use of the Internet is spreading

Age is a less important factor than is commonly assumed. According to a 1997 US study by McKinsey, for example, 43 per cent of highly paid 35–44-year-old men had used the Internet in the preceding month. This compared with only 20 per cent of 18–24-year-old men, reflecting, perhaps, lower use of the medium at work by this age group.

Gender has become less important. McKinsey also found that 21 per cent of 25–34-year-old women earners used the Internet, compared with 26 per cent of working men of the same age. By 1998, more than half of US net users were female.

According to research company IDC, the number of net users will have risen to 327.5 million by the end of 2000, up from 150 million in March 1999. In 1995 there were just 20 million users. IDC predicts that interactive television and mobile phone Internet links will boost this figure to half a billion by 2003.

The UK is catching up with the USA in terms of Internet usage. A poll in March 2000 from another researcher, ICM, showed that 45 per cent of British adults were online, compared with 29 per cent a year earlier. A further 38 per cent anticipated getting 'wired' (connected) as the access costs continue to fall. The figures suggest that the UK is now into the 'early majority' stage on the classic diffusion of innovation model shown in Figure 7.15.

Figure 7.15 also illustrates that as the number of connected users grows, so does each user's use of the medium: experimental browsing leads to serious information-gathering and ultimately online purchasing.

The speed at which users progress through these stages depends on a number of factors, including the quality of the connection. Many business users have high-speed links, but elsewhere response times can be annoyingly slow, prompting users to switch to other media.

IDC puts the value of e-commerce in 1999 at $111.3 billion, and predicts e-commerce will be worth over one trillion (1000 billion) dollars by 2003. But until web sites are faster to use, more reliable and have more functionality, e-commerce will not achieve its full potential.

A recent survey of UK web sites found that almost half the attempts to access some of the UK's most popular electronic banking sites failed, while on other sites it took over a minute to download a page. There was a big difference between sites: 99 per cent of visits to HSBC's site were successful, compared with only 57 per cent of visits to Citibank's.

Research by leading UK academics Lockett and Littler in 1997 discovered some of the characteristics of early adopters of a related innovation, direct banking by telephone. For example, early adopters tend to be opinion leaders and be more receptive to change than non-adopters. For them the 24-hour availability of direct banking far outweighed the perceived complexity and risk.

There are obvious parallels for Internet-based product and service delivery. Contrary to popular opinion, the availability of products at the right price, convenience, time-saving and customer service are far more important determinants of a customer's propensity to shop online than the security issues associated with giving credit card details over the Internet.

Security and privacy are issues, but users are usually willing to trade them for some perceived economic or other benefit.

When you need asynchronous communication at a distance

Unlike a sales call, a web-based communication can be carried out at any distance. This carries particular benefits for geographically dispersed markets and those where the cost of sales visits is prohibitive.

'Asynchronicity' means that those communicating do not need to do so at the same time. So, for example, an organization can provide Internet banking throughout the night without having to pay staff for working antisocial hours. Likewise, an e-mail request for product support can be answered when the local staff are next in the office.

> *... much of the real potential of the Internet is to facilitate interactive communication in order to better understand customers and personalize the offering.*

But Internet communications can be synchronous when required. For example, you can provide a button on a web site offering the option to 'talk to a representative'. A user clicking on this button opens a live telephone or video link while still viewing the web page. Such facilities will soon be standard.

When you need interactivity (and the interactions are programmable)

As the Dell example illustrates, much of the real potential of the Internet is to facilitate interactive communication in order to better understand customers and personalize the offering. But most UK web sites are currently little more than 'brochure-ware' – online versions of product brochures – as a 1998 study of Times 500 companies by US firm Cambridge Technology Group reported:

> We found that the vast majority of those organisations surveyed were not engaging in any form of interactive marketing. Their web sites were merely operating at the most basic level, providing passive information. Almost half of the web sites we visited did not request any personal details from visitors. Of those that did, only a tenth asked for anything more meaningful than name and phone number. It seems that most UK organisations have failed to grasp the basic elements of salesmanship [sic], that is talking to, and more importantly listening to, customers.

Interactivity on a web site is different from the interactivity of a telephone conversation or sales visit, in that the interaction is with a computer rather than a person. A web site is an appropriate channel for high-volume, repetitive interactions where a computer can be programmed to perform the task.

To take the Dell case again, configuring a computer is one of the few tasks where expert systems have matched their early promise. It is the kind of well-specified task that computers are good at, but, given the detail and complexity involved, is cumbersome and error-prone for humans. Computers are also good at arithmetic, and the customer can see the price of a package as they add items to the bundle.

But other interactive tasks – configuring a complex software package such as an accounting application, for example – are still best performed by humans. This explains the continued dominance of face-to-face selling in software development and consultancy services, for example.

When sight and sound are adequate

In the main, the web is currently a medium of two-dimensional static words and graphics. This is expanding, as bandwidth issues are addressed, to include sound and video, and will no doubt expand further still in the future. But its current limitations make certain products less appropriate for sale over the net. These include clothes, where the customer may wish to feel the fabric or try the item on. But routine or repeat purchases of clothes – jeans or underwear, for example – are being targeted for Internet sales.

When you can benefit from low variable costs

The electrical components company RS Components, traditionally a catalogue seller, is growing its customer base through its web channel without having to send out yet more catalogues. The variable cost of the Internet as a communication mechanism can be relatively low.

For most media, the more specific the targeting of a campaign, the higher the cost per thousand. Billboards are seen by a lot of people, only some of whom are relevant to the campaign. A mailshot is expensive but can be very specifically targeted. But once a web site exists, and assuming that Internet users can be motivated to look at it – an important assumption, as the Amazon case illustrates – the variable cost of the interaction can be very low.

But developing the web site and related back-end software is a major fixed cost. Fortune 500 companies spend between $800 000 and $1.5 million just to get their web sites up and running, according to a survey from US research organization Gartner.

This balance between fixed and variable costs is appropriate for organizations where volumes are high. Parcel company UPS, for example, claims it makes considerable savings – 30 cents per customer per day in telephone operator time – from the 60 000 customers who check the status of their parcel delivery online every day.

Delivery of 'infoware' products and services

'Infoware', which can be encoded as 0s and 1s, can be delivered electronically down a telephone line. Examples include weather reports, share prices, books and reports, news, software, music and videos. But even physical products often have an 'information surround' where value can be added to the core product. The IT industry, for example, uses the Internet extensively for providing product support.

Newspapers provide an interesting example of infoware. Newspapers compete with a variety of media: television and radio for news, magazines for advertisements, telephones and faxes for immediate weather forecasts.

The vertical integration of the newspaper, integrating journalists, editors, printing and distribution in one organization, may break down under the new threat of electronic news distribution – perhaps along the lines illustrated in Figure 7.16.

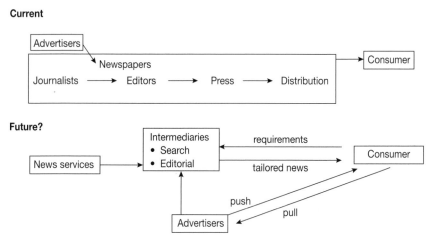

Fig. 7.16   Individualization and industry restructuring: news provision

New online intermediaries are providing an alternative link between news origi-nators and the customer, collecting information from the customer on what news they are interested in and packaging a response.

The CNN web site has an addition called Custom News which allows you to personalize the news you receive. Yahoo!'s Full Coverage service takes a mix of Reuters feeds and links to other sites to provide a viable first port of call for news. Advertisers can pay for their products to be advertised along with relevant news stories – Manchester United football kit along with a match report, for example. Or the customer may ask for product information – a 'pull' request.

The newspaper's position as a remarkably cheap means of distributing vast quantities of information appears secure for the time being, but the market is already changing. Fewer young people read newspapers, turning instead to other sources of news and infor-mation. In the UK, for example, they can find house advertisements at www.uk-property.com, jobs at www.jobworld.co.uk, cars at www.exchangeandmart.co.uk, and weather reports at weather.yahoo.com.

So far the newspapers are not finding the Internet a lucrative channel for their tradi-tional integrated product. *The Times* in the UK offers a full annual service for £100, but regards its web site primarily as promotional and experimental. Respectable levels of advertising revenue have been growing for some time though.

When privacy and security concerns are not dominant

Users' concerns about security are inhibiting the use of the Internet to actually place orders. These concerns are being addressed through initiatives such as the secure electronic transactions (SET) protocol for credit card payments, but to date it tends to be either relatively low-value items or strong brands trusted by the consumer which are being paid for over the Internet.

> **Users' concerns about security are inhibiting the use of the Internet to actually place orders.**

Users also have concerns about the privacy of the information they provide. But as already noted, security and privacy concerns tend to be outweighed by the benefits of price, convenience, service levels, product availability and so on – the traditional ingredients of the shopping experience. So addressing the mundane issues of Internet speed and quality of web sites will be as important to the future growth of the Internet as the higher-profile security issues.

Summary

Integrated databases provide the means by which information is co-ordinated and distributed within the organization, and the Internet allows this information to be electronically disseminated to customers and, in return, added to. The Internet is a new communication channel with distinct advantages and disadvantages over the alternatives. It is not appropriate for every customer interaction, but has sufficient uses to be irrelevant to no company, and so important to others that it is fundamentally reshaping their industries.

The Internet is just one approach to wide area networking based on a particular set of standards that has evolved over time. As such its long-term future is difficult to predict. Some believe that, in time, it will be replaced by other standards designed to cope with the high-volume, high-value electronic commerce with which the Internet still struggles. But it has already performed an important role as a powerful prototype showing the potential for interactive communication of electronic information. As it moves beyond this initial role, every business leader needs to think ahead to what the Internet's place will be in their organization's future channel mix.

We can all be sure of one thing. In future, the most powerful brands will be customer-centric. Successful companies will know the customer better and will be the customer's advocate. E-commerce is simply an enabler that makes this more possible than it has ever been before.

E-commerce has given consumers what they want: speed, choice, control and comparability. Companies that want to thrive in the twenty-first century had better be alive to this new customer empowerment. Business leaders, be warned: no big organization can adapt to e-commerce without your leadership.

Checklist for CEOs

*Chief executive officers should evaluate the usefulness and efficacy of their organizations'
marketing efforts using the checklist below.*

Do you know:

- how customer motivation and behaviour
differs between market segments?
- what kind of relationship is important to
your customers?
- how 'involved' customers are with your
products?
- what 'quality' means to customers?
- what are the most important factors
driving 'satisfaction'?

- what you must do to be 'distinctive'
from competitors?
- what most causes your customers to try
competitors?
- how loyal your customers are?
- how strong your brand is?
- what your market image is?
- how changes in the above will affect the
bottom line?

---

*And if their organization is to survive and thrive in this new electronic world, the business
leader needs to ensure that:*

- their organization has excellent
products;
- their organization is quick to innovate;
- they re-engineer the organization;
- they throw out some legacy business
models;
- they understand that the customer is
king;

- they understand 'marketspace' as well
as marketplace;
- they ask themselves why anyone with
expertise in e-commerce would join and
stay with their company.

Interview: Ben Maddocks, global relationship director, PricewaterhouseCoopers (PwC)

How PwC has reorganized around key customers

*PricewaterhouseCoopers is the leading global professional services firm. It was formed
in 1998 through a merger between Price Waterhouse and Coopers and Lybrand. The
merger triggered a strategic review of the way the combined firm managed its relationships with its key clients around the world. Ben Maddocks is a global relationship
director in PwC's global technology industry group.*

All CEOs of note who are doing their jobs properly rate managing and maintaining
their organizations' relationships with their top-tier strategic customers as their
number one priority. Indeed, it should be the biggest blip on their radar screen.
They don't need to put the same effort into all their customer relationships, as only

a proportion of them are strategic, and there might be some customers they should probably get rid of. But they must ensure that they have in place strong teams of senior, credible, experienced people to help them manage their strategic relationships.

Too many CEOs are locked into the mindset that key account management is product-driven, and in the UK and Europe it is still perceived to be a sales and marketing activity. Consequently many key account managers are too junior. Key account management is really about managing and transforming client relationships at a very senior level and requires a great deal of hard work and a high degree of expertise and experience from the people managing those relationships. These days there is a view that becoming increasingly service led guarantees success. But building up the kind of knowledge culture necessary for true relationship management requires more than a Lotus Notes network. Too many companies instinctively reach for technology, when it is the active involvement of everyone in the organization that is critical to the success of both knowledge management initiatives and, through those, deeper customer relationships.

I joined PwC as global relationship director in September 1998, two months after the merger. I used to work on the consultancy side of Price Waterhouse before leaving to become CEO of a global technology company. I report in to the global technology industry group leader in Boston. The seniority of the role is very important when you are trying to build relationships with blue-chip client CEOs. PwC has global relationship partners and directors performing a similar role to mine, spearheading the global relationship management programme for our top 200 clients.

In common with many of the organizations I have spoken to over the past two years we are spending lots of time on market and client segmentation. These days leading organizations are extremely keen to identify their top-tier customers and treat them differently from the rest. The best organizations assign a 'client director' or some equivalent to manage each of those strategic relationships.

My role falls under our Client Service Executive (CSE) programme – our version of key account management. Before the merger each of both firms' lines of service had account management programmes in place. We introduced CSE roles post-merger, when the enormous size of the combined firm made it increasingly vital to develop and maintain strong relationships with our strategic clients. The strategic imperative brought about by the merger was how to put together two world-class professional service organizations and position ourselves as the number one firm while heading off the competition and ensuring that we attracted or retained the biggest multinational organizations. We work with many of the world's top companies to whom we need to represent the firm's cross-line of service and cross-geographic capability.

There is a lot of discussion about how you organize for key account management. Many organizations still organize themselves around products and geographical area. But we have added an industry dimension which allows us to focus on the client in order to build a level of knowledge and expertise about their business which really adds value. In professional services, in particular, where knowledge is the name of the game, you need to be ahead of the client the whole time if you're going to give them the benefit of all your understanding, knowledge management and learning, so that they are constantly refreshed with 'best in class' experience.

The challenge for CEOs is to manage and co-ordinate 'virtual teams' out of the industry, geographic and product silos to provide the best possible service to top-tier clients.

Within our global relationship management programme we have established a model called Crossing the Bridge, which is designed to transform the relationships we have with our strategic clients from reactive to proactive. Rather than just responding to client briefs, proposals or tenders – being a supplier, in other words – we want to move towards becoming a strategic partner, working alongside clients to help shape their agendas and manage change.

So we aim to have a range of relationships, from being a pure supplier providing service solutions, through offering strategic consultancy-type advice – on flotations, shareholder value, portfolio planning and so on – to strategic partnering. Strategic partnering involves seeking to maximize the revenue streams of both our firm and our clients by addressing future issues, anticipating and planning for change. Sometimes strategic partnering involves creating alliances and consortia involving third parties. The difference between this and strategic consultancy is that the client pays for consultancy, whereas in a partnership everyone gains financially.

Strategic partnerships are arguably more secure than pure supplier customer relationships, and less prone to suffer as a result of marketplace volatility. But they demand a lot of work and performance needs to be continuously monitored.

Nurturing global relationships often means managing the client account much as you would one of your own business units. You need a dedicated team responsible for the relationship, a team to handle consistent high-quality delivery of the service around the world, and global relationship partners or directors who act as chairmen or CEOs of those relationships. And it is crucial that you get the right calibre of people, with the right skills, experience and seniority, to carry out those roles.

Crossing the Bridge is already showing significant results for us. We have transformed a 30-year relationship with one client from one based largely on audit and tax to a much more intimate strategic partnership which is sponsored by the client CEO and executive committee.

The benefit to the client is greater satisfaction, increased revenue and reduced costs. And our revenue from that client has grown by over 200 per cent within the past year.

Any CEO will tell you he wants to 'own' the relationship with his strategic customers, but that is more easily said than done. Any major organization will have a number of major suppliers and no one supplier can have a monopoly on the relationship with any given customer. For everyone to benefit, you have to bring together the various teams and identify joint targeting opportunities.

References and further reading

Ansoff, H. I. (1965) *Corporate Strategy*. Maidenhead: McGraw Hill.

Cambridge Technology Group (1998) *UK Organisations Fail to Grasp New Internet Opportunities*. Cambridge, MA: CBT.

Lockett, A. and Littler, D. (1997) 'The adoption of direct banking services', *Journal of Marketing Management*, 13, 791–816.

Millman, A. F. and Wilson, K. J. (1994) 'From key account selling to key account management', in *Tenth Annual Conference on Industrial Marketing and Purchasing*.

8

Creating consonance:
positioning and branding the organization

*Backed up by his or her board, it is clearly the job of the CEO –
as 'corporate brand manager' – to act as the catalyst and
transform the organization's marketing strategy, and then to
proactively manage the company brand to ensure that the
organization can deliver customer value consistently.*

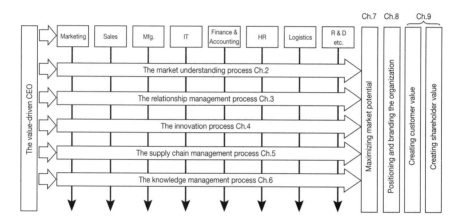

Fig. 8.1   Model of the value-creating process and relevant chapters in this book

Oscar Wilde wrote that a cynic is someone who knows the price of everything but the value of nothing. He may well have been talking about the attitude many business leaders have towards their companies' brands and, indeed, the way they manage the company brand itself.

As customers become more and more demanding in a business environment where competition is fiercer and innovation faster than ever before, the key challenge facing CEOs and their boards is how to continuously add value to the products and services they sell. The more enlightened business leaders know that they will not achieve this through the traditional 4Ps approach to marketing: customer value is created through the company's systems, people, processes and alliances – alongside its products and services.

Under the 'pan-company' marketing approach propounded in this book, the customer has to be involved in as many of the organization's processes as possible. No single department can effect that nor guarantee the customer will have a consistent experience in his or her dealings with the various departments. Backed up by his or her board, it is clearly the job of the CEO – as 'corporate brand manager' – to act as the catalyst and transform the organization's marketing strategy, and then to proactively manage the company brand to ensure that the organization can deliver customer value consistently. (For an insight into the need for strong corporate branding, turn to the interview at the end of this chapter with Ian Ryder, recently of Hewlett-Packard, and now vice-president, brand and communications, at Unisys.)

Brand marketing in transition

It is only relatively recently that senior managers have started talking about brands as assets and brand equity as a major component of their company's value. If anyone is in any doubt about the value of brands, they need do only two things: look at what CEOs are prepared to pay for top brands, and observe the extent to which the market capitalization of brand-led companies exceeds the value of their tangible assets.

During the 1990s there was a spate of acquisitions by consumer goods companies to increase their product portfolio and accelerate their geographic expansion. In many instances, they paid large premiums for the companies they acquired, as Table 8.1 illustrates.

Table 8.1   Acquisitions and balance sheet values

Acquiring company	Acquired company	$\dfrac{\% \ Balance \ sheet}{Acquisition}$ Value
Grand Metropolitan	Pillsbury	15
Nestlé	Rowntree	16
Cadbury Schweppes	Dr Pepper	33
United Biscuits	Verkade	34

Nestlé paid £2.5 billion for Rowntree, though the company's balance sheet value was only £0.4 billion. While this premium reflected the potential value of Rowntree's distribution, its customer relationships and branding know-how, the largest share of the premium was for its confectionery brands – Kit-Kat, After Eight and Polo mints – which Rowntree's management had carefully nurtured for decades. Each of these brands now carries the Nestlé brand name, and their distribution outside the UK has increased dramatically, as one would expect under the ownership of this powerful multinational.

Coca-Cola attributes only about 4 per cent of its value to its plants, machinery and locations. The real value of the soft drinks giant lies in its intangible assets, and first among these is its brand. Likewise, the microprocessor company Intel, which makes more profit than the world's ten biggest PC-makers combined, believes that 85 per cent of its worth lies in its brand equity and intellectual capital: the brand name, patents, know-how, its people and processes.

It is a misconception to think that brands are all about soft drinks and soap powders. The speakers at a recent *Economist* conference on brands came from an impressive range of world-class organizations, such as Hilton Hotels, Whirlpool, Federal Express and BP. They all talked about how their businesses had prospered by embracing the most modern thinking around brands. And brand preferences are becoming increasingly marked in business-to-business markets. Dell Computer and Andersen Consulting are both very good examples. Michael Dell started his company in the back of his garage as an 18-year-old entrepreneur in 1983; Dell Computer in the USA now sells more desktop PCs to corporate clients than IBM (see case study in Chapter 5). Andersen Consulting, within five years of repositioning itself in the IT-led change management marketplace, had increased its turnover from $800 million to $2.5 billion. The firm ran the largest ever business services advertising campaign on television, a first for a management consultancy selling multi-million-dollar services.

> *At the heart of the matter is the fundamental shift in what customers perceive as value, and this is challenging the way that business activities create customer value.*

In simple terms, a brand is an entity which offers customers (and other relevant parties) added value based on factors over and above its functional performance. These added values, or brand values, differentiate the offer and provide the basis for customer preference and loyalty. Traditionally, marketers have used the marketing mix – the 4Ps of Product, Price, Place and Promotion – to position the brand, and created brand values around a coherent set of policies for each of these Ps. Over time, the marketing community's knowledge of the effect of these various stimuli on customer perceptions increased and brand managers became 'brand engineers', manipulating well-tried stimuli to achieve predictable levels of customer value and generate superior profits.

Brand values and customer value

As we noted earlier, business leaders' key challenge today is how to add ever more value to the products and services they sell in the face of product commoditization, faster innovation, growing competition and more demanding customers. For many, corporate life is a treadmill of constantly squeezing time and cost out of their business only to discover that customers reap all the benefits of the management's hard work. The future for these firms will be one of relentless reengineering, eroding margins and extreme uncertainty.

At the heart of the matter is the fundamental shift in what customers perceive as value, and this is challenging the way that business activities create customer value. Since the Second World War, customers have relied on a familiar and trusted brand name as the antidote to the perceived risk of the product or service failing to provide its basic functional benefits. And, at a psychological level, a trusted brand minimizes the risk that the image created for customers using the product or service will fall short of that desired.

The business market has not been immune to this psychological risk either: we have all heard of the now-dated expression, 'You never get fired for buying IBM'.

In essence, brand values were a promise of sameness and predictability. But new ways of coping with risk have changed all that. As we discussed in Chapters 5 and 7, business buyers are now much more inclined to develop partnerships with suppliers which involve closer relationships and more sophisticated purchasing processes. And in consumer markets, 25 years of consumerism, higher disposable incomes and continuous improvements in product performance and reliability have led to more confident, less risk-averse customers. Unfettered by the need to manage downside risk, customers are increasingly discriminating between products and services on the basis of positive added value. The promise of sameness and predictability is no longer a strong enough brand proposition to meet customer expectations, as Heinz conceded when it announced its intention to supply supermarkets with own-label baked beans.

> *In the search for superior customer value, business leaders are realizing that their company has to touch customers in myriad ways, which go far beyond marketing communications about products and services.*

In the search for superior customer value, business leaders are realizing that their company has to touch customers in myriad ways, which go far beyond marketing communications about products and services. For example, they have to wow them through the company web site and in the tailoring of products and services they sell over the Internet. They also touch them in call centres and on helplines for product advice and complaints. Customers use each of these experiences to evaluate and test the company's image and reputation, its ability to deliver against expectations. The business leader needs to develop an integrated approach to these endeavours if he or she is to deploy the organization's assets and capabilities effectively. To achieve this the context of the brand has to change to embrace culture, know-how and organizational systems and processes – as well as products. Traditional brand-building activities are unlikely to create value without such a transformation in strategic marketing thinking.

The value gap

In the early twenty-first century, we are witnessing a growing gap between brand values and customer value. Customer value increasingly stems from processes outside the remit of marketing, such as customer relationship management and supply chain leadership, as we discussed in Chapters 3 and 5 respectively. When the value offered to customers does not meet their expectations, a company faces a stark choice: change or fail. Mercedes-Benz in the USA is a case in point. The car marque has long been one of the world's most powerful brands in terms of engineering quality, luxury and exclusivity. But by the early 1990s, the range no longer met customers' perceptions of good value and they were not willing to pay Mercedes-Benz's prices. The quality of the cars had not slipped, they were no more expensive to buy or own than before, nor did the brand have the disassociative connotations that the makers of Rolls-Royce and Porsche experienced during the early 1990s when conspicuous consumption fell out of fashion.

Mercedes lost its following in the USA to a competitor whose brand appeared to lack credibility in the relevant market segments. But customers quickly recognized that Toyota's Lexus offered better perceived value for money. This superior value stemmed from Toyota's breakthrough developments in manufacturing, which allowed it to produce the cars more cheaply, in conjunction with excellent design and customer care.

In an unprecedentedly frank interview, the then CEO of Mercedes-Benz acknowledged that his cars were over-engineered, and he began to address the problem. He stated his intention to change the company from being a producer of luxury cars only to an exclusive, full-line manufacturer offering high-quality vehicles in all segments. Mercedes was forced to look beyond the traditional 4Ps of brand management as its definition of 'premium' positioning was no longer working.

The value-driven business leader must continuously question his or her senior management team about how customer value is appraised within their organization. They also need to be satisfied that the company's value proposition or brand is both competitive and closely aligned with the value their key customer segments expect.

Customer value and the organization

Today's customers are highly sophisticated and confident in their ability to decide between products and suppliers' offers; these days they need much less brand reassurance to validate their choices. In most markets, the customer can choose between a large number of high-quality products made by renowned companies. In the modern economy, value is no longer exclusively created by marketers branding what their company wishes to produce. Rather, long-term value is created through the relationships customers develop with their trusted suppliers over a period of time.

The customer believes they have got value when the perceived benefits they receive from something exceed the costs of owning it. These components of customer value are represented in Figure 8.2.

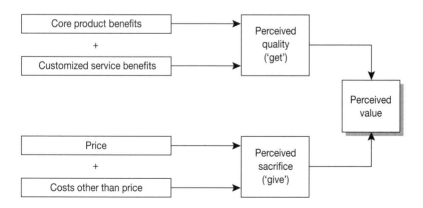

Fig. 8.2   The components of customer value

In many consumer goods markets, brands can no longer command premium prices or even shelf space purely by virtue of advertising-generated awareness and affinity. The price of a brand is no longer what customers pay for it. The real price includes everything the customer has to do to realize its value: time and money spent searching for the right product and sales outlet, travel and purchasing costs, consumption and disposal costs.

Our research into the components of customer value in business markets shows business customers use similar criteria when evaluating, selecting and buying from suppliers. These criteria fall into two broad groups:

1   *Qualifiers.* These are the product- and service-related attributes; the 'fitness for purpose' of the supplier. These attributes are simply a given and function only as qualifiers since any number of suppliers will meet the technical specification. The product no longer differentiates.

2   *Differentiators.* The problem-solving and relational capabilities of the supplier. Suppliers without a solid reputation in these key areas are screened out. But though reputation is essential, it alone does not guarantee success. The main basis for differentiating between suppliers has become: who will make the best partner over time and how can they customize their service, systems and programmes for us?

The price of a brand is no longer what customers pay for it.

When we questioned business customers about the price they paid for strategic services and capital equipment, it was clear that price was not the overriding factor in their decision to buy. More important was the supplier's ability to align their own organization – its people, products, services and processes – to add value to the customer's organization.

Taking this broader view of value – and customizing it – is transforming the marketing agenda. Let us look at how the former CEO of First Direct transformed the perceptions of customer value in the banking world.

How First Direct creates customer value

Kevin Newman, the former CEO of the world's first telephone bank, had a very clever vision of how to create customer value in his bank:

I believe that in going forward [at First Direct], three things need to be developed. We have to be utterly low cost. We must be able to individualize the manufacturing process and recognize that all our customers are individuals. Thirdly, we must build a strong brand as people need to identify with institutions they can trust.

Since opening for business in October 1989, First Direct representatives have signed up over 850 000 customers for their telephone banking services. Without a branch network to support, First Direct's staff costs are about half those of a typical retail bank and an efficient information system has been instrumental in keeping these costs down.

Information technology is critical for accessing the bank's online customer database, which is the hub of its operations. An automatic call distribution system routes customers' calls to unoccupied operators across its four call centres. Each banking representative has instant access to each customer's accounts and business history. The same representative can complete all day-to-day transactions, such as balance enquiries, electronic payment of bills or a transfer of funds between accounts, without having to transfer the customer. For more specialized information, such as loans and mortgages, customers are transferred to trained advisers. In most instances, the full range of traditional banking services is offered in a friendly and efficient manner – 24 hours a day, 365 days a year – for the price of a local telephone call.

These components of customer value delivered by First Direct's banking representatives can be summarized in the customer value monitor shown in Figure 8.3.

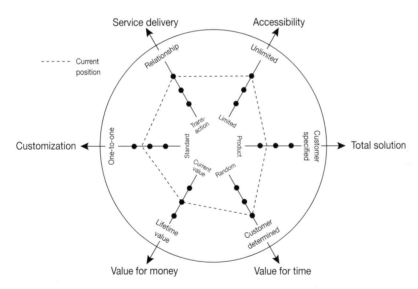

Fig. 8.3 The First Direct customer value monitor
Source: © Knox and Maklan (1998)

What sets First Direct apart from high street banks are the perceptions its customers have of a convenient, well-informed service which provides access to a broad range of financial, travel and information products in a speedy and business-like fashion.

Because the bank can provide superior customer value, it enjoys a level of customer retention and loyalty that is second to none. Some 97 per cent of First Direct customers remain with the bank year-on-year and about one-third of its new customers are referred by these loyal customers.

Customer value and business integration

As products become more sophisticated and customers' demands for service and performance grow, few companies, if any, find they can offer a total solution to what customers require. The traditional brand marketing response to these demands is to add more and more levels of service to augment the product offer. But this tends to create complexity and cost rather than value. IBM's experience in the early 1990s, before Lou Gerstner arrived to turn it round, is a good case in point. The company was the leading exponent of 'solution selling' during the 1960s and 1970s and its methods were widely copied by companies such as Xerox. It created a company brand based on its product line, augmented with layers of added value services and systems support. The positioning of the IBM brand was about being the IT manager's supporter, and the selling proposition was about certainty and predictability. But the infrastructure needed to deliver that promise proved unequal to the challenge of client server architecture: leaner competitors unbundled IBM's offer and created real or *de facto* alliances that delivered more powerful solutions at lower prices and with better service. Novell, for instance, the 1980s start-up, took the local area computer network (LAN) market from IBM in a few short years. Operating through a vast network of Novell-trained third-party distributors, it proved much more agile and competitive than the total solution brand.

> **Business leaders must accept the need for and drive the introduction of new models for differentiating their organization's offer, or they will find themselves increasingly irrelevant both to their customers and their peers.**

Marketing today creates value by integrating the company's suppliers and manufacturing processes to create value-adding business systems, as we discussed in Chapter 5. The structure of alliances and processes needed within the supply chain to create the total customer experience is beyond the ability of product management.

Competition and company positioning

Chief executive officers and their boards are increasingly acknowledging that competition is based on supply chains rather than the efforts of their individual company, its product portfolios battling head to head with those of adversaries. This understanding has profound implications for how the company is organized to create and deliver customer value. At the heart of this transformation is the strategic requirement to shift marketing from a purely departmental approach, positioning and selling product lines, to a pan-company activity that positions the entire company in the supply chain. Business leaders must accept the need for and drive the introduction of new models for differentiating their organization's offer, or they will find themselves increasingly irrelevant both to their customers and their peers.

Marketing the organization

Marketing the organization or a strategic business unit requires a very different approach from the conventions of 4Ps product marketing. There are a number of very good reasons for this.

1   The organization's good name and reputation is at stake rather than the name associated with a product or service in a particular market. As the portfolio increases or the company diversifies into different markets and scale and operational complexity increase, the risk of a service or product failing becomes magnified.

2   Managing the reputation of the organization or business unit is much more challenging than managing a single product, since it is constructed by customers from multiple reference points which extend well beyond the products and their projected images. The key elements of a company's reputation derive from its commitments, values, ethics, policies and practices. Neither individual marketing managers nor the product portfolios they manage have the necessary scope or authority to commit the entire organization in these areas or to manage the full range of stakeholder relationships necessary to build a reputation.

3   As we have already discussed, customer value is created through the company's systems, people, processes and alliances, alongside its products and services. Most of these value-adding elements, other than the products and services themselves, are usually outside the domain of the marketing department.

Although the risk associated with developing a pan-company approach to marketing is greater than traditional product marketing, the rewards can be dramatic. As the context of marketing widens to include this broader set of capabilities, it opens up opportunities to align processes – both within the company and deep into the supply chain – in a way hitherto simply not considered. These aligned processes then become central to strategic decision-making.

In marketing and positioning their organization, business leaders need to consider four components: reputation, product/service performance, product and customer portfolio, and networks. Again, First Direct neatly illustrates how to interpret customer value across the entire organization, as illustrated in Figure 8.3 showing the First Direct customer value monitor.

How First Direct positioned its brand

The First Direct brand aims to communicate and deliver a no-frills, inconvenience-free approach to banking more in tune with customers' lifestyles than the traditional high street bank. Customer feedback through surveys suggests that First Direct is achieving these brand objectives: customer satisfaction levels are running at over 85 per cent, compared with less than 60 per cent in a typical retail bank. Commercially, the telephone bank is very successful, enjoying a return on equity of over 25 per cent and an equally healthy return on investment.

How has First Direct managed to create these brand values and position itself as bank of choice in the minds of its customers? Let us analyze the four components of the First Direct brand using the positioning monitor shown in Figure 8.4.

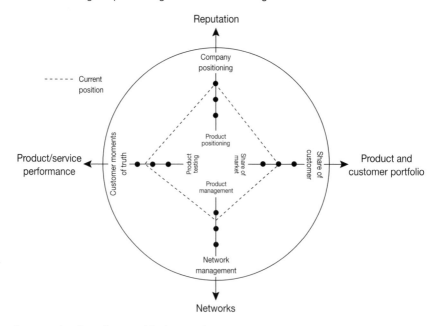

Fig. 8.4   The First Direct positioning monitor
Source: © Knox and Maklan (1998)

1 *Reputation*. The First Direct brand is not seen as depending on any one product. The company's reputation is built on the complete portfolio of its activities and values. It engenders trust and commitment by being flexible, responsive and accessible, as well as highly competitive. All aspects of the company's operations contribute to this positioning: it is not a by-product of the marketing efforts behind individual brands.
2 *Product/service performance*. This component is to do with the way customers perceive the bank's products and service delivery. It is about the 'moments of truth'

customers experience in their day-to-day dealings with the bank and its representatives. The relationship customers have is with the bank rather than individual representatives, but the representatives' thorough training and knowledge of the customer's usual needs, which is instantly accessible through information technology, means that the company culture is very customer-orientated and keen to serve. The relationship is based upon 'listening and serving' rather than 'selling financial services'.

3 *Product and customer portfolio.* In building up its customer portfolio, the new customer team rejects about 50 per cent of applicants. The profile of its existing customers is young professionals working in metropolitan areas who tend to make extensive use of the bank's product portfolio. The bank's strategic focus is to balance share of spend targets, by encouraging existing customers to spend more across the bank's product portfolio by cross-selling and up-selling, and growing market share from new customers generated by referrals.

As a result of matching customer and product portfolios, the bank generates superior profits. A journalist has estimated the average balance of a First Direct customer to be ten times higher than that of a typical high street bank, while the overall transaction costs are 60 per cent less. The bank makes money on 60 per cent of its customers compared with 40 per cent at the average British bank.

4 *Networks.* To help deliver its service, the bank uses a number of IT providers for transaction clearing, card service processing and credit scoring. Likewise, the management team has developed its product portfolio through establishing networks both within the HSBC group, which owns it, and among external insurance and assurance companies. But these networks of relationships are not overtly branded. Over time, the network could become part of the company brand proposition, so that when you 'buy' First Direct, you get access to a large number of value-added partners.

Overall, the First Direct brand is positioned to offer outstanding customer service by skilfully managing each customer's 'moments of truth' with an individualistic style that is both respectful and open. Thus, the strength of the brand lies in its customer relationship management capabilities and the service values the senior management team has inspired its staff to support and believe in.

As former CEO Kevin Newman said: 'We like to think that we are not really in banking but distribution. We just happen to supply financial products.'

Positioning and branding the organization

As the First Direct example illustrates, the marketing mix and the positioning of the company brand are determined by its reputation, the performance of its products and services, its product and customer portfolios and the network of relationships it has developed in the supply chain. Clearly, you can place a different emphasis on each of these components according to how you wish to position your company and the nature of the competition.

Table 8.2 shows how airline brands in the UK have positioned themselves at the corporate level.

Table 8.2   The positioning of airline brands in the UK

	British Airways	*Virgin Atlantic*	*easyJet*
Reputation	Reliable, predictable	Challenging, exciting, unconventional	Cheap
Product and service performance	Extensive routes, range of service, excellent recovery from problems	Limited routes, innovative services	Fit for purpose, few routes
Product and customer portfolio	Strong business class sub-brand Focus on long-distance business traveller	Trade on corporate name mostly, target Virgin-likers	Corporate brand focused on budget traveller paying for own trips
Networks	Emerging global alliances deliver world-wide capability Airmiles scheme a major part of loyalty strategy	Focused on Virgin to appeal to Virgin-likers	Not as part of the brand

British Airways aims to be the choice of the highly profitable, long-distance business traveller. It is ruthless in its determination to keep its hold on the business's most profitable customers and, its current problems notwithstanding, is creating the world benchmark for reliable global travel. It delivers an effective and predictable service to time-obsessed business travellers, provides a comfortable and convenient business-class service, and has a network of relationships integrated into the brand proposition to meet customers' global needs. If it can extend its business processes to its partners, it will lead a powerful global network with unrivalled reach and capabilities. But BA may continue to find its new low-priced brand extension, Go, difficult to integrate into its strategic positioning.

Virgin Atlantic Airways, referred to by some marketers as the 'challenger brand', has wisely avoided trying to become a 'mini-BA', a strategy that was unsuccessfully attempted by Mercury when it was the challenger brand to British Telecom. Virgin Atlantic's appeal is more emotional than BA's and its service performance reflects this: massages, free ice creams, baseball caps on flights and so on. It seems to appeal to those disposed towards the Virgin brand as a whole and all that it stands for. This concept will be much harder to extend to business partners, and you wonder about its ability to compete for business travellers should the industry consolidate into a number of global players.

The 'no frills' proposition is not new in the airline industry and many early successes have closed down – none with more publicity than Laker's SkyTrain. Nonetheless, easyJet offers a highly credible brand positioning: limited but effective and low cost.

The company brand should consist of a coherent set of credentials that add value through the supply chain. These credentials are forged by the senior management team when they determine policy around the company's marketing mix, and by the effectiveness with which the policy is implemented and measured. Formulating and implementing policy requires cross-functional teamwork, as Table 8.3 illustrates.

Table 8.3 Positioning the company brand: the marketing mix

Component	Policy	Team activities
Company reputation	• Identity (how we see ourselves) • Image to customers and others • Culture development	• Mission, values • External and internal communications • Stakeholder relationships
Product and service performance	• 'Moments of truth' in the customer purchasing cycle • Customer relationship management	• Product and service design • Delivery-execution • Customization • Continual improvement
Product and customer portfolio	• Share of customer spend • Share of market	• Market segmentation • Competitive response • Customer segmentation and purchasing patterns
Networks	• Aligning business systems and processes	• Alliances and partnerships • Co-branding/marketing • Customer-sharing • Information-sharing

The 4Ps approach to marketing remains central to product and sales strategies, but the company marketing mix is more appropriate in an environment where customer value is created through the activities of the entire organization. But these company credentials – or what the company is known for by customers (and other related parties) – are only sustainable if the core processes that run end to end through the company (as we described in Chapter 1 and which appear in the value-creating process figure at the beginning of this and every chapter) are suitably aligned. So it is the positioning of the company brand in conjunction with its core processes that creates and delivers customer value throughout the organization.

The company brand should consist of a coherent set of credentials that add value through the supply chain.

The company marketing mix we have described here provides the business leader with a methodology for aligning processes. Once the processes are aligned, the proposition moves deep into the organization because process leaders and their teams understand the priorities that determine customer value among their important customer segments.

Many organizations in the West have recast their activities from being driven by discrete business functions to cross-functional, value-adding processes. The core processes which deliver value to customers will vary industry by industry and company by company. We have highlighted five in this book which we view as being representative – market understanding, relationship management, innovation, supply chain and knowledge management. But the methodology discussed in this chapter works across most process designs.

Let us look at two examples where the positioning of the company brand and its core processes are closely aligned.

How First Direct aligns its brand and core processes

The brand values of First Direct are delivered through very effective customer relationship and knowledge management processes. Both processes support a positioning based upon product/service performance (customers' 'moments of truth') and a company-wide reputation (culture, identity and image development), as we have already identified in the customer value monitor (Figure 8.3) and positioning monitor (Figure 8.4). Arguably, these processes represent the investment priorities for the CEO, and it is critical that he or she ensures that these processes are aligned. Continuous innovation and supply chain management are less well developed within the bank, as Figure 8.5 shows.

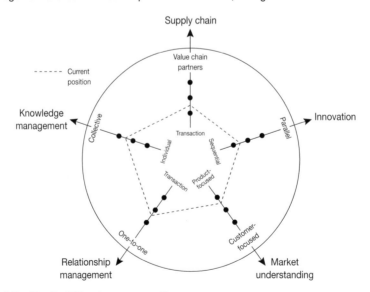

Fig. 8.5   The First Direct process monitor
Source: © Knox and Maklan (1998)

As market understanding grows within the bank, and the management teams develop their innovative capabilities to meet a wider set of their customers' needs (in both financial and non-financial areas), stronger alliances, new modes of distribution and networks will be needed within the bank's supply chain.

The challenge facing the bank's new CEO and his board is to develop the supply chain process to enable these more complex relationships, from suppliers to end customers, to be managed effectively.

To quote former CEO Kevin Newman again:

> The mode of distribution is changing – at the moment we definitely see it as person to person over the telephone. Do we believe that people will bank electronically over the next ten years? We are not fussed about how quickly or by which means our customers choose to access all or part of their banking electronically. The elements for us are: when they do so, what is the role of our bank and how do we deliver competitive advantage in this environment? We must always remember that our 'moments of truth' are the telephone contacts with banking representatives. Creating value in an electronic world will be a key issue in the future of First Direct.

From buns to buildings: how McDonald's builds its brand

Retail franchise brands in fast food, printing and car repair businesses are built upon effective supply chains and knowledge management. McDonald's provides an excellent example.

McDonald's derives most of its customer value from branding and food preparation, supported by first-class supply capabilities (from buns and burgers to new store design and build). Marketing at McDonald's is as much about supporting training and company brand developments as it is about the 4Ps of its product portfolio.

The McDonald's brand positioning consists of:

- reputation – family fun, value for money, hygiene;
- performance – consistency in taste of food, speed of service, cleanliness of restaurants;
- portfolio – clear product portfolio strategy based upon burgers, fries and soft drinks and a customer portfolio of families with young children;
- networks – Disney for joint promotion;
- (co-branded) – Cadbury's flake in its ice cream desserts (UK). Coca-Cola has been introduced through branded founts and paper cups.

The McDonald's service model and its business process design has been well chronicled. While all its business processes are important, McDonald's does not have close customer relationships nor is it particularly innovative. Though it conducts extensive market research, its market understanding is supported neither by sophisticated customer segmentation practices nor by a differentiated approach to its consumer marketing. However, it deems knowledge management and extensive training across the whole organization to be essential to sustaining its brand values and business growth. In the USA, McDonald's Hamburger University is the centre of training for management and staff across the franchises.

To support training in the workplace, every senior manager around the world has a special affiliation with one or more restaurants in order to share their experiences and knowledge with retail management and staff. In fact, some senior managers spend extended periods of time in the regions operating a franchise or a group of McDonald's-owned restaurants, to ensure that best practices in product and service performance are continuously improved through their leadership.

Dell Computer is another organization which aligns the positioning of its corporate brand with its core processes, as the case study in Chapter 5 illustrates. The combination of supply chain efficiency and customer relationship management has been a real differentiator in what is one of the world's toughest markets. The company is very innovative too – not in terms of its products, but in terms of the way it manages its supply chain and the resulting rapid time to market. The company's web site now allows customers to configure their computers directly, taking even more time and cost out of the system. By defining its business on the basis of business processes, the Dell brand remains unique and continues to add value.

The CEO and marketing management

In Chapters 1 and 2 we examined in some detail the role marketing plays in the 'pan-company' approach to doing business. But it is worth reiterating here in the context of how the CEO should brand and position his or her organization.

The value-driven business leader must continuously question their company's investment in marketing. In some organizations, particularly those serving the mass customer market, marketing budgets can equal total net profits. As marketers find it more and more difficult to achieve breakthroughs in customer value, CEOs should be reviewing not only how judiciously marketing budgets are spent but also how effectively marketing is organized within their company.

It may be that the traditional approach to product marketing and the functional structures usually associated with this are no longer appropriate and are destroying rather than creating value. A sequential approach to processing customer feedback through marketing and sales departments may be costing the CEO dear in terms of time to market, customer defections and missed opportunities.

In today's flat-structured organization, end-to-end process management encourages the involvement of customers at one end and suppliers at the other. Neither the marketing department nor sales should act as the final arbiter of customer needs or market developments. Similarly, supply chain partners must have access to all parts of the organization; purchasing should not impose itself between supplier and company. The traditional marketing department, perversely, can act as a barrier to the marketing of the company brand if it does not support process management in this broader approach to delivering customer value.

It has become almost a truism that marketing is too important to reside in the marketing department alone. While a small marketing department staffed by specialists will continue to add value to the organization, marketing as a philosophy and a way of thinking must live within everyone in the organization and be lived by everyone. The CEO can act as a catalyst for this transformation by instigating a strategic review of the positioning and branding of his or her company. If they use the three-stage audit suggested in this chapter (customer value monitor – positioning monitor – process monitor), it should become clear just how pervasive marketing principles are in appraising customer value and the lead which the marketing department provides. The audit should also reveal how closely the company's positioning and delivery of brand values are aligned with the value expectations of key customer segments.

Although many of the value-adding processes discussed in this book fall outside the remit of the marketing department, they will manifest the effects of marketing. In a process-based company, the CEO should be able to see the degree to which the marketing department has adapted to the new challenges. If they cannot, then they may want to think about restructuring their marketing and sales teams to strike a better balance between their functional tasks and involvement in cross-functional processes.

Summary

A brand is not just a name on a product or service. Successful brands are valuable assets since they create customer preferences among their target markets and deliver superior profits. But as customers become much more confident in their own ability to decide between products, the value-driven business leader must challenge how brand marketing is implemented in his or her company.

In the early twenty-first century, there is a growing gap between brand values and customer value as the latter stems increasingly from activities and processes outside the remit of marketing management. To close this value gap, the business leader should be questioning how customer value is assessed and interpreted across the organization.

Is customer value created and marketed across a broad set of company capabilities, such as its people, processes and supply chain networks, or is there an overdependence on branding its products and services?

As the context of marketing widens to become a pan-company activity, the business leader needs to manage the company brand proactively to position it effectively in the supply chain. This positioning depends on aligning processes so that customer value can be delivered on a consistent basis across the company. A methodology which enables the CEO and his or her senior management team to position their company brand and align these processes is outlined in this chapter.

The CEO's decisions on investment priorities in core processes effectively determine their company's positioning and the competitive nature of the offer. In today's economy, marketing is too important to be left to the marketing department alone.

Checklist for CEOs

Chief executive officers and their teams should ask themselves the following questions.

- How is customer value appraised within our company?
- Is customer value in our company created and marketed across a broad set of capabilities, including people, processes and supply chain networks, or is it overdependent on branding its products and services?
- What is the level of our customer defections?
- Could our time to market be shorter?
- Broadly, how much of our company's value is accounted for by our brand equity?

- Is our company's positioning and delivery of brand values aligned with what customers expect?
- How is marketing organized within our company? If it is primarily a functional department, does it act as a barrier to marketing the company brand?
- How big is our overall marketing budget compared with our total net profits?
- How judiciously are our marketing budgets spent?

Interview: Ian Ryder, vice-president, brand and communications, Unisys (and former director of global brand management, Hewlett-Packard)

How Hewlett-Packard built its corporate brand

Ian Ryder is vice-president, brand and communications at Unisys. At the time of this interview he was director of global brand management at Hewlett-Packard (HP), based at the company's headquarters in Palo Alto, California. Hewlett-Packard, a $43 billion technology company, has recently undergone a radical transformation from a hardware to a service provider. It spun off Agilent Technologies, the technology business that was the genesis of HP, and HP now concentrates on computing, imaging and printing. Ryder's role was a new one, and it involved driving strategy development, core values and positioning the HP brand around the world.

Business leaders need to bear in mind three key statistics. One, up to 40 per cent of a company's image and reputation stems directly from the CEO. Two, between 70 and 75 per cent of the company's stock price derives from the company's reputation. And three, in nearly every case a company's intangibles, including brand equity and intellectual capital, brand name, patents, know-how, people and processes, are its largest asset, representing over 50 per cent of its capital. Unless CEOs understand corporate branding, they could usefully look for another job, because they won't be around for too long.

Corporate brands have always been important. Nine out of the top ten world brands are corporate brands, the exception being Marlboro. But while consumer goods companies have long recognized the fact, business-to-business organizations have been slower to catch on. Eight to ten years ago many of them resisted the idea of corporate branding, believing it to be tangential to their real business. But IBM and Microsoft are now in the top ten and there is a growing recognition of the necessity of having a strong corporate brand.

But very few companies manage this hugely important asset. This is extraordinary when you consider the requirement in most companies to show return on investment on fairly low-value assets. The approach to managing the corporate brand has traditionally been one of 'tight and light' management – 'how cheaply can we do this?'.

This was the case even in a major company like Hewlett-Packard when I came back just over four years ago. I spent much of my early days proselytizing to senior management around the company about the importance of corporate brand management.

Corporate branding should be central to strategic decision-making, and the CEO, with his or her umbrella vision, is the only person who can make that happen. No one should even try to start developing the corporate brand unless the CEO is behind it. Companies like Sony have been working hard on their corporate brand for many years. In such organizations the CEO inculcates the organization with the understanding that everyone has to own the brand. He or she acts as the figurehead, and then they need someone in a role like mine, with the knowledge, skills and capabilities to drive and develop the strategy and ensure the systems and processes are in place to deliver it.

The cross-functional pan-company approach to marketing is common among consumer goods companies. But it reflects a major shift in the thinking of business-to-business firms. There has been a big operational review of marketing at HP as part of the 'reinvention' of the company. Hewlett-Packard's new positioning is 'performance through invention', and the company's key processes, including market understanding, are like cables within that sheath.

In the reengineered company marketing is a way of thinking and behaving for everyone. But I neither believe nor accept the flip idea that 'marketing is too important to be left to the marketing department'. Marketing is what any company is all about. While everyone in the company needs to be 'in marketing' as a discipline, you still need a marketing function staffed by experts – just as you need a finance function even though everyone in the company has some kind of financial management responsibility.

The CEO is essentially the corporate marketer – the equivalent of the traditional market trader with goodies on his stall shouting out to passers-by. But someone needs to own marketing and provide skills and direction – and that should be the marketing department, headed up by a marketing director, VP (vice-president) of brand management, or the equivalent.

And the goal, the culmination of all these people's efforts, the Holy Grail, is effective brand management with the objective of creating a company for customers. The only reason any company is in business is because it has customers. That's a truism, but it is easy to forget.

I don't believe the gap between brand value and customer value is growing: to me they are one and the same thing. A customer derives value from a brand, just as they always have, but the components of that value and how the brand delivers the value is changing. What has also changed is the number and range of attributes on which today's more sophisticated customers test a brand. It is the CEO's job to ensure that all those attributes are up to scratch – and that is part of corporate brand management.

The key fundamental component of a company's reputation – and therefore its corporate brand image – comes from a grounded, effective and competitive product or service. If a customer has a bad experience or buys a bad product, they don't give a damn about the company's commitments, values, ethics, policies and practices.

For 60 years Hewlett-Packard's entire reputation was built around its products. Other factors are increasingly coming into play as competition intensifies, but products and services remain firmly at the centre. Likewise, while the supply chain is playing a bigger role in companies' competitiveness, companies are still battling it out head to head at a more fundamental level. And again, customers are still basing their purchase decisions primarily on basic product/service functionality; only when they are satisfied with that do all the other image and reputation elements come into play. The big difference today is the number of elements that the customer is including in his or her definition of product/service functionality.

References and further reading

Knox, S. D. and Maklan, S. (1998) *Competing on Value: Bridging the Gap between Brand and Customer Value.* London: Financial Times Pitman.

Delphine Parmenter *et al.* (1997) 'First Direct: Branchless Banking', INSEAD Case No. 597-028-1.

Levitt, T. (1986) *The Marketing Imagination.* New York: Free Press.

Christopher, M. (1995) 'From brand values to customer value', *Journal of Marketing Practice* 2 (1), 55–66.

Wayland, R. and Cole, P. (1997) *Customer Connections: New Strategies for Growth.* Boston: Harvard Business School Press.

9

Delivering the goods: creating stakeholder value

There is a common and explicit assumption that customer value drives shareholder value. But there is also a view that shareholder value drives customer value. A better approach is to consider shareholder value and customer value together, as they are mutually dependent.

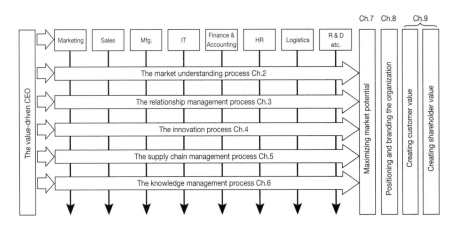

Fig. 9.1   Model of the value-creating process and relevant chapters in this book

Most business leaders would acknowledge that creating 'value' is a major source of competitive advantage. Yet, though the term 'creating value' is bandied around constantly, people seem unable to agree on either what constitutes value or how value relates to stakeholders.

In Chapter 3 we looked at companies' numerous stakeholders, categorized them into six market domains and outlined a framework for relationship value management. This chapter explores how business leaders can create value for their three key groups of stakeholders as outlined in the relationship value management framework: customers, employees and shareholders.

Customer value, employee value and, ultimately, shareholder value are the three critical areas of value creation. Though many organizations recognize the importance of stakeholders, few actively develop formal strategies which address these critical value areas in an integrated way.

Customer value

A business leader needs to consider four key issues relating to customer value:

* the nature of 'the offer' a company makes to its customers;
* the value proposition framework;
* the use of relationships to increase customer value;
* the value of customers to the company.

Start from the customer's perspective

Value is part of the total offer that surrounds a product. The work of US marketing expert Theodore Levitt in this area was instrumental in developing the concept of customer value creation. He recognized that it is not what companies produce in their factories that competes, but 'what they add to their factory output in the form of packaging, services, advertising, customer advice, financing, delivery arrangements, warehousing, and other things that people *value*' (Levitt, 1983).

As such customer value is an inherent part of the product which the company can actively manage to benefit the customer. In fact customers are not buying goods or services, but rather specific benefits and value from the total offering. This total offering – or 'the offer', as it is commonly called – represents the value that customers get when they buy goods or services.

Customers buy products or services to solve problems, and they value their purchases according to their perceived ability to do this. So improving a product or service is a way of differentiating that product or service and thus adding value in customers' eyes.

A CEO needs some sort of structured framework or methodology to review his or her organization's existing and potential 'offer' to customers. One useful approach is the value proposition framework.

Building the value proposition

The term 'value proposition' is sometimes used in a general sense to refer to any activity which adds value to customers. But it also describes a specific approach to value developed by consultants McKinsey and Company.

Figure 9.2 shows the value proposition framework or 'value delivery sequence'. It emphasizes that business leaders need to shift from the traditional view of the business as a set of functional activities towards an externally oriented view of the business as a form of value delivery. It builds the idea that customers buy promises of satisfaction and they only buy products because they are of some value to them.

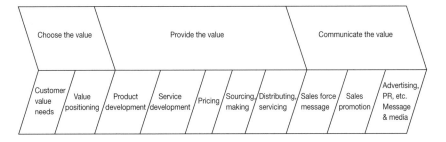

Fig. 9.2 Value proposition framework
Source: Based on McKinsey and Company

McKinsey consultants Bower and Garda (1996) stressed that marketing strategy should be directed 'first – factually, constantly, resolutely and imaginatively – to the customer and his or her needs, rather than the product given to the marketer to sell'. The traditional physical process sequence of 'make the product and sell the product' is replaced by the value delivery sequence which depicts the business from the customer's perspective rather than as a series of internally oriented functions.

The value delivery sequence comprises three key steps: choose the value, provide the value and communicate the value.

1   *Choose the value.* Customers select products and services because they believe they offer superior value. Companies need to understand changing customer needs – the forces driving demand, customer economics, the buying process *and* how well the competition serves those needs, particularly in terms of their products, service and the price they charge.
2   *Provide the value.* Organizations need to develop a product and service package that creates clear and superior value. This involves focusing on product quality and performance, service cost and responsiveness, manufacturing cost and flexibility, channel structure and performance, and price structure.
3   *Communicate the value.* Organizations need to engage in promotional activity to persuade customers that the value they offer is better than that of the competition. This involves not just sales promotion, advertising and the sales force, but also providing outstanding service in a way that the target audience recognizes.

It has been suggested that companies wishing to implement a value proposition approach should adopt a three-step sequence.

1   Analyze and segment markets by the values customers desire.
2   Rigorously assess opportunities in each segment to deliver superior value.
3   Explicitly choose the value proposition that optimizes these opportunities.

But success is not a simple matter of choosing a value proposition: it rests on the thoroughness and innovation that go into developing the value proposition and communicating it throughout the organization. Creating the right culture to do this is not easy, but once the culture is right it is very difficult for competitors to replicate it, and as such it becomes a source of sustainable competitive advantage.

Use relationships to increase customer value

Many companies have poor relationships with their end-consumers. Think of yourself as a consumer for a moment. You will no doubt have had unhappy experiences when buying a range of consumer durable products. For example, you may have been motivated to buy a car as a result of a promotional campaign by a car manufacturer, only to be disappointed by the subsequent lack of interest by the dealer in rectifying faults that occurred within the warranty period. You may have been let down even further when seeking redress directly from the manufacturer to find they are totally uninterested in engaging in dialogue with you.

> *Building better relationships with customers through offering superior service is one way to create competitive advantage.*

But within the motor car sector, radical changes in customer service, distribution and marketing – not least the direct approach pioneered by Daewoo – are now prompting other manufacturers to look at ways of developing closer relationships with their customers.

Building better relationships with customers through offering superior service is one way to create competitive advantage. Customers have increasingly sophisticated requirements and demand ever higher standards of service. Many major companies have now woken up to the need to improve customer service in order to compete in today's highly competitive service environment. They recognize that warranties, unconditional service guarantees and free phone-in advice centres are critical to creating customer value.

General Electric provides a good example.

How General Electric builds customer relationships

General Electric's (GE) Appliance Division in the USA is a good example of an organization which has built a closer relationship with its end-consumers through establishing a major call centre. General Electric's Answer Centre is widely regarded as one of the best in the world. In setting up the call centre in 1981 GE sought to 'personalize GE to the consumer and to personalize the consumer to GE'. Unlike most manufacturers, which avoided any contact with the end-consumer, GE took the unusual step of giving its phone number to customers. Over the past 19 years the Answer Centre has evolved into an increasingly important relationship marketing tool: the current network of five call centres receives several million calls each year. Consultants Robert Wayland and Paul Cole have outlined how GE's Answer Centre has contributed to increased customer relationship value in three key areas:

First, resolving immediate problems results in a probability-of-repurchase rate of 80 per cent for the previously dissatisfied customer, as compared with 10 per cent for the dissatisfied but uncomplaining customer and 27 per cent for an average customer. In other words, by making it easier to reach the company and by responding effectively, GE gets more opportunities to convert dissatisfied customers and to strengthen relationships. Second, contact with the centre significantly increases customers' awareness of the GE appliance line and their consideration level. Finally, the knowledge that is generated through customer interactions provides valuable input to the sales, marketing, and new product development processes. (Wayland and Cole, 1997)

Companies can build customer value by offering customers a wider range of channels. These may include direct sales, sales through indirect channels, such as distributors or brokers, and Internet sales using electronic commerce (e-commerce). The Internet affords considerable opportunities for building one-to-one marketing systems, offering a differentiated service for every individual customer who comes on to the system using information gained from electronic interactions with customers. The business may even be able to respond instantaneously to customer enquiries. We discussed the opportunities that e-commerce has opened up to the value-driven CEO in Chapter 7.

Companies can offer an individual tailored service by phone, mail, face-to-face or via the Internet. RS Components, which we also discussed in Chapter 7, chose the latter approach.

How RS Components has tailored its approach

International distribution company RS Components has shifted its focus to individualized relationships. Its electrical component catalogue weighed 4 kilos, was 20 cm thick and featured over 100 000 products. Upgraded quarterly and dispatched to over 150 000 account customers, the cost of the printed catalogue prompted the company to switch to a CD-Rom version and then an Internet site.

With a direct presence in 13 countries, the company's ability to find and service customers was constrained economically by the costs associated with a catalogue-based business. Today, the Internet gives it global reach, with virtually no engagement costs.

Customer personalization is a major feature of the Internet site. The site is driven by questions such as job, industry and product interests. On entering the site each customer is greeted by their own welcome page featuring tailored editorial, advertising and new product alerts relevant to them.

The site has been designed to provide individualized relationship marketing. For example, customers can directly access 10 000 documents in the RS technical data library. With its customer service, personalized operation, downloadable technical information and navigation tools, it clearly offers customers an improved value proposition over the old paper catalogue.

RS Components states the site is significantly exceeding its sales expectations.

The relationship between a company and its customers does not *have* to be personalized (that is, involve direct person-to-person contact with the customer) but it must be individualized. For the relationship to be individualized, the business needs to develop IT systems that 'know' the customer and then extend that knowledge throughout the enterprise. If the business develops a 'corporate memory' of the customers it is dealing with, whenever the customers contact it (and whomever within the organization they contact) they will feel that the business knows all about them. The relationship is then continually strengthened through ongoing interactions. What is more, customers are likely to build an emotional bond with an organization that has invested time in the relationship, and they may be unwilling to invest their own time again with competitors.

The company's perspective of customer value

The company must also understand the value to it of its customers. 'Customer lifetime value' is closely related to the economics of customer retention, and is an output of, rather than an input to, value creation.

Customer lifetime value emphasizes customer retention. Improvements in customer retention of just a few percentage points can dramatically improve profitability, as research by US strategy consultants Bain and Company demonstrates.

> **The company must also understand the value to it of its customers.**

Bain showed that a 5 per cent increase in customer retention leads to a considerable rise in net present value profits – up to 125 per cent for a credit card company and 50 per cent for an insurance broker (see Figure 9.3). It is not easy to obtain a 5 per cent increase in customer retention, but even a 1 per cent increase could yield considerable profit improvements. Moreover, the cost of customer defection is very high: research has also shown that it can cost as much as five to ten times more to find a new customer than to keep an existing one.

Retaining customers is so profitable because:

- sales and marketing and set-up costs are amortized over a longer customer lifetime;
- customer expenditure increases over time;
- repeat customers often cost less to service;
- satisfied customers provide referrals;
- satisfied customers may be prepared to pay a price premium.

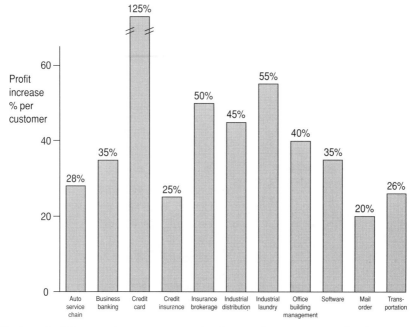

Fig. 9.3   Profit impact of a 5 percentage points increase in customer retention for selected businesses
Source: Bain and Company

To calculate a customer's real worth a company must look at the projected profit over the life of the account. This is the expected profit flow over a customer's lifetime; the longer they stay, the more profits they bring to the company. For example, a credit card company will probably lose money if a customer defects within the first year. But if a customer stays with the company for more than three years, then the costs of administration are low compared with the revenue, and the profits start to accrue.

But marketing directed at retaining customers can be expensive and needs to be closely evaluated against results – not all customers are profitable. Within a portfolio of customers, typically some will be profitable, some will break even and some will be unprofitable. So increasing customer retention does not always increase profitability, and in some cases increasing the retention of unprofitable customers actually destroys value.

It is important to understand the relative profitability of different customer segments, so that the biggest effort to keep customers can be directed at those segments that are presently or potentially the most profitable. But unprofitable customers may be valuable in their contribution towards fixed costs, therefore companies should be very cautious in the way they allocate fixed and variable costs to ensure that customers who make a contribution are not simply discarded.

Shareholder value

Business leaders have been concerned with creating shareholder value ever since the ownership of organizations moved from an individual to a wider basis. The growing power and influence of the City in the UK and Wall Street in the USA has driven many company boards to regard the creation of shareholder value as their primary business focus.

> *In Britain and the USA, maximizing shareholder value is widely accepted as being top management's major goal.*

Not all organizations have shareholders, but most organizations of any size have some external owners. So while we consider commercial organizations with shareholders here, much of what follows is relevant for other organizations too.

A lot of what has been written about shareholder value focuses on measurement and places inadequate emphasis on the role of the customer in achieving it. In Britain and the USA, maximizing shareholder value is widely accepted as being top management's major goal. But some observers believe that overemphasis on shareholder value disadvantages other stakeholders and results in weakened brands, diminished job security, higher unemployment, poorer products and services and, ultimately, reduced shareholder value.

Measures of shareholder value

Academics Ian Cornelius and Matt Davies (1997) have summarized the five principal strategies that can lead to the creation of shareholder value. These are as follows:

- increasing the return generated on existing capital invested;
- investing more capital where the rate of return exceeds that required;
- divesting assets which generate a return lower than that required, thus releasing capital for more productive use;
- extending the period over which returns above the required rate are generated;
- reducing the cost of capital.

Cornelius and Davies emphasize the need to adopt a 'value-based management' approach that stresses creating and maximizing the wealth of shareholders in every aspect of the business. Managing the key financial variables, or 'value drivers', is essential to this, and these include:

- the opening amount of capital invested;
- the rate of return generated on capital;
- the rate of return that investors require;
- the growth in the value of capital invested;
- the time horizon over which returns are expected to exceed those required by shareholders.

During the past few years there has been considerable emphasis on the tools for measuring the creation of shareholder value. A summary of the main shareholder value measures and their proponents is shown in Table 9.1. These approaches are known by a number of acronyms, such as EVA™ (economic value added), SVA (shareholder value added) and MVA (market value added). Anyone interested in the technical measurement issues relating to these different approaches should read the report by Cornelius and Davies listed in the references at the end of this chapter.

Table 9.1　Shareholder value measures

Company	Shareholder value product
LEK/Alcar Consulting Group	Shareholder value added (SVA)
Stern Stewart and Company	Market value added (MVA)
	Economic value added (EVA™)
McKinsey and Company	Various methods
Marakon Associates	Various methods
Braxton Associates	Cash flow return on investment (CFROI)
The Boston Consulting Group	Cash flow return on investment (CFROI)
	Cash value added (CVA)
Holt Value Associates	Cash flow return on investment (CFROI)

Source: Adapted from 'Metric Wars', CFO, October 1996.

There is an ongoing debate as to the best technique for measuring shareholder value, but business leaders *must* consider shareholder value creation in the context of the strategic fundamentals of the business, and particularly how it relates to customer value.

Shareholder value and customer value

There is a common and explicit assumption that customer value drives shareholder value. But there is also a view that shareholder value drives customer value. A better approach is to consider shareholder value and customer value together, as they are mutually dependent.

Figure 9.4 shows a customer–shareholder value framework outlining four positions of different value combinations. The bottom left-hand corner of the framework represents a position of low customer value and low shareholder value. The 'value destroyer' organization creates low levels of

> *... business leaders must consider shareholder value creation in the context of the strategic fundamentals of the business, and particularly how it relates to customer value.*

customer and shareholder value compared with its industry peers. Fisons plc, the UK mini-conglomerate described in the case study in Chapter 3, is a good example of an organization which alienated both customers and shareholders in the mid-1990s.

In the bottom right-hand corner is the 'customer hero' which focuses on high levels

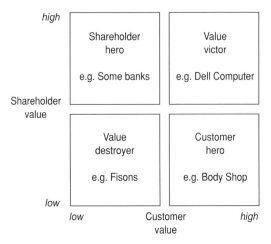

Fig. 9.4   The customer–shareholder value matrix

of customer value but does not necessarily achieve high levels of shareholder value. This group includes organizations that may provide inappropriate or unnecessarily high levels of customer service at a price that may damage their business performance. The Body Shop is a good example.

In the top left-hand corner is the 'shareholder hero' organization, whose primary focus is to increase shareholder value. This may, however, be done at the expense of the customer, through failing to invest in new product or service development or to continue to improve.

Some UK banks, despite strong shareholder value performance, do not rate nearly as highly in terms of customer value as other UK retail service providers. Ultimately this position may be untenable unless the organization is protected by some proprietary capability such as a product patent or a monopoly which enables it to disenfranchise customers without a long-term impact on shareholder value.

Mike Sommers, a former marketing director of Prudential Retail and TSB Bank, succinctly sums up this situation. Writing in *Marketing Business*, he stated:

> With one exception, I don't know what any bank's customer proposition is; I can't think of any distinguishing characteristics. Banks are so busy sorting out their technology and optimising their narrowcast 'relationship' approaches that their broadcast brands are withering into the commoditised environment they should most seek to avoid. (Sommers, 1999)

In the top right-hand corner is the 'value victor' group – organizations which understand the interplay of customer value and shareholder value and manage their activities so as to maximize both.

Dell Computer, mentioned throughout this book, is once more a good example. For many years the computer manufacturer has scored highly on customer service compared with its peers, but it has also seen outstanding shareholder performance.

Not surprisingly, we advocate this 'value victor' approach and advise the business leader to build strategies with both customer and shareholders in mind.

Employee value

Two key market domains discussed in Chapter 3 – the recruitment market and the internal market – have an impact on the value that employees add to the business. We will consider these two markets together. The extent to which companies create employee value through the way they recruit and manage their staff will ultimately have a significant bearing on customer and shareholder value.

The value employees add to business success is tied closely to the way they are selected, trained, motivated and led. Examples abound of businesses failing or succeeding as a consequence of ineffective or effective management of their people. The expression 'our employees are our greatest asset' is increasingly common – but more often than not is a platitude. If CEOs and their boards were more proactive in recognizing employees' contribution in winning and keeping customers, they would substantially enhance their firms' competitive performance.

Recruiting the best employees

Annual employee turnover is as high as 150 per cent in some service businesses. This obviously represents a significant cost to the company in terms of advertising, interviewing time, administration, interview – and, possibly, relocation – expenses and training. There are also opportunity costs because of reduced productivity during the handover from an experienced employee to a new recruit or when a situation is vacant for a period of time. Estimates suggest that the cost of replacing an employee is 50 per cent of their annual salary.

With the costs of recruitment so high, it is becoming increasingly important to find employees who not only have the necessary skills and competencies and match the profile that the company wants to portray to its customers, but who are keen and likely to stay. So the employee value process begins at recruitment.

Potential employees need to be given realistic expectations of the job from the outset. Press advertisements, brochures and information supplied by third parties must accurately reflect the job requirements and the company environment. Otherwise the result will be disillusioned employees, low employee retention and poor word-of-mouth referrals.

Selecting employees

Companies must choose their recruits carefully if they are to be successful and gain competitive advantage. The values and motivations of potential employees must be in keeping with the organization's service ethic, therefore suitability should not necessarily be based on technical skills, which can be taught later, but on psychological characteristics.

Selection techniques range from the traditional interview, through self-assessment, group methods and assessment centres, to the increasingly popular psychometric tests.

Psychometric testing is an effective way of identifying the personality profile of people who are likely to be successful in delivering service quality and developing relationships with customers. Traditionally used more for management and graduate jobs, organizations are now using these techniques for a wider range of .positions, including administrative, secretarial and manual jobs. This reflects the importance that companies are now placing on the 'emotional content' of front-line positions.

> **Companies must choose their recruits carefully if they are to be successful and gain competitive advantage.**

Essential to understanding how employees add value is to recognize the different roles they play in the organization. Customer-facing employees can only function effectively with support from others in the company who, though they do not come into direct contact with the customer, nevertheless play a very important role and directly influence the service ultimately provided to customers. By viewing people as a value-adding element, companies can direct the appropriate level of attention towards maximizing the impact of their activities and motivating and rewarding them to make the desired contribution.

Employee development

Research has shown that employees who are unclear about the role they are supposed to perform become demotivated, which in turn can lead to customer dissatisfaction and defection. So new employees must be carefully prepared for the work ahead of them, as their early days in a company colour their attitudes and perceptions towards it.

Those organizations lacking a strong service ethos may need to implement a major change management programme aimed at all employees. Development programmes aimed at instilling a customer consciousness and service orientation in employees are increasingly being referred to as internal marketing – an issue we discussed in Chapter 3.

The basic premise behind internal marketing involves getting employees to recognize the impact of their behaviour and attitudes on customers. This is especially important for employees who are as close – or closer – psychologically and physically to customers as they are to each other. Their skills and customer orientation are critical to the way the customer views the organization and, therefore, help determine their future loyalty.

Some of the best examples of change management programmes are to be found in the airline industry. Both Scandinavian Airline System (SAS) and British Airways reversed their fortunes during the 1980s. Faced with declining profits, increasing customer complaints, employee dissatisfaction and mounting competition, both airlines launched a series of programmes to refocus employees on customers. As such, employees were involved in helping to turn their companies around.

Employees were trained to develop new attitudes towards customers by emphasizing that the airline was in business to satisfy the needs of the customer. In turn, the company made employees feel wanted and cared for, building on the principle that those who are looked after will pass on this caring attitude. The success of this new direction for both airlines was manifested in greater customer and employee satisfaction and increased profits. But such programmes have a limited life. Both airlines now face a further challenge to improve the motivation of their employees. As noted in the case study in Chapter 3, BA is in the throes of a major change management programme for all its employees aimed at improving motivation and commitment.

The Disney Corporation operates a similar scheme. Employees are rigorously trained to understand that their job is to satisfy customers. Employees are part of the 'cast' at Disney and must constantly ensure that all visitors ('guests') to their theme parks have a highly enjoyable experience. Strict dress codes, rules of conduct and training are maintained in order that employees 'live the brand'.

Employee empowerment

Employees need to be involved and empowered to use their discretion in order to deliver a better quality service. There are various forms of empowerment, from 'full' empowerment, where employees have absolute power to do whatever is necessary to satisfy the customer, to milder forms – essentially 'suggestion' involvement.

Empowerment means creating the right culture and climate for employees to operate in. Employees need the knowledge that allows them to understand and contribute to organizational performance, and the power to take decisions that influence organizational direction and performance. Au Bon Pain, a chain of bakery cafés on the east coast of the USA, illustrates empowerment in practice.

How Au Bon Pain empowers employees

Au Bon Pain has focused on empowerment as a means of growing employee value in its bakery café chain. Managers were empowered to significantly alter processes, procedures, store layout and other policies, in order to develop service quality and marketing activities designed to build stronger relationships with frequent customers.

These changes led to significant performance improvements. Staff turnover in one of the Boston stores has dropped to 10 per cent per annum for entry-level jobs compared with an industry norm of about 200 per cent. Absenteeism has plummeted and sales have soared as customers develop a relationship with counter staff. Productivity has increased greatly and employee headcount has been considerably reduced. Under the Partner-Manager Programme at Au Bon Pain employees can earn double the industry average wages and the manager of an outlet can earn up to $160 000 a year. The type and quality of employees has changed radically, and word of mouth creates strong demand for jobs at all levels in the chain.

Many companies have sought to introduce a culture of empowerment, but many have failed. One of the barriers is middle managers feeling threatened by delegating power and authority to subordinates. Equally, some staff are reluctant to take on such responsibility and believe that making decisions is a manager's responsibility.

The advantages of empowerment can include a faster and more flexible response to customers' needs by confident and well-informed staff. In fact, where service does fall down, there is evidence that if the problem is resolved promptly and to the customer's satisfaction by trained, empowered staff, the customer's perception of service quality actually rises.

But organizations should weigh the benefits of empowerment against increased labour, recruitment and training costs, and view it as a long-term investment in employees. It will not be the answer for all companies, and the pros and cons need to be carefully assessed.

Integrating employee, customer and shareholder value

Towards the end of the 1990s business leaders became preoccupied with assessing company performance. Concerns over the need for improved market metrics led to joint initiatives and research by a number of UK and USA organizations. The 'Marketing Metrics' project in the UK, for example, is a research programme involving a number of organizations, including the Marketing Society, the Marketing Council, the Institute of Practitioners in Advertising, the Sales Promotions Consultants Association, London Business School, Cranfield School of Management and the Marketing Science Institute.

We examined a number of different market metrics in Chapter 7. But most companies have not yet reached the stage where their marketing strategies, focused on maximizing long-term profitability, can be rigorously measured. And only a handful of companies worldwide have sought to develop metrics to understand the linkages between employee value, customer value and shareholder value and how they contribute to corporate success. But new and improved metrics to measure performance across the business will increasingly be used by business leaders in the future.

There is growing recognition of the links that exist between leadership, employee satisfaction, employee retention, customer satisfaction, customer retention, sales and profitability.

There is growing recognition of the links that exist between leadership, employee satisfaction, employee retention, customer satisfaction, customer retention, sales and profitability. Academics and consultants have developed a number of 'linkage models' or 'employee-customer-profit chain models', but perhaps the best known is the 'service profit chain' developed by the Harvard Business School.

Sears, Roebuck and Company, the leading US department store, is an outstanding exemplar of the use of the service profit chain measurement approach. Sears, one of the great turnaround success stories of the 1990s, has undergone a radical transformation. Much of its success is attributed to rigorous measurement systems which track employee attitudes and their impact on customer satisfaction and profitability. Critically, management has aligned around the metrics and there is widespread understanding throughout Sears of how this model works.

How Sears developed 'best-in-class' metrics

In 1992, Sears, Roebuck and Company reported massive losses of $3.9 billion on sales of $52.3 billion. Arthur Martinez was appointed to head the merchandise group and he streamlined the business, closing 113 stores and terminating the 101-year-old Sears catalogue, a household institution in the USA. He also changed the service strategy, focusing on women who were the most important buying decision-makers. As a result, in 1993 Sears reported a net income of $752 million – a dramatic reversal of fortunes for such a mature company.

Martinez set up task forces to define world class status in each of four categories – customers, employees, financial performance and innovation – to identify obstacles and to define metrics for measuring progress. The task forces spent months listening to customers and employees, observing best practice in other organizations and establishing measures against objectives. Gradually it became apparent that the company needed a model to show direct causation from employee attitudes, through customer satisfaction to profits. Sears needed to know how management action, such as investment in sales force training, would directly translate into improved customer satisfaction, retention and higher revenues. What was required was a measurement system around the employee-customer-profit model.

Sears defined a set of measures based on its objectives, which were to make Sears 'a compelling place to work, to shop at and to invest in'. Relationships between changes in key metrics were identified using advanced statistical techniques.

The results were impressive. Direct links were identified between employee measures, customer measures and revenues, so total profit indicators for the company could be established. Employee attitudes towards the job and company were found to be critical to employee loyalty and behaviour towards customers, while customer impressions directly affected customer retention and recommendations. After further refinement, the model is now used to predict revenue growth: a 5.0 unit increase in employee attitude drives a 1.3 unit increase in customer impression, a 0.5 unit increase in revenue growth and a quantifiable increase in store profitability.

Sears had to change the behaviour of its senior managers and encourage them to take responsibility for the company's culture and understand how this affected revenues before it could successfully implement the service profit chain model. In addition, employee rewards needed to be aligned to the model for financial and non-financial measures. The results have been impressive: employee satisfaction at Sears has risen by 4 per cent, customer satisfaction has risen by almost 4 per cent, and more than $200 million in additional revenues have been achieved through this value creation process. A further benefit has been the streamlining of IT – from 18 separate legacy databases to a single, integrated system.

These relationships were modelled by CFI, a leading US consulting firm specializing in econometric modelling. Sears Roebuck's confidence in the CFI data was such that it computed, depending on the type of managerial role, between 30 per cent and 70 per cent of executive compensation from these measures. In terms of shareholder value, the total return to investors between September 1992 and April 1997 was 298 per cent – again a remarkable improvement for such a mature business.

Not every organization will be able to be as sophisticated as Sears Roebuck, but all business leaders should be aiming to improve their companies' performance metrics.

 ## Checklist for CEOs

Some key questions for CEOs to consider.

Customer value

- **What is our value proposition?**
- **How do we rank ourselves in terms of the process for value creation in the following areas: choosing the value; providing the value; communicating the value?**
- **Do we rigorously assess opportunities in each segment to deliver superior customer value?**
- **Do we understand the existing and potential lifetime value of our customer segments?**

Employee value

- **Do we place sufficient emphasis on creating employee value?**
- **How do we rank ourselves in terms of recruiting the best employees?**
- **How do we rank ourselves in terms of selecting employees?**
- **How do we rank ourselves in terms of developing employees?**
- **Have we placed enough emphasis on empowering our employees?**

Shareholder value

- **What technique do we use for measuring shareholder value and are we satisfied that it is an appropriate measure?**
- **Do we consider shareholder value in the context of customer value?**
- **How do we rank ourselves in creating shareholder value compared with our major competitors?**

Employee-customer-profit chain metrics

- **Do we understand the role of employees and customers in driving shareholder value?**
- **Is it appropriate for our organization to develop an employee-customer-shareholder linkage model now, or in the medium term?**
- **Do we acknowledge the role of leadership in creating employee, customer and shareholder value?**

Summary

Much of what has been written on value creation has focused primarily on the company and its customers. Insufficient attention has been paid to other stakeholders and how they should be considered within an organization's total value creation process. The role and interdependence of employees, customers and shareholders should be of particular importance to the CEO and his or her team, who should review the situation regularly.

Interview: Jim Brooks, head of corporate planning, RMC Group

How RMC creates value for its stakeholders

RMC is the world's largest producer of ready-mixed concrete, the world's fifth largest producer of aggregates and the world's twelfth largest producer of cement. It also sells a range of specialist concrete products. It has a wide range of customers, from governments and large commercial contractors, through small local house builders, to private individuals. A public company for some 40 years, its current market capitalization is £2.2 billion. It recently bought Rugby Cement Group in the UK for £900 million, an acquisition which will add value to customers through enhancing the product range. Jim Brooks joined RMC in 1970 and became head of corporate planning in 1996.

RMC has always been customer focused – you don't achieve international market leadership without being so. But we also focus on creating sustainable long-term shareholder value – or maximizing return on investment – with the emphasis on the 'long term'. Anyone can boost short-term returns. But we don't milk markets, we don't push short-term margins up, because that upsets customers and damages the business as a result. We try to ensure that we offer good value to customers. Shareholder value and customer value need to be considered together, as they are mutually dependent, rather than one driving the other. Shareholder value reflects the performance of the company – and the company doesn't exist without customers.

RMC has always taken a long-term approach. We are an asset-based business: we have large investments in mineral resources and in fixed plant and equipment on between 25- and 50-year timescales. To make those kinds of investments we are in a market long term, which means we have to take a long-term view of the market.

We have recognized the links between leading market positions, employee satisfaction, employee retention, customer satisfaction, customer retention, sales and profitability for many years. Indeed, understanding those links lies at the heart of our culture, and drives our focus on delivering consistent long-term returns. You have to look at creating value for customers, employees and shareholders together. High staff turnover leads to a dysfunctional relationship with customers and hence with shareholders. These three key stakeholder groups are totally interlinked.

Many of our employees have spent most of their careers with RMC – and we pride ourselves on the tremendous loyalty to the business. Peter Young, our CEO, has just retired after 39 years with the company, and there are employees in every sector and at every level, from senior and middle management, through supervisory to operatives, with 40 years or more service in the company.

You reap what you sow: treat employees well, trust them, involve and empower them, and they remain motivated and loyal. We work hard to create an attractive environment for people to work in. We have always been at the forefront of management development and training for all levels of employees. And because we are servicing local markets, the business is heavily decentralized, and there is trust, autonomy, ownership and responsibility at every level. That gives us a key edge in terms of retaining customers: employees know the market inside out, and customers see a consistent uniform face. That's particularly important given the fact that we operate in cyclical markets. And we build relationships at all levels: the interface between us and our customers involves a wide range of people.

Consequently we are very close to our ultimate customers, the contractors and builders. But we have to have such close relationships because our product has a finite shelf-life, so our business is all about meeting the needs of local markets.

In keeping with the long-term nature of our business, we want long-term relationships with our customers. We make sure we target our offer to each customer, and we work very hard at product quality, delivery and service in what is an increasingly competitive market. We have a huge number of live accounts in all the countries where we do business – there are more than 8000 in the UK alone – and we monitor those very closely so that we can react quickly when there is a problem. All the feedback surveys we do are very focused on individual customers. But we want repeat business: one sale is not enough. And that comes back to our long-term approach. We have achieved, retained and enhanced our number one position in the world by continuing to make a sustainable offer to our customers.

Customers have to be made to feel they are being properly and fairly treated and that they have proper service levels. We know we are only as good as our last performance, our last delivery. You can never slack on your commitment to customers. We are constantly striving to improve our service performance, for example, and we can now give customers information on their delivery by satellite tracking. And the quality of our products is always of the highest.

It's all about doing the simple things consistently well. In a competitive environment you can't take anything for granted.

References and further reading

Bower, M. and Garda, R. A. (1996) 'The role of marketing in management' in Buell, V. P. (ed.) *Handbook of Modern Marketing*. New York: McGraw-Hill, pp. 1–10.

Clark, M. (1999) 'Managing recruitment and internal markets: a relationship marketing perspective', draft working paper, Cranfield School of Management. (Part of the section on employee value draws on this work and is used with permission.)

Cornelius, I. and Davies, M. (1997) *Shareholder Value*. London: FT Management.

Levitt, T. (1983) *The Marketing Imagination*. New York: Free Press.

Payne, A. F. (1999) 'Creating customer, employee, and shareholder value', draft working paper, Cranfield School of Management. (This chapter is based on a shortened version of this working paper and is used with permission.)

Reichheld, F. F. and Sasser, W. E. (1990) 'Zero defections: quality comes to services', *Harvard Business Review*, September–October, 105–11.

Sommers, M. (1999) 'Getting the customer into the boardroom', *Marketing Business*, May, 28–31.

Wayland, R. E. and Cole, P. M. (1997) *Customer Connections: New Strategies for Growth*. Boston: Harvard Business School Press.

Index